Contemporary Issues in Development Economics

D1807513

This new collection of articles puts the very latest issues in economic development under the microscope, exploring them from a variety of perspectives.

Beginning with an assessment of the current state of play in development, the authors move forward to examine neglected issues such as human development, gender, brain drain, military expenditure and post-colonial theory. While analysing the problems of external debts, technology transfer and new theories of international trade, the relationship between developing and developed economies is fully explored. The book also examines the important topics of financial reform, structural adjustments and the role of the IMF in the new financial architecture.

The highly respected contributors subject these critical issues to thorough analysis with suggestions towards resolving some of these problems, making this an indispensable book that researchers and students of development economics cannot afford to miss.

B.N. Ghosh is Professor of Economics at the University of Science, Malaysia. He is also Director (Hon.) of the Centre for the Study of Human Development, Leeds, England and Editor of the *International Journal of Human Development*. B.N. Ghosh is the editor and author of several books, including *Global Financial Crises and Reforms: Cases and Caveats*, also published by Routledge.

Routledge studies in development economics

Contemporary Issues in Development Economics

**Edited by
B.N. Ghosh**

Routledge
Taylor & Francis Group

LONDON AND NEW YORK

First published 2001
by Routledge
2 Park Square, Milton Park, Abingdon, Oxfordshire OX14 4RN

Simultaneously published in the USA and Canada
by Routledge
711 Third Avenue, New York, NY 10017

First issued in hardback 2014

Routledge is an imprint of the Taylor and Francis Group, an informa business

© 2001 Selection and editorial matter B.N. Ghosh; individual chapters
© 2001 the contributors

Typeset in Times New Roman by Exe Valley Dataset Ltd, Exeter

All rights reserved. No part of this book may be reprinted or
reproduced or utilised in any form or by any electronic, mechanical,
or other means, now known or hereafter invented, including
photocopying and recording, or in any information storage or retrieval
system, without permission in writing from the publishers.

British Library Cataloguing in Publication Data
A catalogue record for this book is available from the British Library

Library of Congress Cataloging-in-Publication Data
Contemporary issues in development economics / edited by B.N. Ghosh.
     p.   cm. -- (Routledge studies in development economics ; 20)
   Includes bibliographical references and index.
   1. Economic development. I. Ghosh, B.N. II. Series

   HD82 .C574825 2001
   338.9--dc21   00–045950

ISBN 13: 978-1-138-86629-4 (pbk)
ISBN 13: 978-0-415-25136-5 (hbk)

Contents

Tables

Figures

Contributors

M.R. Aggarwal is Professor of Economics, Department of Economics, Panjab University, Chandigarh, India. He was also the former Director of the Indian Council of Social Science Research (Northern Region).

John Asafu-Adjaye is Lecturer in the Department of Economics, University of Queensland, Brisbane, Australia. He has extensive working and consulting experience in Papua New Guinea, Brunei, Indonesia, Philippines and China.

Masudul Alam Choudhury is Professor of Finance and Economics jointly with the Department of Finance and Economics, King Fahd University of Petroleum and Minerals and the School of Business, the University College of Cape Breton, Sydney, Nova Scotia, Canada. He is also the Director of the Centre of Humanomics and the Editor of *Humanomics.*

B.N. Ghosh is Professor of Economics, School of Social Sciences, University of Science, Malaysia, 11800 Penang, Malaysia and former member of the Senate. He has provided short-term consultancies to various organisations including the University Grants Commission and the United Nations Development Programmes. Prof. Ghosh is the Director (Hon.) of the Institute for the Study of Human Development at Leeds, England and the Editor of *International Journal of Human Development.*

Rama Ghosh is Lecturer in the Department of Economics, DAV College for Men, Sector 10–A, Chandigarh, India.

G.S. Gupta is Professor of Economics and Finance, Indian Institute of Management, Ahmedabad, India. He is a consultant to several organisations including Government of India, Reserve Bank of India, National Academy of Administration, Resource Management Corporation (US) and International Cooperative Alliance, British Council.

George Kadmos is a Doctoral Researcher in the Department of Economics, Curtin University, Australia.

Ozay Mehmet is Professor and Development Economist in the Norman Peterson School of International Affairs, Carleton University, Ottawa, Canada.

Shankaran Nambiar is Lecturer in Economics, International College at Penang, Malaysia where he teaches on the University of Sydney programme. His areas of specialisation are: institutional economics and economic development.

Phillip Anthony O'Hara is Associate Professor of Political Economy and Director of the Global Political Economy Research Unit in the Department of Economics, Curtin University, Australia. He is the Associate Editor of the *Review of Social Economy* and the Editor of *Encyclopedia of Political Economy* (Routledge, 1999). He is also on the Editorial Board of Ashgate Publishers' series on *Alternative Voices in Economics.*

Randy Stringer is the Deputy Director, Center for International Economic Studies, School of Economics, University of Adelaide, Australia. He was also an economist with the FAO (United Nations) during 1990–6.

Gale Summerfield is the Director of the Office of Women in International Development and Associate Professor in Human and Community Development at the University of Illinois at Urbana Champaign, USA. Her areas of specialisation are: gender aspect of economic reforms, economic developments and the regional development of China and Vietnam.

Prefatory note

Some of the pressing contemporary issues in development economics have been in existence for many years. In fact, some of the issues like human development are indeed as old as human civilisation. But these issues were recognised formally very late, and only since the inception of development economics as a special branch of mainstream economics in the 1950s. Unfortunately many of these basic issues could not be resolved during the last century, while some other issues have indeed become problematic in the current century.

The basic purpose of the present volume is to examine some of the central issues in the economic development of Third World countries. The issues presented here are fundamental to human development, resource allocation, technological progress and international interactions between developing and developed countries. The development implications of such interactions have not yet been sufficiently understood by all. Hence, the need for such a volume.

There are myriad contemporary issues that currently confront development economics. This book, however, focuses mainly on those issues which are very basic and those which are related to the political economy of international development and underdevelopment. I am sure that the volume presents most of the more important issues in these areas of development economics.

In the preparation of the volume I have incurred intellectual indebtedness to many. I am thankful to the contributors who in spite of their busy working schedule have written valuable pieces for this volume. My thanks are also due to Abdul Hamid Abdul Wahab, Executive Officer, for his impeccable secretarial assistance and to Ms Marina Cheah for typing out a portion of the manuscript. However, none of them is responsible for the errors that might have crept in.

B.N. GHOSH

Introduction

There are indeed many ways of considering contemporary issues in development economics. These issues can be looked at from the perspective of economic backwardness of domestic economies in terms of policy failures and/or implementation failures or resources inadequacy and/or sub-optimality in the allocation of resources. The problems that arise out of domestic market failure and/or government failure are generally manifested in increased degrees of unemployment, inflation and poverty.

In the open and exposed economies of the Third World, economic backwardness or the slow rate of economic development in many of these less developed countries (LDCs) is a result of international forces which are generally working against these countries. In the context of the new international economic disorder, the developed countries (DCs) are able to manipulate things in their favour and against the LDCs which have less bargaining power in the international political market.

A close look at the development of development economics will make it abundantly clear that many of the important issues relating to the development of LDCs have either been willy-nilly neglected or have not been satisfactorily resolved. These issues have both domestic and international ramifications. For instance *food security* is predominantly a domestic issue, and the issue of *debt trap* for LDCs is basically an international one. However, some issues which originated primarily as domestic issues do also have international manifestations and ramifications. These issues, among others, are *technology transfer, brain drain, human development* and so on.

The contemporary issues in development economics pertain more to the international issues, though these might have been basically experienced as micro-issues for domestic economies of LDCs. Prominent among these issues are human development, brain drain, gender and development, food securities, external debt, technology transfer and the role of the IMF in the context of the *new financial architecture* that the present world monetary system is attempting to build up. However, the issues that are adumbrated here are not the only issues, but these are of course the major ones. It should be clear that the contemporary issues are not the very recent issues. Some of the issues have arisen since the inception of development economics in the 1950s and some issues have cropped up subsequently with the temper of time. As Ghosh's chapter on the 'Development in development economics' reveals, there have been occasional paradigm shifts in development economics. In the initial stages, it was responsible for many theoretical innovations in devising theories and models of development for the poor countries. However, in later years, more particularly in the 1970s, it was realised that the blind application of western growth models was not only inappropriate but also harmful because these caused enormous maldevelopment in LDCs. It was also the decade when one could discern the growing economic domination of DCs over LDCs through trade and aid, and the increasing debt burden of these countries. It was realised that, in reality, trade was not an engine of growth but was a mechanism for immiserising growth (Bhagwati 1958).

After the 1980s, many contradictions were found in simple economistic paradigms of development, and there was an apparent failure of the conventional theories of development. The new international economic order lost its momentum, and was regarded by many scholars as a system of new international economic disorder. Contrary to expectation and earlier promise, less capital and less technology flew to LDCs. In the words of W.A. Lewis (1984), development economics was completely in the doldrums. As a matter of fact, economic underpinnings of the development paradigms came under serious scrutiny once again in the 1990s with the feminist movement taking the lead (O'Connell 1997: 119–20). The earlier notion of *women and development* was subsequently replaced by the more comprehensive notion of *gender and development.*

Be that as it may, the issue of *globalisation* was the most publicised and confused slogan of the last decade and it is feared that MNC-led globalisation may unleash a regime of unequal competition between DCs and LDCs.

However, in spite of various rhetoric and slogans, the primary focus in the last decade shifted from the question of underdevelopment to the problem caused by maldevelopment. The issue of human development attracted the attention of social scientists and policy-makers. It was realised that development does not necessarily mean that one should have more, but that one should be more. As A.K. Sen asserts, the scope of development economics in the past was very narrow, concentrating too much on growth and too little on development (Sen 1983 and 1989). Development economics has been less successful in characterising development involving human capabilities, qualities, freedom, justice and equalities.

However, the construction of human development indices to measure human development has been a significant innovation in recent years. Masudul Choudhury's chapter on 'Human development, military expenditure and social wellbeing' makes a conceptual and empirical treatment of human development in terms of the prevailing human development indices and a new interactive index called the social well-being function. The chapter concludes that there exists a dire need for developing an interactive index of human development explaining the political economy of complex relations of development at the grass-roots level. The human development indices (HDI) are found to be linear composite measures which cannot explain the socio-econo-political and institutional forces that predominate the process of globalisation. The chapter also questions the supposed inverse relation between military expenditure and social well-being which has been the basis of the IMF's generalised inference. In fact, the flow of official development assistance has not increased to LDCs in spite of a decline in military expenditure; rather, presumably, there has been a decrease in social well-being in the crisis-ridden developing countries.

Related to human development, more particularly to the development of high-quality manpower (HQM), is the problem of brain drain from LDCs. It is a phenomenon of one-way migration of HQM from LDCs to DCs. This crucial manpower is employed in strategic industries and positions, and the migration of this strategic manpower causes enormous dislocation and loss to LDCs. The chapter by B.N. Ghosh and Rama Ghosh on 'The problem of brain drain' analyses the causes, extent and the consequence of brain drain from the developing economies. According to them, the problem of brain drain is a part of the explanation of economic backwardness and reverse transfer of technology. The loss, as a result of the migration of HQM, is more overwhelming than the gain from foreign assistance from the DCs. The reverse transfer of technology, in this sense, can be looked upon as a more detrimental dimension of brain drain.

The problem of brain drain is generated and intensified by the deliberate neo-imperialist policy of DCs which are still exploiting the LDCs under the new garb of aid and assistance. The exploitation continues unabated in the sense that while in the pre-industrial revolution period the imperialist countries drew physical capital from the colonies, in the post-industrial revolution period they are drawing away HQM without paying any compensation. The surplus extraction still continues and is intensified from LDCs by the DCs. Brain drain is responsible for the intensification of international inequality in the matter of distribution of HQM.

Another dimension of human inequality is manifested in the social reconstruction based on sex differences and is commonly known as gender inequality. Since the 1970s, the issue of gender and development has become a lively issue in development economics. It is generally argued that differences in material endowments and earnings are often due to the existence of a gender gap. The ownership and control of property is a crucial determinant of economic differentials between men and women (Aggarwal 1994).

Gale Summerfield's chapter, 'Gender and development: transforming the process', examines gender issues in the process of development. She concentrates on the shifting focus on gender and development since 1970. Whereas in the 1970s the main focus was the status of women in the developing countries and the study of impacts of policy changes on women, it gradually shifted to the study of the active role of women in development and the relative disparities between men and women. The chapter then explains the more recent key themes in the realm of women and development, including culture and identity, migration, property rights, socio-economic securities and so on.

In a very meaningful way, the issues of gender inequality and human development can be said to be interrelated with the issue of food security. In Southeast Asia, Latin America and sub-Saharan Africa, women farmers produce more than half the basic food. However, their contributions are often downplayed by male chauvinists. Be that as it may, the importance of food security can hardly be overestimated as the most important basic necessity for human existence and development.

Randy Stringer's chapter on 'Food security in developing countries' examines in this context the issues relating to entitlements for food, progress in food security, food security and poverty, food security and sustainable development and related issues. The concern for food security is growing in every type of country in the modern world, for food is not only a basic necessity but also a strategic item. And as such, in many countries, the incorporation of the issue of food security has become part and parcel of general development planning. Growth strategies are focusing more and more on the promotion of diversified farming and agrarian activities, and new technologies are being developed not only to increase food production but also to lower the cost of food production. All this is important because, in spite of economic growth, in many countries calorie consumption per capita went down during 1995–97 as compared to 1979–81, and the percentage of undernourished population increased in many countries of Asia, Latin America and sub-Saharan Africa. The present picture is indeed gloomy, but there is still hope in the sense that there are enormous possibilities both for increasing production through increased intensive cultivation of old land and extension of cultivation of new land and also through better systems of distributive management. For poor countries there is of course a limit to the buying of food from foreign countries using borrowed money on a long-term basis because these countries are already in the *debt trap,* and debt for consumption is generally regarded as unproductive in nature.

G.S. Gupta's chapter, 'External debt, government expenditure, investment and growth', reveals that external debt and debt servicing of many developing countries have overtaken the rate of growth of the economy during the last two decades. While Latin America and Caribbean regions are heavily indebted, the sub-Saharan Africa region tops the list in terms of debt to GNP ratio. The middle-income developing economies are highly indebted and their debt to GNP ratio is the highest.

The debt crisis has been coupled with serious internal social dislocation in many of the Third World countries, and this was partly caused by the policy of loan-pushing by the developed rentier nations in the 1970s (Basu 1991). The regime of *finance capital* which pushed up the so-called aid and assistance to developing countries was found to be unjust in many ways. This was one of the reasons why the poor countries demanded a higher share of trade than aid. However, a better access to trade is not the panacea, for trade is often based on unequal exchange.

As is well known, the pure theory of international trade established the superiority of free trade over restrictive trade practices. M.R. Aggarwal's chapter on 'The pure theory of international trade, globalization, growth and sustainable development: agenda for the future' asserts that in the context of market imperfection in trade, the state has to play an important role, but its role in the desired direction has remained rather insignificant. The growth of regionalism is an important development in recent years which gives larger opportunities for the member countries to expand their trade. The unrestricted growth of MNC-led trade may be dangerous for ecological balance and sustainable development in LDCs. Trade liberalisation indeed has to be done with care and circumspection; the new capitalist slogan of globalisation is bound to unleash the forces of unequal competition between DCs and LDCs. Here comes the positive role of the domestic state and international economic order to develop and diffuse environment-friendly technology to maintain sustainable development. Trade and technology are closely interrelated. Trade is not merely a channel for physical goods and resources, it is also a channel for knowledge and technology.

Shankaran Nambiar's chapter, 'Knowledge, technology transfer and multinational corporations' examines the phenomenon of technology transfer from the viewpoint of the economics of knowledge. The chapter analyses the knowledge that is useful for the formation and transfer of technology. In this context, the role of MNCs is explained in the generation and transfer of technological knowledge. Nambiar also considers issues relating to the channels of technology transfer, the loss of information that technology involves and the impact of globalisation.

Along with global transfer and exchange of technology, there takes place global financial transfer and exchange. The IMF is the central regulator and coordinator of the world financial system and obviously its role is very crucial for the smooth functioning of the world financial system. In their chapter, 'The International Monetary Fund: functions, financial crises and future relevance', George Kadmos and Phillip Anthony O'Hara have critically evaluated the role and functioning of the IMF in the light of its changing organisational dynamics and the real-world operation of global financial crises. While the IMF has been successful in many respects, it has also failed in many areas. In the future, the IMF's efforts should be directed at ensuring that the financial system is progressing in the right direction and that the fault line, if any, is detected and rectified as early as possible. The future relevance of the IMF will depend on its ability to act as a global central bank and to perform the roles of monitoring and supervision, cooperation with and assistance to nations, policy formulation and implementation and to effectively create a new financial architecture that serves all types of countries, developed and developing, equally well.

The issue of economic development is also closely related to the problem of environment. John Asafu-Adjaye's chapter, 'Economic development and environmental problems', reviews the debate on the trade-offs between economic development and environmental problems. He concludes that economic growth is necessary to achieve both economic development and a cleaner environment. However, this process does not occur automatically. The chapter argues that in countries that have obtained low levels of environmental pollution, institutions have played a significant role. The chapter also presents policy responses to reduce national and global level environmental degradation.

Environmental pollution is a global problem, and whether globalisation will increase it or not is anybody's surmise. Ozay Mehmet in his chapter, 'Globalization as Westernization: a post-colonial theory of global exploitation', observes that western capitalism is too pro-capital and too exploitative to fit in the Global Village. Therefore, globalisation of capitalism has worked as a tool of global inequality. The author has made a number of sane suggestions to reform the system of globalism to suit the countries of the Third World. These reforms include regulation of trade and capital movement, introduction of the system of empowerment and entitlement, universalisation of basic worker rights, introduction of international social policy and democratisation of world institutions like the IMF, WTO and the World Bank. In fact, global development must evolve from multi-cultural global consent.

References

Agarwal, Bina (1994) 'Gender and command over property: a critical gap in economic analysis and policy in South Asia', *World Development,* vol. 22, no. 10.

Basu, Kaushik (1991) *The International Debt Problem, Credit Rationing and Loan Pushing: Theory and Experience,* Princeton Studies in International Finance, no. 70, Princeton.

Bhagwati, Jagdish (1958) 'Immiserising growth: a geometrical note, *Review of Economic Studies,* June.

Lewis, W.A. (1984) ' The state of development theory', *American Economic Review,* vol. 74, March.

O'Connell, Helen (1997) 'The 1990s: new alliances, new directions', *Development,* March.

Sen, A.K. (1983) 'Development: which way now?', *Economic Journal* vol. 93, pp. 745–62.

—— (1989) 'Development as capability expansion', *Journal of Development Planning,* vol. 19, pp. 41–58.

1 Development in development economics

B. N. Ghosh

Introduction

After the Second World War, the poverty and backwardness of some of the world countries became extremely conspicuous. Many reasons, including colonial exploitation, devastation by war, war-induced inflation and the like, could possibly be said to be responsible for such a sad state of affairs in many countries. It is precisely at this time that the subject of development economics (DE) came into being to study the problems of backwardness and underdevelopment of these nations. To be precise, DE started as a sub-discipline of economics in the early 1950s. However, over the decades it had a number of paradigm shifts, and the enthusiasm and gusto with which the subject took off in the 1950s and through the 1960s became somewhat mellowed in subsequent decades.

The basic objective of the present discussion is to make an assessment of what has really been learnt about development economics in the last fifty years or so. The discussion here is organised into five sections. Section one outlines the *differentia specifica* of development economics, followed by a taxonomy of basic theories of development and underdevelopment in Section two. Section three gives a brief analysis of the paradigm shifts of DE from the 1950s to the 1990s, and the visible change in the trajectory of DE will be discussed in Section four, and Section five will make some parting observations.

Differentia specifica of DE

Development economics was basically designed to theorise on economic backwardness of the less developed countries (LDCs) and apply the theoretical knowledge to the analysis of particular problems of underdevelopment, low income and poverty, and to find ways and means to solve these problems. The generalisations in DE are often based on hypothesis testing of microeconomic case studies (Stern 1989: 599).

DE is indeed a blend of many types of issues and questions, including the analysis of causation and its perpetuation, and policies towards solution of a host of problems relating to underdevelopment. The epistemic basis of theories of DE in general has been the broad manifestation of the syndrome of poverty and underdevelopment prevalent specifically in LDCs. The purpose of DE has been mainly to study the phenomenology of underdevelopment, and to prescribe appropriate policies to eradicate it. Theorising on development has been based on the study of the symptoms and diagnosis of economic backwardness. Theories developed by development economists have encompassed the theoretical underpinnings of empirical facts drawn across the board from socio-econo-political realms of life of many poor countries.

However, over the years, the area of investigation of DE has transgressed the boundaries of pure economics, and has trespassed into the fields of other allied disciplines. This is the reason why DE is often regarded as the *subject of trespass*. As a matter of fact, the fine line of demarcation of DE became increasingly blurred in the decades following the 1950s. At the present moment, it is indeed very difficult both conceivably and observably to pinpoint the precise scope and ontology of development economics. The subject has become over-expanded so much so that almost any type of study under the sun can be brought conveniently within the analytic umbrella of DE. Although this has produced certain positive externalities for the subject, it has also been responsible for its lack of specialisation, direction and focus. Be that as it may, the subject of DE has remained and is still popular especially among the students of Third World countries, though its importance and charisma among the doctoral researches might have been somewhat reduced in DCs, as Arthur Lewis has made us believe (Lewis 1984: 1).

The popularity of the subject at the academic research level has waned perhaps because of disillusionment with the subject as a problem-solving pragmatic discipline. In the early theories of development, there was some sort of permeating optimism that the subject would be able to take the LDCs out of the morass of penury and pauperism (Bhagwati 1984: 24). But nothing of that sort has happened in actual practice in the LDCs. In the words of A.K. Sen, the 'would-be dragon-slayer seems to have stumbled on his sword' (Sen 1983: 745). One should, however, note that while theorising has remained innocuous in DE, things may have gone haywire at the levels of policy formulation and its implementation.

Theorising on underdevelopment and development

Theories and strategies of development of LDCs have been based on theories of underdevelopment which were developed mostly in the 1950s and 1960s. There are basically two strands of thoughts and theories explaining economic backwardness: (i) structural-cultural theories and (ii) linear stage theories.

Structural-cultural theories seek to explain underdevelopment in terms of structural factors such as rigidities and inelasticities in the supply of factors, sub-optimal occupation structure, and the inability of the economy to respond to price mechanisms to increase agricultural output and thereby to contain inflation. Underdevelopment in these countries is also explained in terms of market imperfections and sub-optimal allocation of resources. The structural-cultural models also view institutional rigidities responsible for the proliferation of dualism of various types, such as sociological dualism (Boeke), ecological dualism (Geertz), financial dualism (Myint), techno-logical dualism (Higgins) and foreign enclave dualism (Myint) as important constraints for economic development. A dualistic structure makes inter-action among the entities difficult, and stands in the way of progress. Myrdal demonstrates how a growing sector generates *backwash effect* for the underdeveloped sector or region. The *spread effect* of growth/development cannot often be absorbed by the backward sector owing to structural-cultural inhibitions and insulation.

Due to structural inflexibilities, structural adjustment necessary for development often becomes impossible. In the context of limited capital, both physical and human, limited or no modern technology, fixed factor proportions existing in backward economics (Eckaus) lead to overt and covert unemployment and underemployment, particularly in labour-surplus economies. All these may end up with the situation of low income, low saving, low investment, and low income again. This creates a system that begets a vicious circle of poverty among poor nations (Nurkse). Lack of adequate stock of capital and of modern technology stands in the way of exploitation of resources which may be abundant in many backward eco-nomies. Considered from a different perspective, limited income, consump-tion and demand are said to be primarily responsible for limited market investment, employment and income. Thus, both demand and supply sides of the vicious circle can substantiate the fact that poverty generates poverty. Hence, the maxim: a country is poor because it is poor.

Socio-economic behaviour of people in LDCs remains highly culture-bound, and the traditional cultural milieu is found to be partly responsible for economic backwardness. People have low aspiration (Mellor) and limited target level of income, giving rise to backward-sloping supply curve of labour, low productivity, unemployment and underemployment. Too much dependence on fate, and metaphysical belief in other-worldly pursuits, coupled with indifference and ignorance of the materialistic economic calculus, creates a mind-set that easily tends to neglect the importance of population control in LDCs. Needless to say, a very high rate of growth of population has been looked upon as a factor primarily responsible for low per capita income and poverty.[1] The low-level equilibrium trap (Nelson) is found to be one of the main reasons for the perpetuation of economic backwardness. Many theories of development have come to the conclusion that sporadic, inadequate and unbalanced sectoral investment cannot give a sufficient boost to creating a situation of sustainable development. Value system, institution and culture can indeed, to a great extent, be regarded as the basic constraints on growth and development.

Another way in which culture is looked upon as an associated factor impeding economic development is the culture of foreign domination and dependency. The international structuralist model has two main versions: the false paradigm version (Todaro 1977: 91–2) and the colonial dependency models (Samir Amin, Gunder Frank, Emmanuel, Dos Santos, Marini and others). The false paradigm version contends that the advice given by international institutions on economic development of the LDCs is harmful. There is a kernel of truth in the paradigm which is being recognised presently by the Southeast Asian countries which recently went for IMF bailout packages. The dependency theories in general have brought home the fact that the so-called backward countries were indeed rich countries in terms of resource endowments, and that the resources from these foreign-dominated colonies (periphery) had been transferred to the exploitative foreign colonial powers (centres). Dependency has created international dualism that has exacerbated the economic distance between DCs and LDCs.

The distinguishing point of many dependency writers is that they treat the social and economic development of LDCs as being conditioned by external forces: the dominance over LDCs by other powerful DCs. As Gabriel Palma asserts, the most distinguishing feature of dependency theory is its focus on the interplay between internal and external structures in the analysis of underdevelopment (Palma 1985: 139). The main line of analysis of the dependency model is based on two approaches: (i) a surplus extraction approach and (ii) an unequal exchange approach. Frank and Amin, among others, show that the present-day LDCs are underdeveloped because their surplus resources have been taken away by the DCs. Emmanuel and others maintain that there is unequal exchange between DCs and LDCs, and that there is a transfer of value from the latter to the former. LDCs are compelled to sell their goods at prices below their values, and purchase goods from DCs at prices above their values. In the international interaction at many levels, the exploitation still continues unabated. In the pre-industrial revolution period, the DCs used to take away resources from their colonies in the form of physical capital, while in the post-industrial revolution period, they have been draining the human capital resources (brain drain) from LDCs (Ghosh 1999: 46).

The second strand of thought explaining underdevelopment is in terms of *linear stage model* mainly popularised by W.W. Rostow (1960). However, prior to Rostow, Karl Marx in his *theory of social formation* pointed out that there were three important stages of social and economic development that one could encounter before entering into the most progressive stage of capitalist development. These three stages were: primitive communism, slavery and feudalism. In a five-fold classificatory schema of stages of growth, Rostow observed that the LDCs were backward as they were not yet prepared to enter into the stage of perceptible development (take-off) due to lack of required level of saving and investment.[2] The LDCs are dominated by traditional societies and some of them were passing through the stage of pre-conditions for take-off. Thus, to Rostow, each country has to graduate through the natural stages of backwardness before it can finally attain the stage of economic development.

The requirements for development are indeed multi-dimensional, and hence, different theories had to focus on different issues and dimensions. However, it is recognised by all that the most essential need for development and growth is capital accumulation and investment, reminiscent of the classical theory of growth. Many economists including Harrod, Domar and Ragnar Nurkse harped on the need for investment for accelerating economic growth. Harrod and Domar's theory provided a formula for measuring growth: growth is measured by the reciprocal of capital-output ratio times the rate of investment (or saving). The formula is handy and simple, and was later on used both as a growth model and as a planning model. The importance of investment lies in the dual functions that it performs: income generation and capacity creation.

The *threshold theory* suggested that investment would have to be of a critical minimum amount (Leibenstein) so that growth-retarding factors like population explosion and so on can be swamped out by the growth-inducing factors. In this connection, Rosenstein Rodan suggested the theory of big push, and Ragnar Nurkse and H. Leibenstein separately put forward the view that what was essential for sustained development was the strategy of balanced growth for making investment in different sectors mutually supportive. Hans Singer, however, maintained that balanced growth doctrine is applicable only to subsequent stages of sustained growth rather than to the breaking of deadlock (Singer 1958: 10). That investment is the kingpin of growth was also acknowledged by H.W. Singer, W.W. Rostow and Robert Hirschman. But Hirschman prescribed the strategy of unbalanced growth, for he believed that investment in some strategically selected leading sectors creates further investment opportunities, and growth gets momentum through a process of communication from growing points to the stagnant points. However, it was soon realised that the debate between balanced growth and unbalanced growth was based on false consciousness, for there are many common grounds between these so-called two strategies. Paul Streeten (1959 and 1963) contended that it was possible to reformulate the choice between balance and imbalance. As a matter of fact, balanced and unbalanced growth need not be mutually conflicting, and an optimum strategy of development should combine some elements of balance as well as imbalance (Mathur 1966: 137–57).

For quite some time, the discussion on saving/investment became a prominent issue in DE. Ragnar Nurkse expressed his note of optimism for LDCs by pointing out that, although these economies contained a huge amount of disguised unemployment and surplus labour, the stock of redundant labour could be utilised for rural capital formation, and disguised unemployment implied disguised saving potential. However, whereas Nurkse prescribed the strategy of shifting the surplus labour from rural to urban areas, Gunnar Myrdal found the strategy to be quite counterproductive, because the industrial sector in LDCs did not have sufficient pull factor, and could not create sufficient job opportunities for rural labour. Some of the LDCs in Asia did emphasise the development of agriculture for food and fibre, but the realisation of saving potential could not be translated into action. Some of the Southeast Asian countries, prominently Malaysia, placed more emphasis on industrial development and followed a Preobrazhensky-type of model of squeezing agriculture. And labour was withdrawn from agriculture for the development of the industrial sector: the Lewis model was in operation. However, this was not a suitable strategy for the labour-surplus economies of Indonesia, India, Pakistan and Bangladesh.

The question then precisely becomes tangential to the choice of technique. The debate between capital-intensive vs. labour-intensive methods of production became a lively issue in the past, and A.K. Sen made an attempt to resolve the debate by pointing out that no technique of production is always distinctly superior to the other and that there is nothing like a once-for-all choice of technique (Sen 1962: 57).

Harking back to the crucial question of investment, the main pressing issue that was identified was: how to increase saving and investment for higher rate of growth (Rostowian take-off)? Nurkse observed that investment was limited by the extent of the market. Chenery and Strout discussed, in their two-gap model, the two constraints to development, namely, saving constraint and foreign exchange constraint. Since endogenous possibilities for augmenting saving and trade were found to be rather bleak, many theories in DE proposed the importance of foreign aid and foreign trade. Trade was regarded as important not only as a channel for goods and services but also as a channel for new ideas and technology. Many countries adopted the twin policy of export promotion and import substitution, and Schumpeterian risk-takers and innovators got the reward (Bhagwati 1984: 30).

Nevertheless, in the process of interaction through the foreign sector, some countries opened up more than the others and allowed different degrees of liberalisation and privatisation through multinational capitalism and foreign direct investment. Although foreign technology could not be transferred fully to the newly industrialising economies for various reasons, improved technology was made available to augment production and exports.[3] All these made it possible to realise a growth rate of between 8 and 9 per cent per year in the Asia Pacific region, which was nothing short of a miracle (World Bank 1993).

There are indeed many reasons why growth rate differs and why some countries lagged behind while some went ahead of others (Denison 1967). Apart from capital stock, technology, high-quality manpower and the like, the role of state has remained a contributory factor to the process of growth and development. On the basis of resource-use efficiency which ensures efficient utilisation of factors of production, and the level of economic growth which ensures effective direction or channelling of resources, the developing world can broadly be divided into mainly three categories: almost stationary or very slow-moving economies, developing economies and newly industrialising economies. These economies have, accordingly, non-participatory or least participatory state, marginal state, and strong and expansive state (Ghosh 1998: 108–12). The marginal, very weak or unstable states (noodle states) in many Asian countries, including India and Bangladesh, have been found to be responsible for the low rate of economic growth compared to the strong visible hands of states of the ASEAN economies which experienced a high rate of economic growth. According to the World Bank (1993), the economic success of the East Asian economies is, to a large extent, due to the strong power of its states. On the other hand, a weak state remains soft not only in policy formulations but also in policy implementation. And government failure and market failure in such economies are primarily responsible for all sub-optimalities and systemic dysfunction.

Countries where economic development or growth has remained sluggish have in general also experienced a poor structuralist and/or institutionalist role of state; but bureaucracy, on the other hand, gained substantially through the activities of rent-seeking (Krueger 1974), and in some countries, including India, it became a dominant class both economically and politically (Bardhan 1989). In contradistinction to it, in the East Asian economies, where economic growth has remained consistently high for a long period of time, bureaucracy has been found to be rather ineffective and weak.

Paradigm shifts in DE

Ever since its inception as a new subject, DE has been pursuing its basic desideratum of amelioration of poverty, increase in employment and income, elimination of diseases, malnutrition and under-nutrition in the world, especially in the Third World, by means of growth and development. It is in this sense that one can say that there is a continuity of purpose and action sustained by DE over the last fifty years. However, in spite of purposive unicity and continuity, DE has been experiencing new challenges and constraints, and the response to these issues and problems has induced paradigm shifts in the subject which will be discussed in the present section.[4]

The 1950s can be described as a decade of *theoretical innovations* in DE. Many theories of development that were put forward during this period attempted to explain the existence of underdevelopment from various perceptual angles, and accordingly suggested remedies to the problem of backwardness and poverty. The approach was simplistic and non-technical, easily comprehensible by planners and policy-makers. The attainment of economic growth was the fundamental objective set for the Third World countries, for it was presumed that economic growth could automatically solve the problems of poverty, unemployment and other associated problems.

The 1960s are often regarded as the *golden period* and a decade of optimism in development economics (Singer 1997: 16–17). Development was more objectively defined as a blend of growth and change. While new theories of growth and development were forthcoming, some of the old theories and issues were refined and reconciled. Influenced by the Keynesian economic theory, a positive role was assigned to the state to manage economic growth and development. It was thought that foreign aid and technical assistance from DCs would be able to make a dent on poverty and unemployment. Many Third World countries initiated economic planning with gusto and grit but the outcome was not commensurate with the efforts. It was soon realised that despite concerted efforts for a decade, and the realisation of around 5 per cent economic growth by LDCs, the basic problem of poverty and inequality in these countries could not be perceptibly reduced. And on the other hand, the economic gap between DCs and LDCs was widening. The optimism with which the decade started off could not be sustained, and a sense of pessimism entered the arena of DE.

The 1970s can be looked upon as a *decade of reappraisal*. The achievement of 5 per cent rate of growth was not sustainable, and poverty and inequality intensified in most of the poor countries.[5] Economic growth as the basic desideratum of DE was challenged by many economists, and it was thought that blind application of western growth models was not only inappropriate but also harmful, for these caused enormous maldevelopment to LDCs. All these called for *limits to growth*.

At the other end of the spectrum, one could discern growing economic domination by DCs through trade and aid. The debt burden of LDCs started increasing, and it was realised that trade was not the engine of growth; rather, it was a mechanism immiserising growth.[6] The negative externalities of large industrial projects in terms of ecological costs looked conspicuously overwhelming. The new international economic order reflected these issues for the first time.

Basic human needs, including education, health and employment and the like, were regarded as the correct components of development and were reflected in the formulation of a *basic needs approach* to development popularised by the World Bank and the UN Research Institute for Social Development.[7] The agenda for employment generation was the main agenda in this development decade. The most significant achievement of this development decade was the realisation that it was distribution rather than production *per se* which was necessary for ensuring the basic needs required for human development.

The 1980s were characterised as a *lost decade* in development economics for many obvious reasons, of which the following remain important: first, in the course of time, many contradictions became evident in the simplistic economistic paradigm of development (Wignaraja 1997: 81–3). Development became unstable and volatile in many countries (Esteva 1998: 46) and there was an apparent failure of conventional theories of development.

Second, the welfare state of the Keynesian type no longer brought any hope for solving the problems relating to underdevelopment and poverty; and at other end of the continuum, there was a smouldering discontent both against capitalism and socialism for their failure to show a viable road to growth and development in poor countries. Third, while the countries in the South were trying to find out alternative driving forces for socio-economic changes in the desired direction, they constantly castigated the North as responsible for their sad plight: the North–South debate became more vociferous and vitriolic. Fourth, the new international economic order lost its momentum, and could be dubbed as a system of new international economic disorder. Contrary to the expectation of people, less capital and less technology flowed to the LDCs from DCs; and there was also a *reverse transfer of technology* from the poor to the rich countries. Fifth, there was an apparent disillusionment with aid and trade as mechanisms for helping the desired process of development. Both trade and aid became means for *surplus extraction* from the poor countries. The temper of the time suggested alternative strategies for people's empowerment, participation and grass-roots development with top-down planning processes, settlement of gender conflict, elimination of, or at least a reduction in, ecological imbalance, and a powerful civil society that could bring about social changes.

Thus, there were indeed many types of debates, conflicts, issues and questions during the decade. But there were no synthesis and solutions in the offing, and neither was there any new consensus on the feasible strategic action and direction. In the words of W.A. Lewis, development economics was in 'a complete doldrums'.

The 1990s will go down in the annals of DE as the decade of *new vision and new direction*. The decade has witnessed attempts for redevelopment after years of maldevelopments in the Third World countries. The entire development process so far based on state planning and patronage came in for serious criticism, and more reliance was placed on the market as an organising mechanism for global relations (Harcourt 1997: 5–8). Privatisation, which was already on the agenda in many developing countries, occupied the front seat in terms of priority. But towards the end of the decade, the limitations of free market mechanism came to the surface with the financial crisis of the East Asian economies. Perhaps it was a new perception. Economic underpinnings of the development paradigms came once again under critical scrutiny with the feminist movement taking the lead (O'Connell 1997: 119–20). Instigated by the Beijing conference of 1995, the whole gamut of issues concerning gender was recast, and the earlier notion of *women in development* was replaced by the more comprehensive issue of *gender and development*.

There has been mounting pressure from the Third World to reform the UN, to democratise the WTO, and to make the international institutions more accountable and transparent in their dealings. It was realised that the old institutions like the IMF and World Bank need structural changes to effectively deal with the financial crisis of the Asian countries. The civil society movement which was prominent in the early 1990s became very positive and innovative in its agenda for action, asking for all-round policy changes both within and without. Globalisation was the most publicised and confused slogan in this decade. It reminds one of the exploitative globalisation of the nineteenth century, and many well-informed groups have been trying to spin away from it because MNC-led globalisation may unleash a regime of unequal competition between DCs and LDCs, and this may be destructive to economic and social development processes. These groups are engaged in achieving self-sufficiency and autonomy while recognising limits to competition in the globalised world. The focus, however, shifted from the question of underdevelopment to the problem caused by industrial development. Human and social dimensions of development, which were emphasised in international conferences from 1992 to 1996, are going to get the upper hand, and are likely to be the basic theme song of DE in the new millennium.

The future of DE

DE, as it appears, has not yet outlived its utility, and economists do strongly feel that there is a dire need for the discipline. If this is correct, then DE has a future. Most of the fundamental prescriptions of traditional DE are still valid today. For instance, what Hans Singer was emphasising as the mechanics of development in the early 1950s (i.e. the importance of a higher rate of saving and investment and the need for changes in the occupational distribution of population for economic development) does still retain its prescriptive value (Singer 1952). As A.K. Sen observes, the broad policy themes of traditional DE are still relevant, and the discipline of DE does have a central role to play in the field of economic growth in developing countries, and its problematic is rather limited (Sen 1983: 753 and 745). Albert Hirschman also believes that conditions for healthy growth of DE seem to be remarkably favourable: the problem of world poverty is not yet solved, but encouraging in-roads to the problem have been and are being made (Hirschman 1986: 3).

Sen has argued that in the past the scope of DE was very narrow, concentrating too much on growth and too little on development (Sen 1983 and 1989). DE has been less successful in characterising development involving human capabilities. Development has to be interpreted in terms of human participation, empowerment, entitlement, justice, equality and freedom. To segregate human consideration from DE is like playing *Hamlet* without the Prince of Denmark. Development does not necessarily mean that one should have more but that one should be more. This concept of development, which would predominate in future, implies human development as opposed to the meaningless amassing of material goods for meta-needs.

To be precise, DE will have to consider the following substantive issues in future which have been rather neglected in the past:[9] (i) the issues and problems relating to human development; (ii) the study of institutions and their dimensions: exogenous/endogenous, functional/dysfunctional, and the capability of the institutions to absorb the shock of market failure which is very pervasive in LDCs (Knight 1991: 21); (iii) various dimensions of technology and technology transfer need to be studied by DE in order to assess their impact on economic development – the causes and effects of low technology equilibrium, and the possibilities for reverse engineering, also need careful study; (iv) it would be imperative to make more detailed analysis of the causes and consequences of government failures and market failures in LDCs. Why is privatisation successful in some countries while it is not extensively practised in others? Why is it that some states can pursue effective development policies and some do not (Bardhan 1988). Development economists need to know the nature, policy and motivation of governments and the rent-seeking bureaucratic behaviour in different types of economies, and the impact of *dirigisme* on development and underdevelopment. Such a type of study analysing the tension between government failures and market failures belongs to the area of political economy; (v) the study of various constructive and destructive dimensions of globalisation on development, including the issues on accountability, equity and democratisation, could occupy quite some time in the new millennium. And along with this would be the need to re-examine the political economy of international institutions and of North–South relations with respect to issues involving human rights, technology transfer, ecology, trade and so on. It is very likely that political economy of development would emerge as a more powerful and promising area of DE for studying the phenomenology of both national and international events.

The aforesaid issues cannot always be properly visualised and appreciated through the dazzling light of formal theoretical analysis, which may blur the vision. These need to be studied by DE through empirical analysis, and microeconomic methodologies may often have to be pressed into service. Moreover, to realise the truth value, the DE may have to cross the traditional boundaries of economics, and thus have to be transcendental and eclectic in approach.

On the question of methodology, DE will have two alternatives to choose from. First, if DE is to be a strong and pure academic discipline, it has to be more sophisticated and rigorous in its approach without being vitiated by soft and simple methodological reductionism. Second, however, if it has to be interdisciplinary, which it is, then it will have many methodological trade-offs. In future, the second possibility seems to be more appropriate for the survival and expansion of DE. As a matter of fact, the disciplinary boundaries between economics and other disciplines cannot be regarded as sacrosanct (Toye 1985: 13).

Concluding observations

In the movie *Casablanca*, the police chief, when something goes wrong, always gives an order to round up the usual suspects. This has somehow become the public attitude towards DE. When something goes wrong, or a specific development objective (say, poverty reduction) cannot be achieved, there is often a general proclivity to put the blame squarely on DE, although, conceivably, it does not have any complicity. Be that as it may, DE is an evolutionary subject, and one can learn many positive lessons from it either as a practitioner, or a policy-maker, or as a researcher. A few of these lessons may be mentioned here by way of *obiter dicta,* which need to be kept in mind while evaluating the performance of DE.

First, no policy, strategy or theory can have universal applicability in analysing development-related problems, and there is no once-for-all solution to the problem of underdevelopment. Second, economic development has many facets and dimensions, and therefore it can be studied from different perspectives: economic, social, political and so on. Third, DE has helped us to understand and differentiate between many myths and realities through its empirical epistemics. For instance, for so long Malthusian theory taught us that overpopulation is the fundamental cause of poverty. However, DE has given us a new insight that in many developing countries poverty is not caused by higher population growth, but that higher population is induced by poverty. Despite economic growth, there may be poverty and social underdevelopment, and even some amount of unemployment and underemployment. We must recognise the unpalatable fact that we have reached the age of the end of full employment, and this seems to be an irreversible phenomenon. Fourth, the issues relating to human development are indeed convoluted issues, and it would be too much to judge the success or failure of DE in terms of its ability to solve human problems. The solution to these problems is a function of political will, resource availability, policy parameters and their implementations, over which DE *qua* DE has hardly had any influence. Economic decisions are essentially political in nature.

In a very controversial monograph, Deepak Lal has asserted that the demise of DE is likely to be conducive to the health of both the economics and the economies of LDCs (Lal 1983: 109).[10] While it is not the purpose of the present discussion to enter into polemical dialectics over this subjective effusion, in view of what has been adumbrated in the earlier section, and from the quantity and quality of meaningful research in the subject, it can be reiterated with the words of Arthur W. Lewis that development economics is still alive and well (Lewis 1984: 10). As an interdisciplinary subject, its umbilical cord is tied with a number of closely interactive social sciences from which DE will be able to draw the necessary *élan vital* for its sustenance. An interdisciplinary subject never dies, though its lustre may fade in the course of time.

It would be rather sacrilegious to contend, as many economists really do, that no good theories or studies are coming up in DE any more, and that the milk cow has already dried up. To get out of this kind of intellectual myopia, one really needs to see the good work being published in academic journals like the *Journal of Development Studies, Economic Development and Cultural Change* and the *Journal of Development Economics*, to name only a few, and also the books on DE from international publishers. The subject is still making significant contributions of a reputable academic standard, and like a lady's word, the final word in development economics should not be taken as the last word.

Notes

1 The positive relationship between population growth and poverty was first brought out by the Malthusian theory of population. The theory propagated the idea that overpopulation is responsible for poverty, unemployment, famine and so on. However, many studies in development economics have brought home the fact that it is poverty which is responsible for higher population growth

2 According to Rostow, take-off will require a productive investment of over 10 per cent of national income. He estimated that a 2 per cent per annum increase in net national product per capita would require a regular investment of 10.5 to 12.5 per cent of the net national product.

3 One of the reasons for the low degree of technology transfer (TT) is the low and limited capability of the local workers to absorb the technology (Ghosh 1998b: 155). Other reasons include the high cost of technology transfer, and in some cases, the technology suppliers are rather reluctant to transfer technology. Our study of TT in electronics, electrical and supportive industries in Penang (Malaysia) came to the conclusion that while the rooting process of TT is quite satisfactory, the diffusion effect of the acquired technology was not very perceptible in Malaysia (Narayanan *et al.* 1994).

4 The major achievements and failures of DE have been elaborated on by many academic journals, see *Development* (March, 1997) and *Development Practice* (August, 1998), among others.

5 For instance, poverty intensified in India and China. In India, poverty increased from 34 per cent in 1960–1 to 52 per cent in 1972–3. Jan Myrdal's study showed that poverty increased in China after the end of the 1960s (Myrdal 1966).

6 For an elaboration on the idea of immiserising growth, see Bhagwati (1958).

7 The basic needs included physical and cultural needs. The basic needs approach can be regarded as social indicators of development. Initially, the following six basic needs were considered: nutrition, basic education, health, sanitation, water supply and housing and related infrastructure (Hicks and Streeten 1979).

8 The UNCTAD Report (1974) observed that US foreign aid to LDCs amount to $3.1 billion in 1970; but the income gained by the United States through brain drain, the seed-corn technology, amounted to $3.7 billion in the same year. The study makes it quite clear that it is really the poor countries which are, on balance, aiding the rich developed countries, and not the other way round (Ghosh 1999: 46).

9 Most of the issues considered here are also elaborated on by J.B. Knight (1991), John Toye (1985), P. Bardhan (1988) and others.

10 Deepak Lal's frontal attack against the *dirigiste* dogma highlighting pro-government controls and anti-price mechanism in the 1960s is no longer valid

now. Moreover, the present-day world has been really experiencing the limitation of free market mechanism, and hence, the need for some amount of government control, supervision and direction. DE has experienced both government failures and market failures. Therefore, a mixed economy type of model in DE seems to be more appropriate; but all these do not imply the demise of DE

References

Bardhan, P. (1988) 'Alternative approaches to development economics', in H. Chenery and T.N. Srinivasan (eds), *Handbook of Development Economics*, vol. 1, Amsterdam: North Holland.

—— (1989) 'The third dominant class', *Economic and Political Weekly,* 21 January.

Bhagwati, J.N. (1958) 'Immiserising growth: a geometrical note', *Review of Economic Studies*, June.

—— (1984) 'Development economics: what have we learned?', Asian *Development Review*, vol. 2, no. 1.

Denison, E.F. (1967) *Why Growth Rates Differ*, Washington, DC: The Brookings Institution.

Esteva, Gustavo and Madhu, Suri Prakash (1998) 'Beyond development, what?', *Development in Practice*, August.

Ghosh, B.N. (1998a) *A Tale of Two Economies*, Delhi: New Academic Publishers.

—— (1998b) *Malaysia: The Transformation Within*, Kuala Lumpur: Longman.

—— (1999), 'Brain Drain', in Phillip O'Hara (ed.) *Encyclopedia of Political Economy*, London and New York: Routledge.

Harcourt, Wendy (1997) 'The search for social justice', *Development*, vol. 40, no. 1.

Hicks, Norman and Paul Streeten (1979) 'Indicators of development', *World Development*, June.

Hirschman, Albert (1986) 'The rise and decline of development economics', *Development,* vol. 3, p. 3.

Knight, J.B. (1991) 'The evolution of development economics', in V.N. Balasubramanyam and Sanjay Lall (eds) *Current Issues in Development Economics*, London: Macmillan.

Krueger, A.O. (1974) 'The political economy of the rent-seeking society', *American Economic Review*, vol. LXIV, June.

Lal, Deepak (1983) *The Poverty of Development Economics*, Hovart Paperback, London: Institute of Economic Affairs.

Lewis, W.A. (1984) 'The state of development theory', *American Economic Review*, vol. 74, no. 1 (March), pp. 1–10.

Mathur, Ashok (1966) 'Balanced vs. unbalanced growth', *Oxford Economic Papers*, July, pp. 137–57.

Myrdal, Jan (1966) *Report from a Chinese Village*, USA: Signet Book Edition.

Narayanan, Suresh, Lai, Yew Wah, Ghosh, B.N., Omar, Ismail and Fatah, Abdul (1994) *Technology Transfer to Malaysia*, Kuala Lumpur: UNDP.

O'Connell, Helen (1997) 'The 1990s: new alliances, new directions', *Development*, March, pp. 119–20.

Palma, Gabriel (1985) 'Dependency theory of underdevelopment', in G.M. Meier (ed.), *Leading Issues in Economic Development,* London: Oxford University Press.

Rostow, W.W. (1960) *The Stages of Economic Growth: A Non-Communist Manifesto*, London: Cambridge University Press.

Sen, A.K. (1962) *The Choice of Technique*, Oxford: Blackwell.
—— (1983) 'Development: which way now?', *Economic Journal*, vol. 93, pp. 745–62.
—— (1989) 'Development as capability expansion', *Journal of Development Planning*, vol. 19, pp. 41–58.
Singer, Hans W. (1952) 'The mechanics of economic development,' *Indian Economic Review*, August, pp. 397–9.
—— (1958), 'The concept of balanced growth and economic development', University of Texas Conference, April.
—— (1997), 'The 1960s: a decade of optimism', *Development,* vol. 40, no.1, March.
Stern, N. (1989) 'The economics of development: a survey', *Economic Journal*, vol. 99, pp. 597–685.
Streeten, P. (1959) 'Unbalanced growth', *Oxford Economic Papers,* June.
—— (1963) 'Balanced versus unbalanced growth,' *Economic Weekly,* April.
Todaro, M.P. (1977) *Economics for a Developing World*, London: Longman.
Toye, John (1985) 'Dirigisme and development economics', *Cambridge Journal of Economics, vol. 9*, March, pp. 1–44.
Wignaraja, Ponna (1997) 'The 1980s: seeds for change', *Development*, March 1997.
World Bank (1993), *The East Asian Miracle*, London: Oxford University Press.

2 Human development, military expenditure and social wellbeing

Masudul Alam Choudhury

Human Development Index

Introduction

What is the Human Development Index? The *Human Development Report* of the UNDP defines it as the statistical measure that indicates the degree to which the experience of development in various countries is contributing to enlarging 'human capabilities and functionings' (UNDP 1998). The underlying assumption is that socio-economic development involves a large and expanding spectrum of factors that are not purely economic in nature as the neoclassical orientation to the study of resource allocation would make us believe. On the contrary, development is the result of a spectrum of interactions among factors ranging from economic to ethical, social and institutional ones, all of which must be brought together in a cogent way within a systems approach to the study of the interactions that ensue as these various factors feedback and interrelate with each other through the universal perspective of a general system.

Background

The study of social, economic and political factors in economic theory is not a new undertaking. Yet the methodological orientation of this body of conceptualization and its application in that light make a substantive difference from the way that ethics is treated in neoclassical economic theory and all those parts of economic theory affected by their intrinsic dependence on economic rationality, marginalism and optimization criteria. The fact of the matter is that the presence of such seemingly, though not essentially, interdisciplinary social, institutional, political and ethical factors interrelate in a vastly interactive way in today's study of global issues and problems.

A good example of the above case is that of financial volatility that recently plagued the global order. Here we find a combination of institutional, political, ethical and economic factors combining to cause the uncertainties that have left so many ruined. If we are to study the so-called economics of trust and honest business ethics as defined in terms of transparency of business activities, structural policy and organizational reform to control wastage and non-performing loans in giant projects (IMF 1999), we must consider preference changes under the effects of appropriate policies. Such preferences are then of the endogenous nature as they give rise to and are enforced by underlying normative issues of reform that ought to be taken up by institutions. On the other hand, the analyst must take stock of the crony capitalism and speculative behaviour of large investors who deal in portfolio investments, move funds at will across national economies and take advantage of the IMF's Capital Accounts Liberalization program (Fisher 1997), the OECD's Multilateral Agreement on Investments, and the WTO's binding clauses affecting TRIMs and TRIPs (SESRTCIC and ICDT 1994).

On the macroeconomic front we note that a $20 billion-plus flight of capital from East Asian economies has led these countries into a long-term instability of costly structural adjustment and downsizing in government spending. The *Human Development Report 1998* (UNDP 1998) points out that even though the fortunate rich have gained from globalization in terms of increasing consumption, this has been to the detriment of the poor:

> The poorest 20% of the world's people and more have been left out of the consumption explosion. Well over a billion people are deprived of basic consumption needs. Of the 4.4 billion people in developing countries, nearly three-fifths lack basic sanitation. Almost a third have no access to clean water. A quarter does not have adequate housing. A fifth have no access to modern health services. A fifth of children do not attend school to grade 5, and so on in the list of deprivation.

To this human deprivation is to be added the spectre of long-term unemployment and falling GDP per capita that has followed the recent financial crisis in many of the East Asian economies even after their two to three decades of economic progress. Structural downsizing of institutions has caused a sudden withdrawal of social services, health services and subsidies to the needy citizens. The result has been increasing poverty levels.

The debt burden has remained almost everywhere too high in the least developed countries. For instance, in the heavily indebted countries of sub-Saharan Africa debt is higher than their GNP levels. These countries spent more in debt repayments than their export earnings. That is, the official development assistance that came into these countries for developmental purposes was reversed in payments of outstanding debt. Even on the face of debt repayment, the debt stock of the sub-Saharan African countries increased by $33 billion. Consequently, we note that a large proportion of the IMF loans paid to these debt-ridden countries is found to reverse in the form of debt payments. The social sector remains impoverished.

Macroeconomic stabilization of the external sector of indebted countries, as well as of those devastated by the incidence of financial turmoil arising from the use of monetary and trade-related policies at the expense of fiscal expansion, has proven to be ineffective and risky. This is particularly due to the unpredictable relationship existing between interest rate movement and the exchange rate volatility in developing countries affected by the financial crisis (Obstfeld 1998). There has failed to be any predictable relationship between these two indicators as short-term interest rate movements are hinged on prime rates set in the industrial countries and by the intent to engender motivation to hold and generate savings at home.

The motivation to hold interest rates high in the face of low exchange rate regimes is once again driving the afflicted countries of East Asia towards their traditional economic growth-oriented goals. Yet it was this very goal that lay behind the cause of the economic and financial turmoil in these countries as economic growth relied predominantly on loanable capital and portfolio investments. Both of these were endemic in causing massive debts and speculative investments rather than real sectoral developments in the national economies. The uncertainty of economic growth as a national policy goal is found to be once again fraught with the spectre of that kind of economic and financial frailty which only recently caused the financial and economic collapse of the East Asian economies even after their two to three decades of unprecedented non-inflationary economic growth.

Besides, economic growth in a neoclassical economic framework means delayed attention to the social sector that may never return if uncertainties ride the crest of future economic change. This kind of marginal substitution between economic growth and distributive equity as a goal of attaining economic efficiency that contests with the goal of distributive equity, has remained embedded in the East Asian economic model. Consequently, macroeconomic stabilization policies in the framework of a growth model of economic recovery lose their effectiveness with the use of monetary and trade-related policies that favour savings and investments of short-term capital at the cost of fiscal policy. Monetary policy favouring the trend to privatization looks for short-run profitability. The result is highly unstable capital flows into speculative and risky portfolios. In Malaysia, for instance, growth-oriented development planning, the accumulation of external debt caused by the pressure of capital-intensive economic expansion, a steep increase in speculative portfolio investments, resulted in the financial crisis of the Kuala Lumpur Stock Exchange. This ultimately caused the unit trusts held by the poor (*Amanah Saham Bumiputeras*) to be steeply devalued in the KLSE. Poverty alleviation and economic sensitivity were not sustained.

Thus we find that the prescribed global economic policies proved to foster an adverse selection game played by national governments and their citizenry as they entered global regimes with long-term binding commitments on policy clauses. The so-called economics of adverse selection in the case of global financial volatility became an interplay of factors affecting malevolent preferences of large speculative investors, the preferences of smaller-scale followers who adopt herding behaviour, of institutional enforcement of the uncertain regimes that ensue, and the costly consequences that adversely affect the long-term economic recovery of nations. Some have identified a problem of 'trilemma' in global financial integration in terms of the goals of greater integration, proper economic management and national sovereignty. It is the national sovereignty that remains in tradeoff with the other two complementary goals (Summers 1999).

The same kinds of implications as mentioned above can be associated with the enormous amount being spent in military expenditure in the Middle Eastern countries in spite of their claim that this establishes stability and thereby economic growth. There are serious implications on social wellbeing that need to be examined here in the light of the alternative allocations of military expenditure that can be realized. Yet one needs to be cautious here, because military expenditure in many of the Middle Eastern countries is a repercussion of the status quo established in the region by the self-interested governments of the West.

Objective

Our objective in this paper is to delineate a general systems outlook on socio-economic development studied by means of the composite human development indices. The composite indexes associated with the Human Development Index (HDI) are the Human Poverty Index (HPI), the Gender-related Index (GDI) and the Gender Empowerment Index (GEI) (UNDP 1998).

We will explain the interrelationship between the human development related indices and these with socio-economic development in the context of studying a holistic system of interactions. This will carried out by means of the social wellbeing criterion function. We will explain this substantive concept and the systemic interrelationships within the framework of the political economy of development, meaning the study of interrelationships among economic, social, ethical and institutional factors underlying the human development spectrum.

Definitions of terms

We will first define the indices related to human development in order to set the scene for the analytical part of this paper.

Human Development Index is the combined index of life expectancy at birth, the adult literacy rate, combined enrolment ratio and the adjusted GDP per capita in purchasing power parity (PPP$). The HDI is computed by UNDP (1998) using the formula,

$$\text{HDI} = (\text{actual } x_i \text{ value} - \text{minimum } x_i \text{ value})/(\text{maximum } x_i \text{ value} - \text{minimum } x_i \text{ value}),$$

where x_i denotes the value for the factor under consideration among, i=life expectancy, adult literacy rate, enrolment rate, adjusted GDP (PPP$). The income variable is discounted at the threshold world average income level. For details one may refer to the Human Development Report.

Corresponding to the formula for HDI is also the *Gender-related Development Index*, GDI. For details in the computation of this measure one can refer to the HD Report.

Human Poverty Index, HPI, is a composite of the following factors:

1   percentage of people not expected to survive to the age of 40 years for developing countries (P_1) (60 for industrialized countries) (P_1);
2   illiteracy rate ('functional illiteracy rate' for industrialized countries) (P_2);
3   economic deprivation indicated by percentage of people not having access to fresh water and health services, and percentage of underweight children under the age of five (P_3).

For developing countries the HPI is computed by, HPI-1=$[1/3(P_1+P_2+P_3)]^{1/3}$. Likewise for industrialized countries, HPI-2=$[1/3(P_1+P_2+P_3+P_4)]^{1/3}$, where, P_4 denotes the rate of long-term unemployment.

Gender Empowerment Measure, GEM, is calculated by the percentage shares of men and women in managerial, administrative, professional and technical jobs, and parliamentary positions, and the shares of earned income in agricultural and non-agricultural activities to average wages and earnings.

Clearly, the issues of health and vital statistics, earning power, distribution in economic opportunities by earnings, empowerment and gainful employment together with both the contribution of such factors to GDP per capita as well as the effect that GDP per capita has on these factors, form a gamut of interconnected variables. Such an interrelationship can be understood with the help of Figure 2.1.

In Figure 2.1, elements such as 'human activities' and 'environment and natural resources' denote boxes of inherent variables. The 'agents' box is shown. The circular flow of arrows denote interactions among agents, variables and the relations formed by such variables.

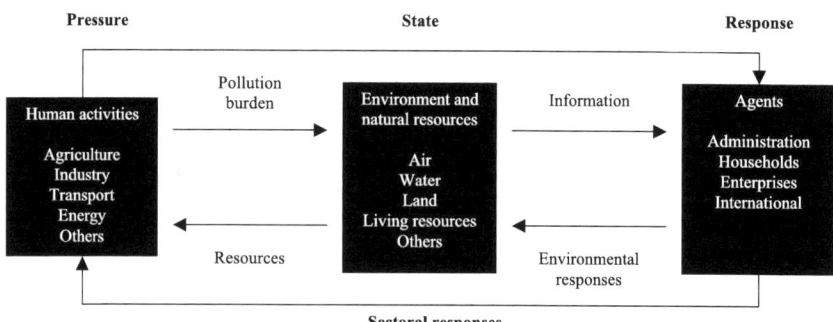

Figure 2.1 Systemic interactions among agents, variables and their relations.
Source: OECD 1994. Environmental Indicators (Paris, France).

The social wellbeing criterion function

The kind of systemic understanding of the organization of change in human interrelations as depicted in Figure 2.1 is referred to by Drucker as 'the society of organizations' (Drucker 1998). However, our concept of an organization is that of a system of regulated and predictable interrelationships among the agents and variables of change. This feature makes the learning process of an organization depend upon continuously emerging complementarity among the interactive factors. Such a knowledge-sharing among agents, variables and their relations is derived from the balancing ingredients of shared welfare, cost-effectiveness and both risk as well as product diversification. The latter reduces unit costs of generating organizational possibilities by extending sharing, creativeness and innovations among agents and projects (Choudhury 1998).

From this underlying principle of universal complementarity (Choudhury 1996) arises the substantive concept of social wellbeing, which we choose in this paper as the criterion for the evaluation of human development. Social Wellbeing Function is the objective criterion function for studying complementarity among the coordinated and knowledge-sharing variables, agents and relations of the organization or the system under examination. Such a mass of interrelationships leads to the simulation of the social wellbeing function through interactions among the variables. Agents, variables and their relations form a general systems approach to the study of the political economy of social wellbeing or human development.

The interactions existing among the variables imply the configurations shown in Figure 2.1. They carry with them the different elements of human development as mentioned earlier. Finally, when the general systems-oriented interactive phenomenon feeds into a discursively human environment in its relationship with the expanding domain of enlarging human possibilities, then a predictable and evolving knowledge-induced objective criterion of the common good is attained. The objective criterion that is formed out of the underlying dynamics of such a 'globally' interactive, integrative and evolutionary system of knowledge-sharing among the variables, agents and their relations, is termed in this paper as the Social Wellbeing Function. A good account of the ethical perspectives of social wellbeing as a deontological function for public policy making is provided by Sen (1991).

Social wellbeing as so understood is a criterion premised on the principle of universal complementarity among the variables, agents and their interrelations. It is thereby a combination of the positive and normative criteria of social evaluation. In the case of human development, the concept of social wellbeing defines the choices that society makes in terms of establishing complementarity among the factors that define the various indexes as defined earlier. The extended context of complementarity is realized by the choices of technology, modes of production, preferences on consumption and the social as well as the institutional framework that enhance these possibilities. The context here is at once of a national and a global one in the midst of the vastly interactive, integrative and evolutionary framework of learning among the knowledge-induced variables, agents and their relations. This kind of momentum provides the inner dynamics of the general systems framework of the interactive, integrative and creatively evolutionary feature that characterizes the social wellbeing criterion.

The concept of social welfare as found in the literature of welfare economics and social choice theory (Arrow 1963) is quite different from that of social wellbeing. That is because of the intrinsic marginal rate of substitution found entrenched in the entire theoretical and hence public policy context of social welfare. Even in the case of public goods in such a neoclassical objective criterion function, the method of resource allocation within public goods and between public goods and private goods is based on the tradeoff principle of marginal rate of substitution between these goods taken up in bundles of contestable goods. This feature of marginalism becomes indispensable in neoclassical resource allocation because it is overwhelmed by the optimization, steady-state equilibrium and price-determination conditions of a social welfare optimization model. This feature remains intact even in the case of a multi-objective general system of constrained dynamic maximization model (Bellman 1957). In the end, therefore, the essential presence and continuous learning by knowledge-sharing that remains as the fundamental causation of interactions, integration and creative evolution of human possibilities, dissipates under the terminal condition of optimality and equilibrium. Human innovation ends (Shackle 1971).

Optimal resource allocation in the case of social welfare, social choice and their applications requires the axiom of economically rational behaviour. Besides, the pre-condition of economic rationality is necessary for the existence of terminal optimal-equilibrium points. In the case of extending such preferences to the institutional context, we learn from the comments made by Whittaker (1987) on Arrow's theory of organization (1974), and from the organizational perspectives of Simon's models of man (1957), that the learning capacity which leads to continuous systemic complementarity by a combination of the normative actions of public policy and their positive effects in the world of organization, remains impervious in social welfare and social choice models. Whereas, they remain pervasive in the social wellbeing model. The only exception in the social wellbeing function with respect to the cessation of continuous learning behaviour and its complementing effect on variables, agents and their relations is for the instantaneous short run. But this is an exceptional case that is of little interest in general equilibrium systems under the effect of knowledge-induction characterizing global issues.

A formal presentation of the social wellbeing function of human development

A formal way of looking at the general systems outlook with respect to the Social Wellbeing Function, $SW(.)$, incorporating human development indices can be represented as follows:

Simulate $\{\theta\} \ SW(h_1, h_2, h_3, h_4)[\theta]$,   (1)

Subject to $h_i = f_i \ (h_j, h_k, h_l)[\theta]$,

where h_r denotes the various human development indices as defined above with, $r = i, j, k, l = $ HDI, GDI, GEM, HP, and $i \neq j \neq k \neq l$.

$f_i(.)$ denotes functional interrelations among the various human development indices as shown.

θ denotes the knowledge-sharing variable. Knowledge appears in the general system as ordinal values assigned institutionally or by systems modelling to the interactions that pervade continuously among agents, variables and their relations.

The appearance of $[\theta]$-value indicates the universal knowledge induction of the human development indices by the underlying knowledge-sharing variable. An example of this is shown in Figure 2.1.

Finer disaggregations of the above functional relations, agents and variables can be obtained by going to detailed levels in the variables that characterize the various human development indices. This presents a meaning of decentralization that arises from finer decision-making and complementary processes with increasingly complex system of interrelationships.

An example of interactions among the h_r-indexes is the following: total HDI can be enhanced by cooperative economic activities generated among genders. A cooperative enterprise between the rich and poor in secondary lines of production and projects ultimately leads to an improvement in skills and human resource development, which thereby alleviates poverty. Increased skills and human resource development in turn increase productive economic activities that lead to higher earnings, more employment and enterprise. Consequently, gender empowerment is attained; increased GDP per capita results. The higher values of HDI in turn feed into more resource mobilization in attaining the same kinds of diversity in the reinforcing cycles of interrelationships.

Yet nothing of this is a sheer automatic market process. Rather, markets are coordinated with the institutional norms and public policies to guide the systemic transformation processes. Every response in terms of enhanced resource mobilization engendering more of the same interactions is the result of the knowledge-sharing process between institutions, agents, variables and their dynamic knowledge-induced interrelationships.

The interactive implications of Figure 2.1 are once again seen here in the context of human development. Every circular flow is marked by the attainment of convergent θ-values that comes about by interactions among many such knowledge values and emerging diversity of human possibilities. These convergent θ-values mark regimes of social consensus on given issues under discourse. The continuity of the circular interrelations at higher levels of realization of resource mobilization is the meaning of creative evolution. Such a creative evolution is to be understood as the ethical relationship of present with future generations as well as the ways and modes of organizing the present generation in terms of its priorities on production, consumption and distribution of a common good. Dynamic relations embedded in creative evolution are thereby both time-induced (intergenerational) and knowledge-induced (intra-generational in terms of prevailing interactions) (Inglott 1990). In this way, a knowledge-induced general systems model gets embedded in the three inherent essentials. Namely, interactions lead to integration; these two lead to creative evolution (thus the IIE-process) (Choudhury 1993a).

Simulation results in a general system of the social wellbeing function

In order to incorporate the principle of complementarity and the IIE-process of the knowledge-induced social wellbeing model we will take the simulation system (1) in the form,

simulate $SW = h_1{}^{a(1)} . h_2{}^{a(2)}$.

We can rewrite this as,

$$SW^{1/a(2)} = SW' = h_1{}^{a(1)/a(2)} . h_2 \tag{2}$$

as a monotonic function of θ-values.

$a(1) = (h_1/SW)(dSW/dh_1)$.

$a(2) = (h_2/SW)(dSW/dh_2)$.

Between $a(1)$ and $a(2)$ we obtain

$$a(1)/a(2) = (h_1/h_2).(dh_2/dh_1) = dlogh_2/dlogh_1. \tag{3}$$

$\theta \; \varepsilon \; [0,10]$

Since $a(1)$ and $a(2)$ are positive parameters influenced by the underlying θ-values, therefore, h_1 and h_2 change in complementary fashion with each other. Let h_1 denote HDI; h_2 denote HPI. Thus expressions (2) and (3) form a complementary system that can be subjected to the underlying θ-values that can assume continuously ordinal values between 0 and 10. This ordinality may be changed for another one. Thus according to the simulation of θ-values with the resulting h_1 and h_2 values determined consequently under a mix of market forces, institutional guidance and public policies, $a(1)/a(2)$ values can be targeted and the simulation of SW', subject to the θ-values and the h_1 and h_2 values, carried out. Normative relations between θ-values and the h_1 and h_2 values would make these variables monotonically increasing functions of θ-values.

To exemplify the simulation process, we assume a starting value for SW' (Indonesia) corresponding to $h_1 = 0.668$ and $h_2 = 0.208$ for the year 1994. The value of $a(1)/a(2)$ is found to be -0.1758 in view of the h-values given by the *Human Development Report 1997* and *1998*.

Next with a proper mix of social and economic policies, institutional coordination in the process of decision-making with endogenous changes in the preferences of households and producers on the nature of goods and services in demand and supply, θ-values get simulated. Consequently, the values of $a(1)/a(2)$ and of h_1 and h_2 vary monotonically with the θ-values. This is done by setting a range of values for $a(1)/a(2)$ by observing the values for $dlogh_2/dlogh_1 =$ (percentage change in h_2)/ (percentage change in h_1) in recent years.

For the period 1994–5, the *Human Development Report 1997* and *1998* yield $dlogh_2/dlogh_1 = -0.0029/0.0165 = -0.1758$ Consequently, the simulated value of SW' is determined. In general we obtain the simulation system,

$$SW' = SW^{1/a(2)} = h_1^{a(1)/a(2)}. \ h_2 = h_1^{-0.1758}. \ h_2$$

For $h_1 = 0.668$, $h_2 = 0.208$, $SW' = 0.208 \times 0.668^{-0.1758}$. We will consider this as our stage 1 of the simulation corresponding to the ordinal value of $\theta = 1$.

In stage 2 for the ordinal assignment of $\theta = 0$, $h_1 = 0.679$, $h_2 = 0.202$, $SW' = 0.202 \times 0.679^{-0.1758}$. Here the choice of θ is below that for the first stage because SW'(stage 2) $< SW'$(stage 1).

Alternatively, in the context of further simulating a normative value of the above-mentioned values, we may choose $dlogh_2/dlogh_1 = 1$. Consequently, for $h_1 = 0.679$, $h_2 = 0.202$, $SW' = h_1.h_2 = 0.1372$. We will consider this to be stage 3 of our simulation corresponding to the ordinal value of $\theta = 3$, for now $SW'(\theta = 3) > SW'(\theta = 1)$.

Such a simulation of the human development values would proceed with other recursive choices in accordance with the human development focus and in the context of prevailing policy/institutional conditions in Indonesia with the knowledge-forming ordinal values being assigned, such as $\theta = \theta^*$.

The computed values corresponding to one such simulation is given in Figure 2.2.

Stage 1:
$[\theta = 1, h_1 = 0.668, h_2 = 0.208, a(1)/a(2) = -0.1758; \ SW'(1) = 0.208 \times 0.668^{-0.1758}]$
↓

Stage 2:
$[\theta = 2, h_1 = 0.679, h_2 = 0.202, a(1)/a(2) = -0.1758; \ SW' = 0.202 \times 0.679^{-0.1758}]$
↓

Stage 3:
$[\theta = 3, h_1 = 0.679, h_2 = 0.202, a(1)/a(2) = 1; \ SW' = 0.1372]$
Here $a(1)/a(2) = 1$ is assumed as a target value for $\theta = 3$,
indicating that poverty index is directly responding to gains in human development index.

Stage 4:
$[\theta = 4, h_1 = 0.681, h_2 = 0.277, a(1)/a(2) = 1; \ SW' = 0.1886]$
etc.

Figure 2.2 Simulation of a social wellbeing function with HDI estimates.

Source: Human Development Report 1999.

Clearly $SW'(\theta=2)<SW'(\theta=1)$; but $SW'(\theta=3)>SW'(\theta=1)$. Also, SW' $(\theta=4)>SW'(\theta=3)>SW'(\theta=1)$, a monotonic increase. These relations point to a non-linear scenario to arise from the simulation of human development as the process proceeds rather than human development being associated with an optimization of the social wellbeing index.

We note in the above simulation of the social wellbeing function of human development that the attainment of target values of the *h*-indices, the post-evaluation of SW'-values, and further creative evolution of similar patterns of change in the IIE framework, depend centrally on emerging θ-values. These simulated θ-values are the result of agent-specific, institutional and scientific relations among the variables (e.g. as in the case of ecology).

In the case of Indonesia we can infer a number of policy directions from the above simulation result in the light of the prevalent conditions (IMF 1999). Table 2.1 points out that between 1997 and 1998 severe decline in output growth has been accompanied by high inflation pressure and external sector imbalance. In the face of high inflation and a plummeting exchange rate, Indonesian interest rates had to be increased substantially.

On the human development front we note that while macroeconomic indicators such as the pursuit of economic growth by export orientation and structural adjustment are policies for attaining high economic growth regimes, the same may not be to the benefit of social wellbeing. Structural adjustment under the IMF policy agenda has always meant a downsizing of businesses and a reduction in subsidy. For Indonesia, such measures have fallen on the common man. Employment and real earnings have declined to record low in recent decades, proving that the goal of economic growth was always fraught with underlying uncertainties, and these have now let up in the face of increased dependence on foreign capital followed by outflow.

Table 2.1 Some critical macroeconomic indicators for Indonesia (percentages)

	1997				1998			
	Q1	*Q2*	*Q3*	*Q4*	*Q1*	*Q2*	*Q3*	*Q4*
Output growth	7.7	6.6	3.3	2.4	−4.0	−12.3	−18.4	−19.5
Inflation	5.2	5.1	6.0	10.1	29.9	52.2	79.7	79.2
Import value growth	11.0	−7.8	−2.6	−10.1	−31.3	−26.9	−31.2	−38.8
Export value growth	10.4	7.5	9.6	2.4	−1.0	−10.5	−6.3	−22.4

Crisis Asian countries:
(billions US dollars)

	1993	*1994*	*1995*	*1996*	*1997*	*1998*	*1999*	*2000*
Net private capital flows	31.9	33.2	62.5	62.4	−19.7	−45.3	−25.7	−11.1
Net direct investment	6.7	6.5	8.7	9.5	12.1	4.9	8.6	8.3
Net portfolio investment	16.5	8.3	17.0	20.0	12.6	−6.5	−3.3	5.9
Other net investment	8.7	18.4	36.9	32.9	−44.5	−43.6	−30.9	−25.4

Source: IMF, May 1999, *World Economic Outlook.*

Much of this is found to be made of portfolio investment (Table 2.1). Net domestic investment remained low and marked a negative outflow.

In the light of human development perspectives as indicated by targets for social wellbeing simulated in Figure 2.1, the Indonesian political economy should focus more on the internal restructuring of resource mobilization by and among the local communties. This calls for opening up domestic production for the large domestic markets, developing enterpreneurship, entitlement and empowerment. This could result in a turnaround in domestic investment and its retention while encouraging foreign direct investment to further enhance entrepreneurship at home. Speculative portfolio investments must be avoided. The capital markets and financial instruments must thus be directed to real economic activities away from speculation. The revenues so generated should then be allowed to flow within the domestic economy through incentives on financing modes and newly developed investment alternatives that are accessible by the local entrepreneurs. Government revenues would be based on an accentuation of incomes and fiscal policies with attention to monetary policy where this can enhance the other policies. There is very little wisdom for Indonesia at this time in repeating the debacle that followed years of blind pursuit of the growth paradigm of growth-led economic development, wherein dependence rather than self-reliance marked the human development future of the citizenry. Poverty alleviation and economic security were not sustainable. The same social and economic scenario has also marked the prevalent status of the *bumiputeras* in Malaysia. Dependence, rentiership and deepening moral hazard caused by economic uncertainty and crony capitalism, rather than self-reliance and entrepreneurship, followed regimes of economic growth (Mehmet 1988).

Comparative examination of trends in the components of human development indices

In the case of simulating progress towards a better human development future in the above social wellbeing treatment, we need to examine which priorities need most immediate attention for Indonesia. Here we refer to Table 2.2.

A comparison of the vital HD-indices and their components for Indonesia with the average for the corresponding medium range human development indices reveals a robust state for the former. A priority area for attention by public policy is the need for improvement in the health of children under the age of 5 years. Hence in our simulation exercise interrelating HDI to HPI-1, the priority of child wellbeing can be one of the critical areas where greater efforts within the Indonesian development plans should be made.

Yet another inference we can draw from the comparative statistics given in Table 2.2, and from the prevailing financial, economic and political turmoil raging in Indonesia, is that sheer human development indices computed as isolated measures from each other cannot answer the nature of interrelation-

Table 2.2 Various human development indices and their components for Indonesia, 1995 (value and percentages)

Indonesia, Human Development Index (value):	0.679	
Life expectancy	64.0	
Adult literacy rate	83.8	
Gross enrolment ratio	62.0	
Adjusted real GDP (PPP$) value	3,971	
Medium Human Development (value):	0.670	
Life expectancy	67.5	
Adult literacy rate	83.3	
Gross enrolment ratio	66.0	
Adjusted real GDP (PPP$) Value	3,390	
Indonesia, Gender-related Development Index (value):	0.651	
Life expectancy	65.8 (F)	62.2 (M)
Adult literacy rate	78.0 (F)	89.6 (M)
Gross enrolment ratio	59.1 (F)	61.3 (M)
Share of earned income	33.0 (F)	67.0 (M)
Medium Gender-related Index (value):	0.656	
Life expectancy	69.7 (F)	65.4 (M)
Adult literacy rate	76.9 (F)	89.5 (M)
Gross enrolment ratio	63.7 (F)	64.9 (M)
Share of earned income	36.4 (F)	63.6 (M)
Indonesia, Gender Empowerment Measure (value):	0.365	
Seats in parliament held by women	11.4	
Female administrators and managers	6.6	
Female professional and technical workers	40.8	
Women's share of earned income	33.0	
Medium Gender Empowerment Measure (value):	N.A.	
Indonesia, Human Poverty Index (percentage):	20.2	
People not expected to survive to age of 40 years	13.0	
Adult literacy rate	16.2	
Population without access to		
Safe water	38.0	
Health services	7.0	
Sanitation	49.0	
Underweight children under the age of 5 years	34.0	
Children not reaching grade 5	10.0	
Real GDP per capita		
Poorest 20% ($)	1,422	
Richest 20% ($)	6,654	
People below income poverty line		
$1.00 a day	14.5	
National poverty line	8.0	

Table 2.2 (continued)

Medium HPI-1 Estimates (value):	N.A.
People not expected to survive to age of 40 years	9.0
Adult literacy rate	19.6
Population without access to	
Safe water	31.0
Health services	13.0
Sanitation	61.0
Underweight children under the age of 5 years	19.0
Children not reaching grade 5	11.0
Real GDP per capita	
Poorest 20% ($)	848
Richest 20% ($)	5,750
People below income poverty line	
$1.00 a day	25.9
National poverty line	15.0

Source: UNDP 1998, *Human Development Report 1998.*

ships among the critical components. The study of such interrelationships in human development indices is important for identifying the feedback cause and effect interrelationships among the critical priority areas for public policy development. One such interactive index that we have proposed in this chapter is the social wellbeing function studied within a systemic framework of interrelationships with respect to human development indices. Subsequently, these indices can be further disaggregated into their components and a more extended general system, adopted with respect to a more extensive specification of the social wellbeing function, can be undertaken.

We note that an important composite index that has not been taken up in the computation of the human development measures is that reflecting the nature of politico-economic analysis. Such an index permits the study of interactions among the composite indices and their variables. Once again such an index can be taken as the social wellbeing function within the general systems oriented specification shown by the expressions in (1). The idea of political economy is understood here in terms of the interactive, integrative and evolutionary features of the IIE-process. In the absence of such features, the composite measures of human development indices remain to be isolated indicators in themselves. They simply indicate the state of human development measures as they are, but have no power of explaining the normative factors underlying goals and directions for socio-economic transformation.

In the case of Indonesia, for instance, such linear composite measures of human development could not point out the social disorder that was brewing just prior to the financial and economic crisis. The brewing social disorder was clouded by sheer socio-economic indicators, as institutional participation of the common citizens in the construction of the future vision of Indonesia remained ignored. A grassroots participatory vision calls for decentralized involvement of all ranks of society in economic, institutional and political processes. Consequently, transparency in economic dealings, the financing of giant projects without the common weal, and the costly way of building Indonesia on risky foreign capital along with the flight of speculative capital from Indonesia, remained hidden in the political hegemony of an autocratic government. The absence of grassroots participation contributed to the subsequent financial, economic and political demise of Indonesia. Thus the absence of a measure in the existing linear forms of the human development indices that could explain the political economy of development did not lend full meaning to these indices for Indonesia.

In the absence of a truly interactive measure of the type shown by the social wellbeing function, the linear forms of the human development indices could not provide both the normative as well as the positive effects of human participation in the national planning of Indonesia (World Bank 1997). In the absence of such an interactive process-oriented measure for evaluation of the economic and political process in Indonesia, the Indonesian government instead took to the enactment of macroeconomic policies. These proved to be those prescribed by the International Monetary Fund. They led the Indonesian economy into a spiral of contraction in subsidy, structural downsizing of economic enterprises, high unemployment, spiralling inflation, soaring interest rates and rigorous fiscal restraint. Monetary and structural adjustment policies that were adopted could not stabilize the exchange rate, price levels and debts in the face of an outflow of foreign capital and foreign reserves. High interest rates together with the political uncertainty discouraged foreign direct investments. In the end, the macroeconomic policies adopted could not tackle the structural problems of development that lay at the grassroots level. The integration of macroeconomic policies with the microeconomic policymaking reduced the usefulness of the human development indices as meaningful indicators for socio-economic development for Indonesia.

Social wellbeing and military expenditure

In this part of the chapter I will use yet another measure of social wellbeing to show that in the context of military expenditure and social wellbeing there has been less than sound result for many of the Middle Eastern countries. I have provided empirical evidence below.

Our objective in this section is to estimate the degree to which any perceptible cutback in military expenditure would have had an effect on increased spending on social wellbeing in recent times. We will measure this relationship between military expenditure cuts and social wellbeing by means of statistical trends in the percentage change in human development index relative to the percentage change in military expenditure. Such a measure is the elasticity of social wellbeing with respect to military expenditure cutback. By investigating such a *sensitivity index* between HDI and military expenditure we will show that the recent observation by the IMF on the existence of an inverse trend between social spending and military expenditure for a sample of countries surveyed does not explain the issue of sensitivity between the two indicators. The IMF conclusion thus remains incomplete and inadequate for policy development relating to military expenditure and social spending in attaining social wellbeing. We need to use more extensive methods to arrive at appropriate results for policy inference.

Present state of military expenditure and social wellbeing in developing countries

Table 2.3 points out that the statistical observation made by the IMF respecting a reduction in global military expenditure in recent years (IMF Survey, June 1999) and its enhanced effect on social spending, cannot be established in terms of the sensitivity relationship between HDI and military expenditure. One would wish the decline in military expenditure to result in an increase of funds made available by the peace dividends for their use in social uplift, including debt relief for the least developing countries (South Commission 1990; Stockholm Initiative 1991). Consequently, a realignment of international relations under the globalization agenda on trade and socio-economic development should have resulted in a development fund for meeting new challenges of social and economic transformation in the developing countries.

The debate surrounding the costs and benefits to the developing countries of globalization has been a vehement one. Today this debate extends from issues relating to the moral duties of the industrialized countries in covering the costs and debacles of uncertainty brought about by privatization and economic restructuring agenda in the developing world to problems of sustainability of development under capitalist globalization (Thurow 1996). The debate can be encapsulated in our measure of social wellbeing.

The social wellbeing measure has its roots in economic theory (Sen 1982). Yet it has not been investigated thoroughly in the literature on ethics and economics, which is the underlying theme of this paper. Consideration of ethics and economics in issues of development is one that turns around deontological consequentialism where Sen (1987) and Rawls (1971) have contributed. The duty-bound stance of morality in promoting social wellbeing of the developing world by development organizations, far from being a self-centered game of Eurocentric hegemony, should in fact be looked upon as a duty that brings common benefits to the recipient and the donor. In the consequentialist perspective, the market process, even in the face of privatization and globalization, should be one that leads towards ethical ways of realizing economic exchange. Examples of such common benefits are to be found in issues of human ecological sustainability on the

Table 2.3 Estimation of elasticities of HDI improvement to reduction in military expenditure, Middle Eastern HDI-countries, 1995

	HDI		Military expenditure (US mill.)*		Military expend. as percentage of GDP		Percentages in HDI	Percentages in military expend.	Elasticity of social wellbeing
	1994	1995	1994	1995	1994	1995	1994–5	1994–95	
Algeria	0.737	0.746	1,249	1,234	2.7	2.5	−99.90	−1.20	83.2500
Egypt	0.614	0.612	2,641	2,417	5.9	4.3	0.33	−8.48	−0.0389
Indonesia	0.668	0.679	2,256	2,751	1.4	1.6	1.65	21.94	0.0752
Iran	0.780	0.758	2,237	2,460	3.8	3.9	−2.82	9.97	−0.2828
Iraq	0.531	0.538	2,628	2,700	14.6	1.8	1.32	2.74	0.4818
Jordan	0.730	0.729	422	440	7.1	6.7	−0.01	4.26	−0.0023
Lebanon	0.794	0.796	301	407	4.4	5.3	0.25	35.22	0.0071
Morocco	0.566	0.557	1,197	1,347	4.3	4.3	−1.59	12.53	−0.1269
Oman	0.718	0.771	1,854	1,840	15.9	15.1	7.38	−0.08	−92.2500
Saudi Arabia	0.774	0.778	13,917	13,215	11.2	10.6	0.52	−5.04	−0.1032
Syria	0.755	0.749	2,358	2,026	8.6	6.8	−0.79	−14.08	0.0561
Tunisia	0.748	0.744	219	369	1.4	2.0	−0.53	68.49	−0.0077
Turkey	0.772	0.782	5,242	6,004	3.2	3.6	1.39	14.54	0.0956

Source: Human Development Report 1996, 1997, 1998.

Notes: *1995 figures are with respect to 1995 prices; 1994 figures are with respect to 1993 prices.

ethical side (Korten 1996) and in sustainable development on the economic side (Brundtland 1987). The resources for both of these goals reinforce those of the other through complementarity between themselves rather than by marginal substitution as found in neoclassical economics (Daly 1992). A range of interactive issues and variables including policy parameters is then found to exist in complementarity among each other within the criterion of social wellbeing (Choudhury 1993b).

In Table 2.3, the elasticity measure, $E_{HDI,M}$, for social wellbeing represented by *HDI*, is given by,

$$E_{HDI,M} = \%(\text{change in } HDI)/\% \text{ (change in military expenditure).}$$

The value for $E_{HDI,M}$ is expected to be negative if the IMF hypothesis of an inverse relationship between social spending and military expenditure for inculcating social wellbeing were to hold. Hence a value such as, $E_{HDI,M} = -0.0389$ (Egypt) would conform with this inference. However, $E_{HDI,M} = 83.25$ (Algeria) does not conform with the IMF's expected relationship between military expenditure and social wellbeing represented here by *HDI*. Many similar country-specific anomalies are found in Table 2.3. See the note at the end of the chapter for a further formalization of the elasticity concept sensitivity introduced here.

Let us make an interpretation of the elasticity of social wellbeing. Although in many cases in Table 2.3 it is true that a cutback in military expenditure is observed to be associated with an increase in *HDI*, yet this is not a generalized fact. In several cases the two indicators are found to have moved up or down together. The elasticity concept provides the degree of sensitivity between *HDI* as a measure of social wellbeing included in which is social spending and military expenditure. The *HDI* being a composite of several social variables would be an appropriate measure to test the hypothesis of an inverse relationship between *HDI* and military expenditure. The IMF has recently tried to draw an observation that global cutback in military expenditure has brought about enhanced social spending. The same would also have been expected of returns from the so-called peace dividends to the developing countries following the end of the East–West détente. The peace dividends were never realized.

According to the underlying hypothesis here we would expect that an increase in military expenditure would be followed by a decrease in *HDI* and vice versa. The elasticity would then be a negative value. However, if the two indicators move together then the elasticity would acquire a positive value. The magnitude of the elasticity value would indicate the sensitivity between both indicators moving together, either upwards or downwards. Because of this anomaly in the interpretation of the elasticity of social wellbeing represented by the percentage change in *HDI* with respect to the percentage change in military expenditure, we infer that there cannot be a meaningful affirmation of the observation made by the IMF. We are examining this question with respect to the issue of sensitivity between the two indicators. The IMF has estimated a slowdown in global military expenditure of 2.3–2.5 per cent of world GDP by the year 1998 (IMF Survey, June 1999). In 131 countries surveyed the percentage share of GDP for military expenditure is found to have remained almost unchanged between 1997 and 1998. The inference that the IMF makes out of this trend is that the slowdown in military expenditure has led to an increase in social spending.

Yet when we study the relational question between *HDI* as a measure of social wellbeing and military expenditure (expansion or contraction) by means of the elasticity measure conveying sensitivity between the two indicators, we cannot ratify the IMF's inference for the sample of countries in Table 2.1. Thus the inference derived from the sample of countries studied by the IMF cannot provide a generalized relationship which the IMF intends in the following words (IMF Survey, June 1999: 187): 'In these countries the reduction in military outlays was accompanied by an increase in spending on education and health care as a proportion of GDP and total spending.' Besides, it is also not correct to conclude in generalized terms that 'education and health care spending fell in relation to GDP between 1993 and 1997' in the Middle East countries (IMF Survey, June 1999: 187).

According to our argument it is the sensitivity of *HDI* to military expenditure that is the important criterion for deriving any relational inference between the two indicators. A mere observation of trends in military expenditure and spending on health and education as percentages of total spending and GDP, is not sufficient to arrive at any meaningful conclusion on the relationship between social wellbeing and military expenditure for the purpose of policy development.

We also note from Table 2.3 that there was no predictive relationship during 1994–5 between military expenditure as a percentage of GDP and a measure of social wellbeing. We can readily note from the relationship given below that no precise inference for policy development on social wellbeing can be made in this regard from the IMF's observation on an inverse relationship between military expenditure and social spending as percentages of GDP.

The quantitative inadequacy of the simple relationship between social wellbeing and military expenditure

To prove our contention relating to the inadequacy of the simple nature of the IMF's observation in explaining the relationship between social spending and military expenditure, we proceed as follows:

Consider the relationship,

$$M/Q = a; \text{ that is, } M = a.Q,$$

where, M denotes military expenditure; Q denotes GDP; a is the (M/Q) ratio.

We rewrite the above expression as,

%(change in M)=a.%(change in Q).

In terms of the elasticity relationship of Table 2.3 we can write,

%(change in HDI)/$E_{HDI,M}$=%(change in M)=a.%(change in Q).

Thereby, %(change in HDI)=a. $E_{HDI,M}$. %(change in Q).

Thus, %(change in HDI)/%(change in Q)=(M/Q). $E_{HDI,M}$.

Since the sign of $E_{HDI,M}$ remains dubious with respect to the variable relationship between HDI and M, as shown in Table 2.3, therefore the relationship between HDI and Q in terms of percentage changes and the (M/Q) ratio also remains dubious. Such a dubious result thereby, does not contribute to policy development relating to social wellbeing.

Conclusion: policy perspectives

We note that the human development indices have been a significant innovation in the computation of measures of development compared to the traditional reliance on the indicator of real GDP per capita. The most important perspective in this regard has been the treatment of ethical issues surrounding poverty, entitlement and empowerment taken up by gender (Sen 1986). Yet when it comes to the explanation of the forces underlying the political economy of development as a complex process of interrelationships among agents, variables and their relations, the human development indices are still found to be linear composite measures. They cannot explain the economic, social, institutional and political forces that ride the crest of the globalizing process in which today's nations are engulfed.

In recent times, the economic and financial turmoil in East Asian economies has adequately proven that macroeconomic policy enactment governed by a predominantly monetarist agenda promoting privatization, economic efficiency, economic productivity and savings regimes with high interest rates and risky investor behaviour at the expense of proactive fiscalism, cannot comprehend the microeconomic social needs that lie at the grassroots (UNDP 1999). Since human development indices focus on the ethical issues of development (Goulet 1995), it is important for them to project both the normative as well as the positive nature of interactions involving the grassroots in every echelon of national planning. A further improvement of the human development indices should be along these directions. We have proposed one such interactive measure in a knowledge-induced framework of the interactive, integrative and evolutionary model of development. Its criterion function was substantively defined as the social wellbeing function.

Our brief examination of the question of estimating the relationship between military expenditure and social wellbeing shows that this is a substantively involved exercise. It cannot be simply established in a straightforward way by observing trends in military and social spending as percentages of GDP. Such an observation has been the basis for IMF's generalized inference on a suspected inverse relationship between global military cutback and social spending. Yet contrary to this fact, the peace dividends that were supposed to flow to the developing countries after the end of the East–West détente did not occur. The flow of Official Development Assistance to the developing countries has not increased so as to enable these countries to maintain their social safety net even in the face of a decline in military expenditure. Between 1994 and 1995, which is our time-period of study, ODA per capita to developing countries changed from a mere US$10.6 to US$11.0, ignoring inflationary effects on these amounts in the recipient countries. For the least developing countries the change in ODA per capita was from US$28.3 in 1994 to US$29 in 1996, being further subject to discounting for inflation (UNDP 1996, 1997).

The social wellbeing criterion used in this paper in terms of percentage change in *HDI* with respect to percentage change in military expenditure is essentially a measure of sensitivity of the relationship between military expenditure and social spending. We arrived at the inference that neither a reduction nor an expansion in military expenditure is a necessary and sufficient cause for betterment or worsening of the percentage change in *HDI*, taken up in all possible combinations in several of the thirteen countries examined in Table 2.3.

A host of important variables are to be considered in understanding the relationship between military expenditure and social spending. This would include the cause and effects of such other variables on the relationship between social wellbeing and military expenditure. For example, defence expenditure may in fact be a necessity for the purpose of internal security of nation states at a time of unresolved regional conflicts, even as the world progresses towards greater economic integration under globalization. There is also the need for additional premiums, perhaps raised by the Tobin Tax on international capital flows, to stabilize the economies that have been battered by the global financial and economic turmoil. In such countries, economic restructuring and fiscal restraints together with the losses to marginal savers in capital markets have caused a substantial decline in social wellbeing despite the cutback in military expenditure.

Thus the relationship between social wellbeing and military expenditure needs to be studied within a complex of conditions, variables and relations. Some of these variables may well be complements to each other rather than being substitutes in relation to defence expenditure for reasons of national security. Consequently, one cannot infer readily that a generalized inverse relationship between military expenditure and social spending is a necessary implication of social wellbeing, as the IMF would otherwise expect us to believe.

Note

The nature of the elasticity of social wellbeing in terms of *HDI* and *M* implies that *HDI* and military expenditure are related to a social wellbeing function of the type,

$$\log (HDI) = E \cdot \log (M) + \text{autonomous coefficient.}$$

That is, $HDI = A.M^E$, with $A>0$ as an autonomous coefficient; $E<0$, if the IMF inference on an inverse relationship between military expenditure and social spending (incorporated in *HDI* as a measure of social wellbeing) is to hold.

Contrarily, in our case of measuring sensitivity between the two variables, *HDI* and *M*, *E* remains a testable parameter, on the basis of which policy development can be charted. The complexity of the relationship arises from the fact that *HDI* and *M* can be together related to variables such as *ODA*, Peace Dividends (*PD*), National Security (*NS*). Through these variables it is quite possible that a general system like the following could engender complementarity rather than substitution between *HDI* and defence expenditure:

$HDI = HDI(ODA, PD, NS)$; $M = M(ODA, PD, NS)$ are functional relations.

$HDI = A.M^E$ would imply that

$HDI(ODA, PD, NS) = A.[M(ODA, PD, NS)]^E.$

Now a system of circular causation equations can result for each of the (*ODA*, *PD*, *NS*)-variables in terms of the other ones, even if any of the two, *HDI* or *M*, were to be targeted by policy goals.

The complexity of the above system will multiply if A becomes institutionally induced as in the case of a technological change parameter. This would likely happen since our variables in the above system of equations are all time-dependent.

References

Arrow, K.J. (1963) *Social Choice and Individual Values*, New Haven, Conn.: Yale University Press.

—— (1974) *The Limits of Organization*, New York: W.W. Norton.

Bellman, R. (1957) *Dynamic Programming*, Princeton, NJ: Princeton University Press.

Brundtland, G.H. (1987) *Our Common Future*, New York: Oxford University Press.

Choudhury, M.A. (1993a) 'A critical examination of the concept of Islamization of knowledge in contemporary times', *Muslim Education Quarterly*, vol. 10, no. 4, pp. 3–35.

—— (1993b) 'Towards a general theory of Islamic social contract', in *The Unicity Precept and the Socio-Scientific Order*, Lanham, Madison: The University Press of America.

—— (1996) 'Why cannot neoclassicism explain resource allocation and development in the Islamic political economy?', in E. Ahmed (ed.) *Role of Private and Public Sectors in Economic Development in an Islamic Perspective*, Herndon, VA: International Institute of Islamic Thought, pp. 17–45.

—— (1998) 'Human resource development in the Islamic perspective', in *Studies in Islamic Social Sciences*, New York: St. Martin's Press, pp. 146–79.

Daly, H.E. (1992) 'From empty-world to full-world economics: reorganizing an historical turning point in economic development', in R. Goodland, H. Daly, S. el-Serafy and B. von Droste (eds) *Environmentally Sustainable Economic Development: Building on Brundtland*, Paris: UNESCO.

Drucker, P. (1998) 'The new society of organizations', in *On the Profession of Management*, Boston, MA: Harvard Business Review Book, pp.115–31.

Fischer, S. (1997) *Capital Account Liberalization and the Role of the IMF*, Washington, DC: IMF, Sept.

Goulet, D. (1995) *Development Ethics, A Guide to Theory and Practice*, New York: The Apex Press.

International Monetary Fund (1999) 'Military spending continues to stabilize; some countries increase social spending', *IMF Survey*, June.

Inglott, P.S. (1990) 'The common heritage and the rights of future generations', in S. Busuttil, E. Angius, P.S. Inglott and T. Macelli (eds) *Our Responsibilities Towards Future Generations*, Malta: Foundations for International Studies.

Korten, D. (1996) *When Corporations Rule the World*, London: Earthscan.

Mehmet, O. (1988) *Development in Malaysia, Poverty, Wealth and Trusteeship*, Kuala Lumpur: The Institute of Social Analysis.

Obstfeld, M. (1998) 'The global capital market: benefactor or menace? *Journal of Economic Perspectives*, vol. 12, no. 4 (Fall), pp. 9–30.

Rawls, J. (1971) *A Theory of Justice*, Cambridge, MA: Harvard University Press.

Sen, A. (1987) 'Economic behaviour and moral sentiments', in *On Ethics and Economics*, Oxford: Basil Blackwell.

—— (1982) 'Rights and agency', *Philosophy and Public Affairs*, vol. 11, no. 1 (Winter).

—— (1986) 'Poverty and entitlement', *Poverty and Famines, an Essay on Entitlement and Deprivation*, Oxford: Clarendon Press.

—— (1991) 'Well-being, agency and freedom', in *On Ethics and Economics*, Oxford: Basil Blackwell.

SESRTCIC (Statistical, Economic and Social Research and Training Center for Islamic Countries) and ICDT (Islamic Center for Development of Trade) (1994) 'The Uruguay Round of trade negotiations: a preliminary assessment', *Journal of Economic Cooperation among Islamic Countries*, vol. 15, nos. 1–2, pp. 1–91.

Shackle, G.L.S. (1971) *Epistemics and Economics*, Cambridge: Cambridge University Press.

Simon, H.A. (1957) 'A comparison of organizational theories', in *Models of Man*, New York: John Wiley & Sons, pp. 170–82.

South Commission (1990) 'North–South relations and the management of the international system', in *The Challenge to the South*, Oxford: Oxford University Press.

Stockholm Initiative (1991) *Common Responsibility in the 1990s, the Stockholm Initiative in Global Security and Governance*, Stockholm: The Prime Minister's Office.

Summers, L.H. (1999) 'Distinguished lecture on economics in government: reflections on managing global integration', *Journal of Economic Perspectives*, vol. 13, no. 2, pp. 3–18.

Thurow, L. (1996) *The Future of Capitalism*, London: Nicholas Brealey Publishing Ltd.

UNDP (United Nations Development Program) (1996, 1997) *Human Development Report,* New York: Oxford University Press.

—— (1998) *Human Development Report 1998*, New York: Oxford University Press.

—— (1999) *Human Development Report 1999*, New York: Oxford University Press.

Whittaker, J.K. (1987) 'The limits of organization revisited', in Feiwel, G.R. (ed.) *Arrow and the Foundations of the Theory of Economic Policy*, London: Macmillan Press Ltd., pp. 565–83.

World Bank (1997) 'Eradicating human poverty worldwide – an agenda for the 21st Century', in *World Development Report 1997*, New York: Oxford University Press.

—— (1998) *World Development Report 1998. Knowledge for Development*, New York: Oxford University Press.

3 The problem of brain drain

B. N. Ghosh and Rama Ghosh

Introduction

The Biblical prediction that 'unto every one who hath shall be given; and from him that hath not, even that he hath shall be taken away' is perhaps best illustrated by the developed capitalist countries' efforts to draw away strategic manpower from the poor countries. Brain drain, representing the outflow of underutilised or overutilised skilled manpower from the low developed countries (LDCs) to developed countries (DCs) *en masse*, and on a regular scale, has received a considerable amount of attention in the literature on economic development of the Third World countries.[1] The problem of brain drain has been made a part of the explanation of economic backwardness and reverse transfer of technology.

The nationalist and internationalist approaches to the problem of brain drain have led to diametrically opposite findings. While to an internationalist, brain migration is a welfare-income-development maximising natural process, to a nationalist, it is a perverse process leading to loss of income, welfare and development, and a widening of international inequality between DCs and LDCs. However, the international political economy aspects of brain drain have not been analysed in detail. Needless to say, the backwardness of the developing countries is the main cause of brain drain, and conversely, it is the brain drain itself which contributes to curbing the development process of these countries. This is so because the outflow of high quality manpower (HQM) constitutes a loss to the sending country in the sense that although such manpower is vitally important in the drama of development of LDCs, it is wooed away by the deliberate neocolonialist policy of the DCs. The losses involved in brain drain have several socioeconomic dimensions.[2] It is an empirical truth that a country following a colonial development policy generates a higher magnitude of brain drain than is otherwise possible.

It is a pity that international trade in beans and bananas has been well documented, but not the import and export of human capital; and while the export of even an ordinary commodity fetches its price, the export of brain power never brings anything back to its owner country. On the contrary, the claim for compensation to the LDCs has just been ignored or willy-nilly brushed aside by the DCs through apologetic theorising by the so-called internationalists to protect the colonial interests.[3] They also design theoretic models to demonstrate that free flow of factors of production, which is a part and parcel of basic human rights, ensures maximisation of income, output and welfare and that, since the LDCs cannot productively absorb the HQM, its outflow does not constitute drain but is simply an overflow, relieving the affected countries of their menacing problem of educated unemployment (Baldwin 1970). However, this type of approach to the problem is based on feather-bedding arguments.

The present chapter seeks to argue that the problem of brain drain is generated and intensified by the deliberate neo-imperialistic policy of developed capitalist countries which are still exploiting the LDCs under the new cloak of so-called foreign aid and development assistance programmes. In fact, brain drain can be viewed as a problem of reverse flow of technology from the LDCs to the DCs rather than the other way round. The exploitation continues unabated but in a different fashion in the sense that, while in the pre-industrial revolution period the capitalist countries drew resources from the colonies in the form of physical capital, in the post-industrial revolution period they are drawing away the human capital resources from the LDCs. The motive and the effect in both the cases remain more or less the same with only small nuances. A strong case can be made for the payment of compensation to the LDCs for the use of their HQM by the DCs. This may be in the form of a consolidated price or the sharing of income-tax to be imposed on immigrants. Whatever may be the *modus operandi* of the payment, an adequate compensation must be ensured by creating favourable international public opinion, pressurising the DCs and by resorting to help from the UN and the socialist-minded group of countries. The LDCs should unite and wage a protracted struggle to end the neocolonialist regime of the developed capitalist world.

Brain drain or brain overflow?

One of the serious misconceptions of our times is the belief that brain exodus from the less developed countries (LDCs) to the developed countries (DCs) represents a single malady. As a matter of fact, different types of migration of high quality manpower cannot justifiably be brought within a single analytic umbrella, though this is what has happened in contemporary literature on the phenomenon of brain drain.

Migration of HQM or brain migration may be due to several different sets of socioeconomic forces. Like the common cold, brain migration is not a single malady, but a loose generic category covering a variety of specific complaints and conditions. The phenomenon of migration of HQM from LDCs can justify the use of the term brain, but we should be cautious in using the term drain. In fact, all brain drain constitutes brain migration, but brain migration does not necessarily constitute brain drain. Brain drain is only a part of brain migration.

For analytical reasons, it is necessary to identify each and every type of brain exodus distinctly. This also becomes helpful for formulating different policies for different types of brain migration. There are mainly four types of brain migration: brain drain, brain overflow, brain exchange and brain export. We have elsewhere analysed these categories in detail (Ghosh and Ghosh 1982).

Brain exchange and brain export do not apparently have any marked repercussions on the LDCs for these are essentially based on quid pro quo. Brain overflow is from the surplus category of HQM, and often helpful for LDCs, to ease the problem of educated unemployment. Brain drain is a one-way permanent migration of productively employed HQM mostly from LDCs to DCs. Needless to say, the outflow of this strategic manpower creates many structural maladjustments and produces enormous negative externalities and thereby retards the process of economic development of the brain-losing country. The gain derived from the brain overflow is more than offset by the loss sustained due to brain drain. The advantages of the phenomenon of brain overflow have often been overplayed by the writers of capitalist countries. As a matter of fact, brain overflow often involves uneducated and semi-educated manpower which is not permitted to inflow by the immigration laws of developed countries (DCs). Thus, the importance of brain overflow as the source of supply of valuable forex in LDCs is gradually declining. But on the other hand, the gravity of the problem of brain drain for LDCs is gradually increasing as these countries have limited stocks of physical capital, HQM and a narrow technology frontier.

The seed-corn technology

In the case of technology formation, needless to say, brain power (human capital) plays a crucial role. 'It is people plus machines that make technology, but increasingly people.'[4] The technology gets embodied in human beings. Physical capital at the most embodies technology of the latest vintage; but human capital embodies both present and future technology. Physical capital also rapidly depreciates and its rate of obsolescence is rather quick. Thus, in the field of formation and use of technology, brain power has an edge over the physical capital.

In a highly developed country, the maintenance and acceleration of growth necessitate a highly sophisticated research and development (R&D) industry which is essentially dependent on team research and organisation requiring not brawn but brain. There has been a noticeable transition in the developed countries from manufacturing to tertiary production and from goods to services of different varieties. In a country like the United States the development of industries, like spacecraft and defence, necessitates continuous research and innovation for attaining the type of supremacy it wants in order to sustain its position as a leading capitalist and a powerful nation. However, the United States is a country of immigrants and much of its strength lies in the contributions of its foreign population absorbed in the mainstream.

The most important item in international intercourse today is not food, fuel or fibre, but transaction in technology. The USA every year exports technology to the extent of $9,000 million but imports only $1,000 million worth of technology. The important countries in the world technology market are Germany, France, Japan and Canada. To correct the structural imbalance created by the rapid spurt in the demand for HQM as against its almost static supply, the USA has to import HQM – the seed-corn technology – from the LDCs. This transaction in HQM is made in such an evasive way that ultimately no price for the use of HQM is required to be paid to the country that supplies the HQM. A strange pattern to purchase indeed.

The imported seed-corn technology is then processed scientifically, pressed into service and exported through multinationals, mainly to the LDCs. Capital exports coupled with the export of technology on a huge scale to LDCs leads at least to three consequences:

1   Through the sale of costly and inappropriate western technology, the dependence of the LDCs on the DCs becomes enhanced.
2   The selling country becomes a rentier nation and gets richer by the fattening returns on investment, and royalties on the export of technology. Every year, the LDCs pay to the United States billions of dollars as dividends, fees and royalty.
3   The multinational corporations assume a more significant role in translating into practice the neocolonial interests of the developed capitalist countries.

In fact, American technology is produced largely by the HQM of the Third World. For instance, during 1958–66, brain drain from India increased eight-fold and a large part of this increase was directed to the USA. In 1967, physical brain drain from India to the USA was 1,425 skilled personnel (Ghosh 1968: 163). Between 1960 and 1976, 420,000 HQM left the LDCs for the DCs. No less than 25,000 people migrate to the DCs every year (UNCTAD 1975). The USA is a mature but still growing nation, having apparently unlimited demand for labour. It should be noted that, at the late stage of development, growth does not become so much machine-based as it is based on human talent, ingenuity and skill. The USA's intake of HQM between 1949 and 1970 increased six times, from 2,517 to 16,492. In this outflow, the percentage share of HQM from developed countries to the USA decreased; but that of the LDCs increased.[5] In the USA, 80 per cent of the research is done by 100 large firms who employ more than 60 per cent of the HQM. Needless to add, the present technological supremacy of the USA would be difficult to maintain if the supply of HQM to America were stopped or reduced. Instead of importing raw materials, the DCs are now importing brain from the LDCs without giving any compensation. This shows that, in international economic relations, the colonial-metropolitan nexus still prevails. The HQM is purchased as raw materials, turned into finished products and sold out to colonies at an exorbitant direct and indirect price. Thus, modern LDCs provide both the sources of raw materials (HQM) and the market for the goods purchased by the capitalist countries like America. This sort of technological imperialism leads to what can be called international 'backwash effect', making the poor areas poorer and the rich areas richer.

The reverse transfer of technology

It is very often claimed by the DCs that capitalist countries have been helping the LDCs by giving them aid and assistance. This apparently innocuous statement has to be taken with a caveat. Let us give it a close look. According to the UNCTAD report, US aid to the LDCs in 1970 amounted to $3.1 billion. As against this, the income gained by the USA through brain drain from the LDCs amounted to $3.7 billion (Government of India 1975–6 and *Mainstream* 1974). This shows that whatever aid is given by the USA to the LDCs is more than compensated for by the brain gain. The highest contribution to the net income gained by the USA is made by developing countries, particularly Asia. In 1970, according to UNCTAD, 3,141 skilled Indian people immigrated to the USA. This represented a loss of $75 million, the per capita cost of a specialist being $5,000. But India received in the same year $55 million as foreign aid from the USA. This shows that India lost more than she gained. Each of the following countries received a milliard dollars' worth of aid after World War II: India, Brazil, Chile, Columbia, Iran, Israel, Pakistan, South Korea, Taiwan and Turkey. But these are also the countries which provided about two-thirds of those professionals who settled in the USA. The USA sends as many experts to the developing countries as she receives from them via brain drain.[6] But the telling tale of exploitation is adequately revealed by the fact that, while the USA does not pay a single buck for the brain obtained from the LDCs, she is highly paid for the services of her experts who happen to be mostly the HQM from the countries. Thus, the leader cunningly rides on the laggards and wins the rat race of the capitalistic game.

The loss sustained by the developing countries on account of brain drain is enormous. As many as 38,000 HQM, who migrated to the United States in 1962–6, represented a loss of $7.6 milliard. Between 1949 and 1961, about 3,922 skilled personnel left India for the USA, and this represents a value of $1,055 million.[7] The UN report states that India relinquished an amount of $1.7 million in the form of brain drain to the USA, Canada and France up to 1966 and this sum amounted to $5.6 million in 1967. The income lost by India per skilled emigrant, under alternative parametric values, is shown in Table 3.1.

Table 3.1 Income lost by India per emigrant

Skill category	Arts, science and commerce graduates	Engineers
High	$30,000	$61,000
Medium	$17,000	$32,000
Low	$8,000	$13,000

Source: UNCTAD, *Reverse Transfer of Technology*, as quoted in *Mainstream*, 16 November 1974, p. 48.

According to the study made by UNCTAD, the cost of an Indian engineer is $32,000, a doctor $44,000, a natural and social scientist $33,000 and a graduate $17,000. On this basis, India can be said to have lost $188,419,000 on account of brain drain of 5,439 HQM between 1958 and 1966. If per capita education cost is taken to be $20,000 as is found in many careful studies, the developing countries' contribution to the USA becomes nearly $45 million every year without corresponding compensation. Thus, the LDCs' assistance to the USA becomes more overwhelming than American aid to these countries. It is in this sense that the concept of reverse transfer of technology from the LDCs to the DCs can be looked upon as a more detrimental dimension of the brain drain problem. Foreign capital investment by the DCs ensures the principal along with the interest; but the outflow of HQM from the LDCs constitutes a permanent loss. Whatever foreign aid is given by the DCs is more than taken away by the shrewd trade practices, unfavourable terms of trade, mounting debt servicing and high royalty charges. As a matter of fact, the reverse flow of technology nullifies the tall claim for neo-imperialist aid to the Third World.

The loss of technology cannot, however, be translated in terms of output, income productivity, for the realisation of the technological potentiality encompasses a variety of considerations. But it cannot be gainsaid that the loss of technology is more harmful than the loss of skill. To the extent to which brain drain involves a reverse flow of technology, the movement of HQM will account for the persistent and ever-widening gap between the rich and the poor areas. It will also reduce the capacity of the LDCs to borrow and assimilate foreign technology. In fact, the USA's export of technology to the LDCs is of old vintage. She never parts with the current technology but rather monopolises the technology of present and future (Timofeyev 1975). The DCs claim that they are trying to help the economic development of the LDCs, but, on the other hand, they enact immigration laws that encourage the flight of skilled labour. These are mutually contradictory activities in as much as brain drain jeopardises the technological base and hence the development tempo of such poor countries. It is a historical truism that no metropolitan country is ever really interested in the real development of the colonies. Had it been a policy to help the LDCs, the DCs would have allowed the immigration of ordinary unskilled labour. But they have altogether stopped the immigration of unskilled labour, and encourage the immigration of only skilled labour. The deliberate government policy facilitated the change-over from proletarian mass transfer to professional elite migration. The process of brain drain has become faster since the change in the immigration laws in many developed countries.

In the field of technology, the western models are promiscuously applied. The software variety of technology transfer from the LDCs to the DCs is denied by the latter on the ground that knowledge is a universal public good. But it is strange that the same notion about knowledge is not entertained by the DCs in the matter of patent which is the embodiment of universal knowledge. Out of three million current patents in the world, the LDCs hold only 30,000. If knowledge is a public good, why do the DCs charge for the export of technology which is based on knowledge? The answer to this question smacks of clear neo-imperialistic design which admits of no humanitarian or moral consideration about the struggle for economic development by the LDCs.

According to an estimate made by a Belgrade expert, over 300,000 experts from the LDCs migrated to the DCs in the early 1960s and most of them took up jobs in the USA and Britain (Adams 1968). To educate these people, the LDCs invested $5 billion. This amount is higher than the amount of aid given by the USA and the UK ($4 billion) to the LDCs during the same period (*Tribune*, October 1982).This once again corroborates the notion of reverse transfer of technology. Brain drain is costing the LDCs annually between $4,000 and $5,000 million. The same amount can be said to be the direct gain of the brain-receiving countries. India's gross loss due to the brain drain of 15,000 persons every year comes to $75 million. However, she gained annually $30 million by way of remittance. Thus, India's annual net loss comes to $45 million. Thus, between 1961 and 1972 the UK, the USA and Canada got brain aid of $4,400 billion from the LDCs. The study made by IDRC, Canada, reveals that the foreign aid of these three countries to the LDCs amounted to only $46 billion. Even if we add the remittances, brain aid still far outweighs the foreign aid (*Tribune*, January 1982).

The DCs encourage brain drain from the LDCs mainly for the following reasons:

1   the workers are readily available 'on tap' without any education expenditure on them by DCs;
2   competent scholars can be had at a cheap rate;
3   during rough times, they can be retrenched, During the mid-1970s, economic recession in Europe forced about 1.2 million workers to return home;
4   employment does not involve any permanent commitment;
5   educational investment of a huge amount of money may be saved;
6   some amenities may be denied to foreign workers; and
7   without HQM, technology cannot be assimilated.

The domestic education system of the LDCs is so designed that people are being prepared for western workshops. These countries also give more value to westernised education and offer better salaries to foreign educated people. There is, thus, a positive temptation to go abroad. Brain drain is partly the result of our faulty education system. Foreign monopoly firms in the UK and the USA persuade the students to study in their countries. Many US firms recruit specialists from abroad. Needless to say, the American supremacy of space technology cannot be sustained without foreign scientists. Many of the Third World scientists are working in NASA and are playing a crucial role in the space shuttle programme. Disparity in domestic emolument structure creates dissatisfaction which is ultimately responsible for the exodus of brain; but such an inequality is produced by a capitalist method of economic awards and punishment.

Harmful consequences

Be that as it may, brain drain from the LDCs has had many harmful consequences (Jolly and Seers 1972: 365–9). Brain drain raises the domestic wage in international professions, but the local professionals' wage remains the same. Hence, inequality is accentuated. Second, for want of HQM, it becomes difficult to properly utilise the modern technology. Third, shortages of skilled manpower create dislocations and bottlenecks. Fourth, brain drain brings about internal migration of HQM from villages to towns. This sort of internal brain drain disturbs unfavourably rural–urban professional distribution. Fifth, the returnees bring in inappropriate technology, wrong models and inappropriate education from abroad. Over 40 per cent of R&D expenses in the DCs are on defence and space research to which brain drain is directed. The spillover effects do not benefit the LDCs. Last, the returnees and foreign experts increase the domestic wage, show preference for foreign items and favour capital-intensive techniques and inappropriate ideologies and policies.

One negative phenomenon in the LDCs, and for which neocolonialism is largely responsible, is the problem of brain drain (Tarabrin 1982:. 271ff.). The drain is caused by the greed of the DCs, which want to accumulate more and more surplus. Students receiving western education do not generally come back home. The reasons are many: inability to find a good job, restricted scope for promotion, possibility of underemployment/unemployment, lack of planning in education and training, conflict with the authorities and so forth. But the crucial reason is the neocolonial policy of buying HQM from the LDCs. In the face of scientific and technical revolution in the DCs, the demand for HQM is very rapidly increasing but not so much the supply. Hence, the wooing away of brain from the LDCs. Capitalist countries are making laws so that skilled foreigners can become naturalised citizens of those countries very easily.

However, it is with the active participation of experts of the LDCs that numerous and costly research and military programmes are being carried out in the DCs. Dean Rusk, a secretary of state of the United States, once admitted that, for the USA, the importance of immigration was determined not so much by the number of the new arrivals as by their quality. Without foreign scholars, the USA could not have entered the atomic age in 1945. It is not surprising to note that 57 per cent of immigrants to America are PhD and Master degree-holders and 33 per cent of the American Nobel prize winners are immigrants. As much as 51 per cent of the brains of the LDCs are engaged in R&D industries in the USA. The cost of training a specialist in the USA is $55,000. America saved $31.3 billion by importing brain from the LDCs between 1949 and 1977. According to the estimate made by UNCTAD, this figure is precisely $100 billion (UNCTAD 1972). The system of brain drain from the LDCs to the DCs is perpetuated by many business firms, industries and companies. Way back in 1913, Lenin foresaw the growth of the system of brain drain among the developed and less developed regions, and we in our times experience its perpetuation.

Brain drain involves the loss of strategic manpower from the key positions in a country. As such, it will create many dislocations and require a drastic organisational change. The losses involved in brain drain, as calculated by Comay, Bowman, Myers, Sjasstad, Weisbrod and others through the present value approach, are found to be very high indeed (Ghosh and Ghosh 1982). The losses involved in brain drain are of many types, e.g. loss of present production, loss of future production, loss of present saving, loss of future saving the emigrants should have made, loss of taxes and loss of potential innovations and so forth. First, the LDCs would experience the loss of valuable skilled personnel. Skill formation in these countries is palpably sluggish although the requirement is really very high. In fact, highly skilled manpower is a rare commodity in any country. These countries are desperately in need of both physical and human capital, and certainly cannot afford to lose strategic manpower. Second, brain drain involves the loss of money invested in education, training and skill formation.[8] At present, there are 250,000 professionally skilled Indians in the USA. Presuming the average education and training cost of a specialist to be $200,000, the loss sustained by India so far as a result of brain drain to America alone comes to $50 billion.

Highly qualified strategic persons are essential for capital and skill formation, education, research and training, infrastructure-building and economic and social development. Thus, by brain drain, the LDCs become losers and poorer and development is halted. Brain drain leads to more and more inequalities in the distribution of skilled manpower in the world. International inequality accentuates because of the fact that, whereas brain drain reduces the income and production of the emigrating country, it makes the economic position of the DCs better off. Myrdal argues that the movement of skilled personnel is harmful to the sending countries, because such economies suffer from the 'backwash effect' as a result of brain drain. The LDCs become more and more backward due to brain drain.

A report prepared by ARE for UNESCO points out that brain drain is an immoral process hampering progress in the developing economies and depriving them of badly needed skilled personnel. Brain drain is morally obtuse in at least two senses: (i) the strategic manpower of the LDCs is wooed away, and (ii) no compensation is paid to the brain-sending countries by the brain-receiving countries. Brain drain damages the morale of those who cannot emigrate. The demoralising consequences erode the socio-psychological milieu and lead to national frustration. The leadership and the creative contribution to science, technology and development, which the emigrating people would have made, are lost by the sending country as a result of brain drain. The indirect costs of brain drain are many. Some of these are: slowdown in production, weakening of administrative and executive structures, rebuilding of skill, apathy of the state to skill formation and so on. By brain drain, the intellectual climate of the country is very much adversely affected. Without the intelligentsia, the idea of progress cannot be spread effectively. Thus, brain drain hampers social development, modernisation and economic growth.

Thomas Romans observes that migration of HQM reduces the average educational level of the country (Romans 1974). The emigration of HQM widens the technological gap and increases the technological dependence of the domestic country. When the process continues, people train themselves at home with the sole aim of ultimately emigrating abroad, and in the process, the national moral value, culture and tradition are neglected. A decline in moral values results in selfishness, careerism and even corruption. All these adversely affect patriotism, national solidarity and creative activity. The loss of critical manpower, which can influence government policies, is a serious loss, particularly for the politically and economically weak developing economies. As a matter of fact, external economies involved in brain drain are indeed very large.

The more skilled the emigrant, the more likely is the possibility of unemployment in the sending country, at least temporarily. The emigration of managerial class will automatically reduce some employment (Romans 1974). If an engineer under whom 15 persons are working leaves the country, all these people become unemployed until his position is filled. There is high complementarity of HQM to other productive resources. The flight of HQM from the domestic economy leads to a reduction in productivity. The loss from brain drain is enormous in the short period. In the long run, the loss of HQM is partly replaced in a growing economy. Brain drain may involve zero-sum game and the propagation of research results may be constrained by patent or by CIA secrecy requirements. Thus, the brain-sending country cannot take any advantage of the superior knowledge of its brain living abroad.

The study by Grubel and Scott (1966) comes out with the observation that international migration of human capital reduces military and economic power by a very small amount in the short-time horizon, and, in the long run, the loss disappears. Only under rare circumstances, brain drain could reduce welfare. However, the short-run loss is more than outweighed by the benefits of emigration. The findings of Grubel and Scott have been challenged by Berry and Soligo (1969), among others. They demonstrated that emigration causes loss to a nation. A similar conclusion is upheld by Weisbrod (1966) and Bhagwati and Hamada (1974). Depending upon the structure and the institutional set-up of a country, brain drain can be said to have varying welfare effects, as observed by Bhagwati and Hamada. Brain drain of highly gifted manpower results in welfare loss for the sending country. Anteny Ward regards brain drain as a manifestation of exploitation of less developed countries by developed capitalistic countries (1975). He observes that over the generations, the majority of emigrants are reduced to an exploited and marginal group in the society. In an empirical study conducted in 1972, UNCTAD calculated income gains to the receiving countries and income losses by the sending countries as a result of brain drain (UNCTAD 1972). The loss is found to be indeed staggering. Aitkin's study demonstrated that brain drain not only reduces welfare but it also redistributes income from unskilled labour to the remaining skilled labour (1968). What is good for the USA is not necessarily good for the whole world, remarks Brinley Thomas.

Harry Johnson's analysis was not able to show any welfare gain as a result of brain drain, though he, as an internationalist, intended to rigorously demonstrate it (1967: 404–5). According to Johnson, the marginal loss will vanish when the supply of professionals increases as a result of their increased price. The conclusion of Johnson is not at all tenable, at least on two counts. First, the increased supply of professionals is not simply a function of enhanced price. Granted it to be so, an increased supply of HQM will once again decrease the price, and, therefore, the subsequent supply. Second, the increased supply of HQM, given the domestic absorbing capacity, will lead to more brain drain which will sustain the net loss of consumers' surplus. Thus, Johnson's analysis could not effectively prove the positive welfare implication of the brain drain process (Ghosh and Ghosh 1982: Ch. 5).

The welfare implications of brain drain can be related to capital that migrants take along or leave behind. If capital is left behind, capital–labour ratio will increase and income gain would be substantially high for the non-migrants; but if capital is taken along, capital loss will more than outweigh the income gain, and, as a result, society will experience welfare loss (Grubel and Scott 1966; Berry and Soligo 1969).

Brain drain involves loss of capital in two senses: (i) loss of gifted, experienced and very highly qualified and skilled human capital, and (ii) loss of physical capital accompanying the permanent emigrants and also the loss of their working capital. It is to be recalled that brain overflow representing unemployed HQM does not involve the loss of capital, for the unemployed brain presumably cannot create any capital or does not have any working capital. If we take the above explanations to be correct, brain drain will make the capital–labour ratio lower in the domestic economy in which case capital loss would more than offset the income gain. It is clear that brain drain reduces a country's total stock of social capital. Therefore, productivity will come down after some time and along with that the wage level, thereby reversing and worsening the position. Our analysis is based on the presumption that the value of an emigrant's capital, both physical and human, is higher than the country's average per capita endowment of human and physical capital. If this presumption is correct, as seems plausible, the welfare loss as a result of brain drain indeed becomes very high. However, the net loss in the domestic economy is apparently more than offset by the increase in the migrants' income. While the domestic economy loses as a result of emigration of skilled personnel, the emigrants themselves gain.

The remittance factor

In the case of brain overflow, there being no question of output loss, the realisation of saving potential will directly lead to net income gain. But, for brain drain, capital loss and hence output and production loss will more than swamp out the income gain. No doubt, the migrants earn more income but there is no satisfactory system to compensate the losses to those left behind. Society does not compensate the losers. Thus, the migration of HQM from the LDCs is not a Pareto optimal situation. True, remittances are repatriated in the cases of brain drain and brain overflow; but the remittances are not adequate, regular and compulsory, specially in the case of brain drain. As our survey reveals, the brain drain is directed mostly to developed countries where the skilled personnel take their families along with them. They do not send substantial amount to their relatives in LDCs, and it is also not possible for them to send a large sum of money after meeting the expenditure for their families and making the necessary savings for the rainy days. It has been observed that a large part of the migrants' income is spent on the education and training of their wards. Brain drain from LDCs is mainly from the upper middle class and rich families. This implies that not only the average cost of living of the migrants is high but that they have had a propensity to spend on conspicuous consumption which not merely reduces the amount of remittances but also reduces the effective saving potentials of their relatives in LDCs out of their remitted amount.

In this context, the findings of two other studies made in India may be corroborative (Mathew 1980). Remittances are a special type of transfer payment in the sense that these are essentially a transfer of personal income used partly for consumption and partly for investment. Very little empirical work has gone into the question of channelisation of the resources arising out of the remittances of productive investment. However, two studies undertaken by the Bombay Chamber of Commerce and Industry in respect of the impact of inward remittances received in certain villages of Kerala and Gujarat have made some interesting observations about the pattern of use of the remitted money.

These studies show that a good part of the remittances are channelled in the form of high expenditure on consumer goods, purchase of durable goods and property, or investment in securities, trade and business including speculation. According to one study, the impact of remittances received in certain villages of Kerala does not seem to have triggered off an era of sustained growth in the state (Mathew 1980). The study, particularly, pinpoints the fact that much of the money flowing into the state from abroad has not been used for productive purposes. Investment in debentures, shares and securities has been almost nil. These observations, thus, indicate that the savings of the Indians employed abroad were not channelised for development purposes according to the national priorities. It can, therefore, be stated that brain drain cannot lead to an adequate compensatory payment to the losers, and it cannot cover the public and private cost of human capital involved in brain drain, even if it partly meets the private cost.

Brain drain deprives the emigration country of the saving and investment which the migrants would have made, had they not emigrated abroad. Presumably, the amount of this relinquished saving and investment is pretty high because these skilled personnel are well within the high-income margin. In most of these cases, surplus was being generated in the economy as wage level fell far short of the level of the marginal productivity of such types of labour. The economy is deprived of this surplus at present and in future, as brain drain occurs. The state exchequer sustains a loss in one more respect. Through brain drain, the government loses a huge amount of tax money each year which would have been contributed to the exchequer by the brains who are generally high-income persons and in whose case tax is much higher than the marginal cost of public goods they consume. Thus, the government is deprived permanently of an important source of net revenue. All these findings unmistakably substantiate the fact that brain drain is not merely a welfare-cum-income reducing phenomenon, but it also considerably hampers the growth process of a low developed country on many counts, one of which is the conspicuous trend of the reverse transfer of technology from the LDCs to the DCs.

With definite plans and programmes, brain drain and brain overflow can partly be converted into brain export. The LDCs may well export consultancy services to the DCs, or may exchange brain for capital, equipment and materials. Instead of sending the surplus HQM individually, it would be more worthwhile to send it as government-sponsored teams, and export the surplus manpower on a regular and systematic basis with prescribed terms and conditions. Export-oriented R&D organisations manned by surplus brain can be undertaken by a brain-surplus country. If export of physical capital can earn income, human capital export should also entitle the sending country to a similar type of return. On this basis, a compensatory brain migration policy may be formulated by the LDCs. Brain exchange may be an important channel for the exchange of knowledge and expertise and cross-fertilisation of ideas and values. When brain export to developed countries is not possible, surplus brain may be sent to those LDCs on exchange or export basis where it is in short supply. Some of the LDCs, for example Africa and Malaysia, still remain the net importer of technical and scientific manpower. What is required is a cast-iron strategy and an organisational network at the state and national levels to promote a planned export of manpower. India, Bangladesh and Indonesia have tremendous potential for the export of human capital in the present century.

Concluding observations: towards a scheme of compensation

There should be a forum for redressing the unjust exploitative development policy of the capitalist world. The LDCs have to wage a historical struggle for emancipation in the real sense of the term and for the compensatory payment from the DCs against the outflow of the HQM. The brain-importing capitalist countries must be pressurised to pay for the brain, in the same way as physical capital import is paid. The migration of HQM should be considered as an item in the balance of payment. The object of compensation would be to offset losses already incurred by a country; whereas the aim is to prevent those losses by regulating abnormal migration of HQM. But compensation has remained a mere idea which has never reached even the stage of preparation of bilateral or multilateral agreements. True, such an agreement has not been formally demanded by the LDCs. The LDCs do not demand compensation perhaps because of the fear that such a demand will reduce their aid from the USA. But it must be understood that aid is in no way connected with compensation for the migration of human capital. It is, no doubt a fact that a large number of brain-sending countries, e.g. Pakistan, Jordan, South Korea, India, Lebanon, Turkey and so on, receive remittances. But, nevertheless, the remittances are irregular and do not cover the shadow price, or private plus public costs of the migrated brain. The earnings in the form of remittances are poor compensation for the lasting and serious loss inflicted by the outflow of HQM.

The question of compensation has never been seriously entertained by the developed capitalist nations. According to them, no compensation should be demanded and paid for the brain whose opportunity cost is zero or which remains unproductive in the country of origin. Such a line of reasoning is entirely preposterous, for it is always the surplus product that a country may be interested in selling out. The people who raise objections against compensation put forward the following points: (i) non-returnees are small in number, (ii) emigrants do not decrease the per capita income of those who remained at home, (iii) emigrants are non-productive, (iv) non-returnees do not worsen the educational situation in the home country, (v) actual loss, if at all, is very insignificant,[9] and (vi) scientists are not ordinary exportable commodities.

The foregoing arguments, needless to say, are gross misrepresentations of the facts and are too weak and tendentious to justify the non-payment of compensation. Rationally considered, there should be no dispute over the question of payment of compensation in principle, although differences may arise in the *modus operandi* of such payment. As payment for human capital import, the government of the recipient country could refund a fixed percentage of immigrants' income tax to the country of origin.[10] Such a tax will have two objectives: (i) rendering some benefits to LDCs, and (ii) discourage brain drain.

The compensatory payment in the form of a tax may be spread over a number of years, or it may be once-for-ever lump-sum exit tax, as in the USSR. A consolidated price for the export of the commodity brain power may also be realised in the exporting country from the outgoing human capital. A surtax may be imposed on the earnings of the skilled emigrants. The income tax collected by the brain-importing developed countries may be routed to the concerned LDCs through the United Nations. Another proposal is that the brain-exporting LDC would levy the tax and the importing DC will collect it. The tax may be ratified by a special treaty at the UN with the provision that the proceeds from the tax would go to the UN to be distributed via UNDP, or to the proposed new UN special Fund for LDCs, to be used for the purpose of development. The estimates of the tax revenue from the surtax were calculated at $500 million from the USA and Canada based on 1976 figures (Ghosh and Ghosh 1982: 137). An alternative proposal was an extension by the developing countries of their tax jurisdiction over income from foreign sources so long as the individuals remain citizens of the developing countries and possibly by an international treaty for some years after their loss of citizenship of the original developing countries. The regular domestic income tax schedule of the developing countries would then be extended to the emigrants, giving them credit, however, for the tax paid by them to the host developed countries in accordance with those countries' normal tax regimes. Several countries, e.g. the USA, the Philippines and Mexico, have already started extending their tax jurisdiction over non-resident citizens; but an international treaty would be necessary to implement this system with its tax credit feature on a general basis. No doubt, imposition and collection of tax on brain drain would involve some amount of difficulty; but that does not make it unworkable in practice. The Third World countries must jointly cooperate to pressurise the DCs to favourably consider the issue of compensation, and, if need be, the interposition of the UN and the socialist-minded countries may be sought in giving the idea of compensation a practical shape.

Notes

1   *Brain drain* has not been properly defined in the literature. It is very often confused with *brain overflow*. While the former is from the employed category, the latter is from the unemployed human capital stock. The literature on brain drain

is fairly extensive. Since it is not possible here to quote the entire body of literature, we mention Walter Adams (ed.) The *Brain Drain*, Macmillan, New York, 1968, which contains a fairly large number of contributions. See also B.N. Ghosh and Rama Ghosh, *Economics of Brain Migration*, Deep & Deep, New Delhi, 1982.

2 The loss can be interpreted in terms of the loss of educational investment, the cost of relinquished alternatives, the loss of life-time income, the loss of interest on invested capital and also the social loss. The external diseconomies involved in brain drain are really very high.

3 Brain drain is sometimes described as an emotive nationalistic nonsense. See Harry Johnson, 'An internationalist model', in W. Adams, op. cit., and 'Some economic aspects of brain drain', *Pakistan Development Review*, Autumn, 1967. Also see E.J. Mishan, 'The brain drain: why worry so much?', *New Society*, 2 November 1967.

4 Modern technology has become increasingly a function of brain power. See 'Summary view of UNESCO's activities in connection with transfer of technology', in International Seminar on Technology Transfer, Seminar Papers, vol. I, CSIR, New Delhi, 1973, p. 52.

5 The percentage share of DCs in the outflow of HQM to America was 70.4 in 1955–6, but it came down to 30.8 in 1970–1; while for LDCs, it went up from 25 in 1955–6 to 69.20 in 1970–1.

6 A report of the Committee on Government Operations acknowledges this fact. See 'Scientific Brain Drain from the Developing countries', Committee on Government Operations, US House of Representatives, 90th Congress, Second Session, 23 Report, Washington, 1968, p. 56.

7 See the calculations made by Jahangir Amuzegar, 'Brain drain: the irony of foreign aid policy', *Economia Internationzale,* November 1968, vol. XX, p. 703.

8 For the extent of monetary loss, see B.N. Ghosh and Rama Ghosh, *Economics of Brain Migration,* Deep & Deep, New Delhi, 1982.

9 Prof. Shearer has put forward such an argument. See J.C. Shearer, 'In defence of the traditional view of the brain drain problems', *International Educational and Cultural Exchange*, Fall 1961, pp. 17–25.

10 The tax proposal is made, among others, by Jagdish Bhagwati. See J. Bhagwati, *The Brain Drain and Taxation II: Theory and Empirical Analysis*, North Holland, Amsterdam, 1976.

References

Adams, Walter (1968) (ed.) *The Brain Drain,* New York: Macmillan.

Aitkin, N.D. (1968) 'International flow of human capital', *American Economic Review,* June.

Amuzegar, Jahangir (1968) 'Brain drain: the irony of foreign aid policy', *Economia Internazionale*, November.

Baldwin, G. (1970) 'Brain drain or overflow', *Foreign Affairs.*

Berry, R.A. and Soligo, R. (1969) 'Some welfare aspects of international migration', *Journal of Political Economy,* September–October.

Bhagwati, J. and Hamada, Koichi (1974) 'The brain drain: international integration of markets for professionals and unemployment', *Journal of Development Economics,* vol. 1, November 1974.

Ghosh, B.N. (1968) *Population Theories and Demographic Analysis*, Meerut: Meenakshi Prakashan, p. 163.

Ghosh, B.N. and Ghosh, Rama (1982) *Economics of Brain Migration*, New Delhi: Deep & Deep.

Government of India (1975, 1976) *Economic Survey*, New Delhi, and *Mainstream* no. 16, 1974.

Grubel, H.B. and Scott, A.D. (1966) 'The international flow of human capital', *American Economic Review*, May.

Johnson, H. (1967) 'Some economic aspects of brain drain', *Pakistan Development Review*, Autumn.

Jolly, R. and Seers, Dudley (1972) 'Brain drain and the development process', in G. Ranis (ed.) *The Gap Between Rich and Poor Nations*, London: Macmillan.

Mathew, T.J. (1980) 'Export of manpower', *Economic Times*, 23 February.

Mishan, E.J. (1967) 'The brain drain: why worry so much?' *New Society* 27.

Patinkin, D. (1968) 'A nationalist model', in W. Adams (ed.) *The Brain Drain*, New York: Macmillan.

Romans, T.J. (1974) 'Benefits and burdens of migration', *Southern Economic Journal*, January

Shearer, J.C. (1961) 'In defence of the traditional view of the brain drain problems', *International Educational and Cultural Exchange*, Fall.

Tarabrin, E.A. (ed.) (1982) *Neocolonialism and Africa*, Moscow: Progress Publishers.

Thomas, Brinley (1972) *Migration and Urban Development: A Reappraisal of British and American Long Cycles*, London: Methuen.

Timofeyev, Anukin (1975) *Aid or Neocolonialism*, Moscow.

Tribune (1982) Chandigarh, January.

Tribune (1982) 29 October.

UNCTAD (1972) *Transfer of Technology and Economic Effects of Brain Drain*, New York: UN.

—— (1975) *Study on Brain Drain, 5th edition*, Manila: UN.

Ward, Anteny (1975) 'European migratory labour: a myth of development', *Monthly Review*, December.

Weisbrod, B.A. (1966) 'Discussion', *American Economic Review*, May.

4 Gender and development

Transforming the process

Gale Summerfield

Introduction

Development is a process that began well before the written record; it takes different shapes in different places and times. Women have contributed to this process as well as men, though their efforts have received less recognition or remuneration. The academic field of economic development is a much more recent phenomenon; it became an area of economic inquiry after World War II, as international trade expanded and many former colonies gained independence. Dissatisfaction with neoclassical emphasis on markets fuelled government planning to increase the pace of development. Policy-makers promoted state planning, employment programs and rapid capital accumulation (Sen 1984; Hirschman 1981). Most development economists focused on growth as necessary and sufficient for development in the early years, rarely noticing the existence of gender disparities in programs and policies.

Inequities in development have been addressed by a variety of social movements over time, but most of them have not been recorded or published. This is especially true for those movements comprised mostly of women (Basu 1995). The first systematic, academic study of these problems was Ester Boserup's *Woman's Role in Economic Development* (1970) that marked the beginning of the multi-disciplinary field of Women in Development (or Women in International Development: WID). Boserup noted that, with development programs, women often do not gain as much as men and may be marginalized from prior opportunities.

In the early years, WID brought together scholars, practitioners, and policy-makers/advocates who focused on the inclusion of women in the development process. Much of the work centered on reporting the status of women in developing countries and then on identifying the impacts of policy-related changes on women – with passive overtones of implied victimization. Gradually the focus shifted to a more active, agency view of women in the process of socio-economic development; strategies and agency became central to the discussion along with more substantial challenges to development models (Aslanbeigui, Pressman and Summerfield, forthcoming; Jackson and Pearson 1998). Relative disparities between women and men replaced the focus on status, and gender analysis and discussion of social constructs accompanied or replaced the concentration on women as a group. Mainstreaming of gender issues in organizations (such as the World Bank and UNDP) became a common goal – though not always a reality, and WID was more frequently referred to as Gender and Development (GAD) (Murphy 1997).

Key themes in WID/GAD have been: employment and income (stressing export processing, microenterprise, and informal sector activities), microfinance, political participation, education, and intrahousehold allocation of time and income including reproductive activities and other unpaid work. More recently, these have been complemented by analysis of culture and institutions, identity, property rights and environmental policy. This chapter addresses these themes in the context of the economic transformation policies (structural adjustment programs, transition of socialist economies to market economies, and the process of globalization) that have been prominent in the 1980s and 1990s. The Asian Crisis of 1997–8 demonstrated that structural adjustment and transition policies continue to be integral components of crisis prevention and management. The chapter concludes with a brief discussion of forward-looking themes including: methodological approaches and increasing multi-disciplinary collaborations; migration and globalization; socio-economic security, caring labor, and macroeconomic modeling; and the process of including the researched at all phases of policy-making and research.

Economic transformation policies and WID/GAD themes

The 1970s were characterized by a growing awareness of the links between developing and more developed countries, calls for a new international economic order, expanding trade and globalization. Although development theory had some success in industrialization, capital accumulation, mobilization of under-employed labor power and planning (Sen 1984: 486–7), corruption and inefficiency were common. Countries that pursued import-substitution stagnated while the export-oriented economies of Asia thrived.

During the 1970–2000 period, countries around the world have increasingly stressed trade liberalization and the use of markets rather than government planning, regulation and other forms of intervention. The governments of highly indebted countries have been forced to accept these policies as conditions for further loans from the World Bank and International Monetary Fund. The former socialist countries of Europe and Asia have undertaken such policies at least partly voluntarily. As policy-makers formulated and implemented reforms, they ignored gender issues or omitted them from the discussion.

During the 1980s and 1990s critiques of the human and gender impacts of the policies gained momentum; by the late 1980s the international financial institutions began to include some discussion of the social safety net and differential impacts of policies on women and men. Despite great regional variation, scholars discovered a striking similarity in gender impacts of restructuring and transition policies.[1]

Employment changes and income

A host of policies – privatization of government-owned firms and para-statals, cuts in government spending, solicitation of foreign investment, devaluations of exchange rates and reduction of tariffs – resulted in different employment opportunities for women and men. Throughout Latin America and Africa, unemployment became a more pressing issue, especially in the 1980s. Even in growing economies, such as China, state firms were compelled to layoff workers as policies stressed cost reduction and increased competition. Around the globe, women were disproportionately represented among the laid-off and unemployed. Export-oriented textile and electronic plants that opened with foreign investment, however, generally preferred to hire women for assembly-line work. The availability of these low-paying, relatively unskilled jobs coincided with demographic changes and the pressures of survival that increased women's labor force participation during restructuring. Only a fraction of the labor force found work in export-processing jobs, and the majority of women hired by these plants were in their teens or early twenties. In countries undergoing reform, women continued to be concentrated in traditional, low-paying sectors. As employment in state firms and government offices declined, millions of women opened microenterprises or worked in small businesses run by their families. Informal-sector work mushroomed since official licenses were expensive and the process of obtaining them was time-consuming.

Scholars who focused on women and men as active agents in the course of economic transformation identified self-owned microenterprises and jobs in companies based on foreign investment (transnationals or joint-ventures) as the main employment strategies associated with the reforms. Women run many of the microenterprises, especially those selling street foods (Tinker 1997; Boris and Prugl 1996). Even when they are not involved in selling food or other products, women are active in their preparation and various home-based activities. Many governments in developing countries take a hostile stance against the informal sector, considering it a relic of the past, a threat to new businesses, and a means of tax avoidance; the bulldozing of vending stalls has been a common practice. Policy-oriented research, however, has stressed the valuable role these activities play in augmenting the income of the poor – improving housing, nutrition and other basic needs of the family even if they don't succeed in getting people over the poverty line. Such informal-sector activity also may help reduce stealing, drug dealing, and sex work. Convinced by these studies, some governments have adopted a more positive attitude toward informal-sector activities, including making formal registration easier, locating markets for stalls in busy locations, providing clean water and trash collection to improve hygiene, and instituting training classes (Tinker 1997).

Opening private businesses in a market environment requires assets or credit (through formal channels, money-lenders, family loans or overseas remittances). Women usually have less access to either; in many countries women do not have the legal right to own a business or property. Many business transactions require some use of credit. Thus, programs to make credit more available, especially to women, have become central to the strategy of governments and nongovernmental organizations. The Grameen Bank in Bangladesh is the most famous organization for providing micro-credit, but numerous variations exist around the world, including many traditional savings clubs. The Grameen Bank approach involves meetings where participants agree to support a list of tenets including family planning; loans can also be made for housing with the requirement that the woman's name must be on the contract as sole or joint owner.

While microcredit programs are an important part of survival strategies in market-oriented economies, they are limited in scope, and researchers have noted serious problems with reliance on this form of development strategy (Hulme 2000; Goetz and Sen Gupta 1996). Loans are frequently given to women who then have the obligation to repay them. Often, however, their husbands use the loans; this may still increase family well-being if the use is productive and the husband makes the loan payments, but it becomes a wasted resource if used for non-productive consumption (such as alcohol). Arguments over the use of the loan have also been associated with domestic violence. Studies indicate that women are most likely to benefit from the loans when they are educated, have cooperative husbands, and have personal access to the market; women who are in worse situations still need other programs (UNIFEM 2000). Little attention has been given to analyzing the circumstances of women whose businesses fail or whose loans are misdirected. Risk is significant; although some microentrepreneurs do much better than they would in formal jobs, others would be better off with the security of a steady income (Tinker 1997; Elson 1995).

A broader-based strategy has developed in response to the needs of home-based microentrepreneurs and to address the problems of microcredit programs. The best known organization is SEWA (Self-Employed Women's Association) of India. Others include Homenet International and Women in Informal Employment: Globalizing and Organizing (WIEGO). These programs provide a full range of support activities, such as preventing the local police from harassing street vendors. They provide an important source of communication, organization and support for home-based workers who would otherwise be isolated.

Political participation

To participate fully in society, a person must have political as well as economic representation. Women rarely hold as many political seats as men;

and in some countries (such as Kuwait) they are still struggling for the right to vote. Quotas for women's participation that are being tried in India at the local *panchayat* level give women more representation. Political quotas have been abandoned during socialist countries' transition to capitalism. In these countries, women face the paradox of being elected less often but now having more voice to make decisions when they are elected. In China, village level elections are leading the way in terms of change and are viewed as key to a more democratic process. Women have held the top leadership positions in some developing countries, for example India, the Philippines, and Pakistan; but they have been relatives of men who have previously been in office. Still, in the USA and other industrialized countries, even women relatives have been less successful at getting elected to high levels.

Women's organizations and NGOs provide an alternative way to power for many women in developing countries. These institutions allow them to address specific issues directly without the requirements of time and money that formal political participation requires. They can overcome or circumvent corruption, a problem common in entrenched political parties.

Education

Formal schooling provides the background, contacts and entrance requirements to opportunities in politics and the economy. With increasing globalization, education is associated with the flexibility to adapt to changing conditions (Hill and King 1995). Knowledge-intensive output is replacing more traditional types of production (World Bank 2000). In developing countries, the marginal social gains from girls' education are at least as high as those from boys' education but the private net benefits may be less, resulting in parents' decisions to provide schooling for sons rather than daughters (discussed further in the following section on intra-household allocation). Alternatives to formal education and reform of learning systems and incentives are current agenda items in this area.

Intra-household allocation

One focus of the gender and development field is to examine how policy and social changes play out within the household. This contrasts to the mainstream economic approach of taking the household as a harmonious unit making decisions through an altruistic dictator (Becker 1991). WID/GAD is heavily influenced by Amartya Sen (1990), who views the household as including aspects of collaboration and of conflict. Income is not always pooled; family members argue over housework, leisure, and spending decisions; and spouse and child abuse occur too often to confirm the model of a fully cooperative household (Sen 1990; Haddad *et al.* 1995). According to Sen, factors outside the household which empower women to make a more visible contribution in society and the household strengthen their bargaining power within the family. Education, employment opportunities and political participation increase agency (Sen 1995). A woman's ability to earn income also provides security for the family, especially in times of economic upheaval associated with economic restructuring. Women's employment is especially important given that female-headed households are increasingly common.

Reform-related changes have given rise to questions such as how home-based microenterprise affects women's well-being and agency in contrast to formal-sector employment. Control of the enterprise including decision-making power, visibility and amount of earnings, and child care arrangements all influence the contribution to women's well-being. In general, expanding capabilities appear to correspond to an expansion of real choices about how to earn income and raise children. Development programs increasingly realize that gender issues must be explicitly addressed at all levels of policy design and implementation; furthermore, a participatory approach to policy design and reform is optimal. Research indicates that women spend a greater percentage of their earnings on children and basic family needs (Blumberg *et al.* 1995). It matters whether the woman is the designated or joint recipient of program benefits or if the husband has exclusive contact with development workers.

Wife abuse is an accepted tradition in many societies. In some countries killing is condoned as an honor crime if adultery is suspected. In others, routine beatings are said to be a sign that a man loves his wife. Women's organizations have become active in opposing honor crimes, dowry-related extortion, rape, and beatings. Female police units have been set up in countries such as Brazil and India so that women can feel more comfortable discussing rape and other problems.

Scholars have begun to study the roles of other individuals in the co-operative-conflict context. Daughters and sons, for example, have different opportunities in many societies. Mothers and fathers may provide education and other opportunities to their sons instead of their daughters because sons are expected to provide for them in old age and have better opportunities to earn a higher income. With economic reforms, higher fees for education, increased opportunities to operate home-based enterprises, and migration of some household members to the city or other countries have increased the school drop-out rate for girls (Summerfield 1997). In the 1990s, a contrasting phenomenon has been observed in some countries (Pakistan, parts of Indonesia during the Asian Crisis, Latin America), where relatively more girls than boys attend school (especially at primary levels). Reasons for this have not been thoroughly investigated but job opportunities for boys or biases from development programs to aid girls' education may be responsible (in Aslanbeigui *et al.*, forthcoming).

Perceptions become distorted by social conventions. Women in developing countries frequently cannot distinguish their own well-being from that of their family (Sen 1990). While some researchers have focused only on the individual, many analyze issues in terms of individuals within the household, the household and the broader community (see Tinker and Summerfield 1999). Indeed, the perception that well-being is tied to conforming to traditions may lead women to pass on hurtful traditions (foot-binding in China or genital mutilation in sub-Saharan Africa) (Papanek 1990). The interplay between policy and family allows development analysts to better appreciate the changing nature of the family and household.

Culture and institutions

Patriarchy and preference for sons run deep in most societies. Such biases are built into the institutional system as it evolves. Job opportunities, legal rights, transfer of property (often patrilineal), residence patterns (virilocal in many traditions) and reliance on sons for support in old age are typical gendered social constructs. At the micro level, the family is an institution that offers support and security at the same time that it reinforces women's secondary role in society through unpaid labor, lack of legal rights (e.g. requiring a husband's permission to work or enter into contracts) and silence on domestic violence against women. Economic transformation threatens the family as a traditional institution; yet little has emerged to replace the family's role in offering security. Family members migrate, divorce becomes more common, diseases such as HIV/AIDS lead to the demise of parents in their prime. Development strategies that address these issues include institutionalizing social security support systems (which also help in crises) that include pensions, unemployment insurance, support for those not in the formal labor market who lose their income during a crisis, and parental leave. The family as an institution needs to be reformulated to permit more equal treatment of its members (Jaquette and Wolchik 1998; Tinker and Summerfield 1999).

Transnational/multinational corporations represent another level of the institutional structure of society; they have evolved over the decades and their influence continues to grow. Transnationals are the prime movers of the globalization process. The structural reforms required by the IMF and World Bank that stress export-oriented industrialization, and repayment of loans from commercial banks and financial institutions have accelerated the process. Companies from the United States and the United Kingdom no longer dominate; developing countries also operate transnationals in other countries. Some postulated that transnationals would replace the nation state as the primary political force, especially since the role of state appears to be shrinking. In 2000, however, the process appears to be more complex. Although market reformers often pose the state and market as oppositional, many development economists stress that a more accurate statement centers on the appropriate role for each. Markets cannot satisfy all social goals, and ethical issues play as much of a role as efficiency (Aslanbeigui and Medema 1998). The proliferation of Western culture and business has generated a critique of post-colonial destruction of existing cultures and a renewed academic interest in identity (Escobar 1995).

Globalization has spurred another area of institutional analysis: new ways of addressing workers' needs. Nongovernmental organizations such as SEWA play a crucial role in the new institutional process. They provide an alternative to formal political participation that is dominated by the wealthy and plagued by corruption. Separate women's organizations play a significant role in addressing women's issues and in building women's 'voice'. In the 1990s, NGOs have been influential in international conferences. Their input, for example, resulted in a program of action from the International Conference on Population and Development in Cairo in 1994, stressing women's education and employment in population planning policies. The meeting of representatives from NGOs at the Fourth World Conference on Women in China in 1995 was the largest gathering of this type. The dynamic interaction of these NGOs holds a significant promise for stimulating relevant policy-oriented research and grassroots activities in the wake of the conferences.

The UN Conferences themselves are an institutional format for bringing topics to public attention and identifying a set of goals for government progress reports. During the 1990s, the environment, population and development, social development, women's issues and housing have been topics for the meetings and follow-up sessions.

One of the greatest disparities between women and men is in ownership of property (Agarwal 1994; Tinker and Summerfield 1999). With reforms that stress privatization and markets, women's rights to own property become even more significant. For joint ownership, women as well as men must sign the contracts. Women's traditional rights to land and housing have usually come through the husband. If he dies or they are divorced, the wife frequently loses her rights to the property. Although sons may maintain rights to property when their father dies, if they are underage, these rights are often not acknowledged.[2] Legal rights must be enforced to guarantee real capabilities and provide security. In 1999, the Supreme Court of Zimbabwe took a significant step backward when it ruled that traditional law would supersede civil law, in effect removing women's rights to property ownership. Critical institutional strategies would use new institutions such as NGOs to handle some of the responsibilities that governments would have addressed and to transform other institutions, such as the family, into more equitable units.

Environmental policy

The accelerating pace of environmental degradation has made sustainability a key aspect of development policies. The environment, however, is still not addressed consistently in policies and analysis (Wee and Heyzer 1995). In addition, while the 'brown' issues of pollution and extinction are compelling, the 'green' issues of environmentally friendly processes should also be addressed. Because men and women have different socially constructed gender roles, they interact with the environment differently. Men are more likely to find work in the forestry industry, for example, while women are more likely to lose their access to fuel wood and vegetation that they scavenge from the forest floor (Ireson 1996). Women are more likely to spend extra time fetching clean water when sources near their homes become polluted. They and their children are more likely to be affected by indoor pollution from inadequately ventilated charcoal stoves, or contamination associated with home-based microenterprises.

Women comprise more than two-thirds of the world's poor and tend to be more vulnerable to natural disasters and associated hunger and famine than men. Traditional discrimination in India has led to later hospital admissions for women during famines, resulting in higher mortality (Kynch and Sen 1983). Targeted feeding programs during famines have been identified with deprivation of girls in order to qualify the family for the program. Alternative strategies include: early intervention by permitting a free press to report problems, democratic political processes that are less tolerant of famine (although endemic hunger often remains a problem), and temporary government work programs that support income and food markets. These work programs during a crisis must be broad enough to reach more than a fraction of those affected and include jobs for women as well as men (Drèze and Sen 1985). Policies aimed at relieving endemic hunger are not gender neutral either since they are introduced into situations where women and girls are disadvantaged; one study indicated, for example, that direct feeding programs had a more beneficial effect on girls' health than programs that distributed food for the family to consume at home (Sen and Sengupta 1983).

Women have been the main subsistence agricultural producers in sub-Saharan Africa for years, and with trade liberalisation policies, they are increasingly the main agricultural workers in countries like China and Vietnam. With increased trade, more fertilizer and pesticides are imported and used. Often protective measures are inadequate; inappropriate use harms the workers, often women, who apply the products, and the consumers of the agricultural output – in the cities or, when they are exported, in other countries. Better labeling in appropriate languages, diagrams and training programs would be useful.

Some environmentally friendly products have expanded with trade liberalization. In particular, growing and exporting medicinal herbs has become a source of income for women in countries like Vietnam (Tinker and Summerfield 1999). Economic crises and cuts in health-care spending have increased the demand for traditional medicines as people switch from using expensive medical clinics and doctors.

Forward-looking themes

Methods and rhetoric continue to evolve. Researchers are increasingly looking for new methodological approaches; especially influential are Sen's capabilities and entitlements concepts and the post-structuralist, post-colonial works by various authors (Sen 1990, 1995; Nussbaum and Glover 1995; Escobar 1995; Jackson and Pearson 1998). Transnational issues overlap with areas of local feminisms, decreasing the projection of 'the other' in both South and North. Multi-disciplinary exchanges are increasing, bringing diverse fields and theories together: for example, art and political economy, or medicine and communications. Poor women help carry out their own surveys instead of being 'the researched' (UNCHS 1996); ordinary people equipped with video cameras tape their own documentaries.

As the field of women, gender and development looks to the future, some themes continue in importance; new issues emerge. The field continues to bring together scholars, practitioners and policy-makers. This is a strength. Policy-oriented research links the academy with the real world and helps practitioners discern whether the cases they are involved with are representative. Women's movements are working for change in many countries, in many different ways. These movements are one reason to keep *women* an integral focus of the field as well as the *gender* disparities.

The focus on women brings in organizational activities and centers on absolute changes in well-being. Gender stresses the crucial area of relative disparities and brings men as well as women into the dialog. At the same time, gender can be used inappropriately by people uncomfortable with women's issues to deflect the analysis away from women or to 'sanitize' it (Jackson and Pearson 1998). Both concepts – *women* and *gender* – are needed for a full understanding of changing capabilities because relative disparities may be shrinking even though absolute levels of 'goods' like education are falling (hardly a desirable outcome) and vice versa.

Economic transformation policies and the process of globalization continue to shape the environment of most of the world's people. The Asian Crisis of 1997–8 illustrates that we can expect crises to recur; to date, the response by local governments and the international financial institutions has relied mainly on the same type of policies observed in the earlier Debt Crisis with slightly more emphasis on the social safety net. Women as well as men need to be actively involved in reforming the international financial architecture so that responses to crises will be more appropriate to the specific circumstances and include an explicit focus on gender aspects (Aslanbeigui and Summerfield 2000).

Globalization affects employment, bringing women and men into more interaction with the market. It contributes to the growing labor-force participation rates of women, though many of the job opportunities are in low-level, low-wage work with few chances for advancement; it also contributes to the growing flexibility, informalization, and contingency nature of the labor force. Financial crises, wars, crime and environmental problems are leading to more focus on socio-economic, as well as political, security (Baud and Smyth 1997; Summerfield 2001). Studies of caring labor and methods of modeling macroeconomic changes with gender included are being examined (Cagatay *et al.* 1995; Grown *et al.* 2000).

Crossing borders reflects the growing interest in breaking the view of 'us' versus 'them.' Migration, between countries as well as from rural and urban areas, is an expanding area of interest as urbanization and globalization accelerate the process. Women are compelled to migrate for remunerative reasons, leaving behind their children and families. Indonesia's experience during the Asian Crisis illustrates that reverse migration, especially in times of economic upheaval, also occurs; in Indonesia during 1997–8, the agricultural sector had to absorb many of the newly unemployed urban residents. The line between more developed and developing countries is less distinct; problems and policies, as well as people, cross borders. Area studies and ethnic studies are finding common themes.

Thus, the paradigm is shifting from the earlier emphasis on growth to human-centered, environmentally aware development policies. Expansion of people's opportunities and capabilities and the security to exercise these opportunities become goals of development in global perspective. This process requires participation from women and men of different classes, ages, and backgrounds at all levels of decision-making and research.

Notes

1 See Beneria and Feldman 1992; Aslanbeigui, Pressman and Summerfield 1994; Bakker 1994; Sparr 1994; Elson 1995; and Pyle and Summerfield 2000.
2 In a recent case in Kenya, when the husband in a family with five adolescent sons died, his brothers claimed the land for their own use.

References

Agarwal, Bina (1994) *A Field of One's Own: Gender and Land Rights in South Asia*, New York: Cambridge University Press.

Aslanbeigui, Nahid and Gale Summerfield (2000) 'The Asian crisis, gender, and the international financial architecture,' *Feminist Economics*, vol. 6, no. 3, pp. 81–103.

Aslanbeigui, Nahid and Steven Medema (1998) 'Beyond the dark clouds: Pigou and Coase on social cost', *History of Political Economy*, vol. 30, no. 4, Winter, pp. 601–625.

Aslanbeigui, Nahid, Steven Pressman and Gale Summerfield (eds) (forthcoming) *Strategies and Policies in the Age of Economic Transformation*, London: Routledge.

—— (eds) (1994) *Women in the Age of Economic Transformation*, London: Routledge.

Bakker, Isabella (ed.) (1994) *The Strategic Silence: Gender and Economic Policy* London: Zed.

Basu, Amrita (1995) *The Challenge of Local Feminisms: Women's Movements in Global Perspective*, Boulder, CO: Westview Press.

Baud, Isa and Ines Smyth (eds) (1997) *Searching for Security: Women's Responses to Economic Transformations*, London: Routledge.

Becker, Gary S. (1991) *A Treatise on the Family*, Cambridge, MA: Harvard University Press.

Beneria, Lourdes and Shelley Feldman (eds) (1992) *Unequal Burden: Economic Crises, Persistent Poverty, and Women's Work*, Boulder, CO: Westview Press.

Blumberg, Rae Lesser, Cathy A. Rakowski, Irene Tinker and Michael Monteon (eds) (1995) *EnGENDERing Wealth and Well-Being*, Boulder, CO: Westview Press.

Boris, Eileen and Elisabeth Prugl (1996) *Homeworkers in Global Perspective: Invisible No More*, New York: Routledge.

Boserup, Ester (1970) *Woman's Role in Economic Development*, New York: St Martin's Press.

Cagatay, Nilufer, Diane Elson and Caren Grown (1995) 'Introduction', *World Development*, vol. 23, no.11, pp. 1827–36.

Drèze, Jean and Amartya Sen (1989) *Hunger and Public Action*, Oxford: Clarendon Press.

Elson, Diane (1995) *Male Bias in the Development Process*, 2nd edition, Manchester: Manchester University Press.

Escobar, Arturo (1995) *Encountering Development: The Making and Unmaking of the Third World*, New Jersey: Princeton University Press.

Goetz, Anna Marie and R. Sen Gupta (1996) 'Who takes the credit? gender, power and control over loan use in rural credit programs in Bangladesh', *World Development*, vol. 24, no. 1, pp. 45–63.

Grown, Caren, Diane Elson and Nilufer Cagatay (2000) 'Growth, trade, finance, and gender inequality', in *World Development*, vol. 28, no.7, pp. 1145–56.

Haddad, Lawrence, Lynn Brown, Andrea Richter and Lisa Smith (1995) 'The gender dimensions of economic adjustment policies: potential interactions and evidence to date', *World Development*, vol. 23, no. 6, pp. 881–96.

Hill, Anne and E. King (1995) 'Women's education and economic well being', *Feminist Economics*, vol. 1, no. 2, pp. 21–46.

Hirschman, Albert O. (1981) 'Rise and decline of development economics', in *Essays in Trespassing*, Cambridge: Cambridge University Press.

Hulme, David (2000) 'Impact assessment methodologies for microfinance: theory, experience and better practice', *World Development*, January, pp. 79–98.

Ireson, Carol (1996) *Field, Forest, and Family: Women's Work and Power in Rural Laos*, Boulder, CO: Westview Press.

Jackson, Cecile and Ruth Pearson (eds) (1998) *Feminist Visions of Development: Gender Analysis and Policy*, London and New York: Routledge.

Jaquette, Jane S. and Sharon L. Wolchik (eds) (1998) *Women and Democracy: Latin American and Central and Eastern Europe*, Baltimore and London: Johns Hopkins University Press.

Klasen, S. (1999) 'Does gender inequality reduce growth and development? Evidence from cross-country regressions', *Policy Research Report on Gender and Development*, Washington, DC: The World Bank.

Kynch, Jocelyn and Amartya Sen (1983) 'Indian women: well-being and survival', *Cambridge Journal of Economics*, no. 7, pp. 363–80.

Murphy, Josette (1997) *Mainstreaming Gender in World Bank Lending: An Update*, Washington, DC: The World Bank.

Nussbaum, Martha and Jonathan Glover (eds) (1995) *Women, Culture and Development: A Study of Human Capabilities*, Oxford: Clarendon Press.

Papanek, Hanna (1990) 'To each less than she needs, from each more than she can do: allocations, entitlements, and value', in Irene Tinker (ed.) *Persistent Inequalities: Women and World Development*, New York and Oxford: Oxford University Press, pp. 162–81.

Pyle, Jean and Gale Summerfield (2000) 'Economic restructuring', in Janice Peterson and Margaret Lewis (eds) *The Elgar Companion to Feminist Economics*, Cheltenham, UK and Northampton, MA: Edward Elgar, pp. 289–302.

Sen, Amartya (1984) 'Development: which way now?', in *Resources, Values and Development,* Cambridge: Harvard University Press, pp. 485–508.

—— (1990) 'Gender and cooperative conflicts', in I. Tinker (ed.) *Persistent Inequalities: Women and World Development*, New York: Oxford University Press, pp. 123–49.

—— (1995) 'Agency and well-being: the development agenda,' in Noeleen Heyzer (ed.) *A Commitment to the World's Women*, New York: UNIFEM, pp. 103–12.

Sen, Amartya and S. Sengupta (1983) 'Malnutrition of rural children and the sex bias', *Economic and Political Weekly*, p. 19.

Sparr, Pamela (ed.) (1994). *Mortgaging Women's Lives: Feminist Critiques of Structural Adjustment,* London: Zed.

Summerfield, Gale (1997) 'The development of economic development: 1980–95', in N. Aslanbeigui and Y.B. Choi (eds) *Borderlands of Economics: Essays in Honor of Daniel R. Fusfeld,* London and New York: Routledge, pp. 92–108.

Summerfield, Gale (ed.) (2001) *Risks and Rights in the 21st Century*, special symposium edition, *International Journal of Politics, Culture, and Society*, vol. 15, no. 1.

Summerfield, Gale and Irene Tinker (1997) 'The family and economic transformation in developing countries: impacts and strategies, a symposium based on issues raised at the NGO forum of the United Nations', Fourth World Conference on Women, Huairou, China, August 30–Sept. 9, 1995', *Review of Social Economy*, vol. 55, Summer.

Tinker, Irene (1997) *Street Foods: Urban Food and Employment in Developing Countries*, New York and Oxford: Oxford University Press.

Tinker, Irene and Gale Summerfield (eds) (1999) *Women's Rights to House and Land: China, Laos, Vietnam,* Boulder: Lynne Rienner Publishers.

UNCHS (1996) *Women's Empowerment: Participation in Shelter Strategies at the Community Level in Urban Informal Settlements*, New York: United Nations.

United Nations Development Fund for Women (UNIFEM) (2000) *Progress of the World's Women*, New York: United Nations.

Wee, Vivienne and Noeleen Heyzer (1995) *Gender, Poverty and Sustainable Development: Towards a Holistic Framework of Understanding and Action*, Singapore: ENGENDER and UNDP.

World Bank (2000) *Engendering Development: Policy Research Report on Gender and Development*, Washington, DC: World Bank.

World Development (1995) Special Issue: 'Gender, adjustment and macroeconomics', vol. 23, no. 11, November.

5 Food security in developing countries

Randy Stringer

Introduction

Food security and hunger are age old problems that endure today. More than 820 million people are chronically undernourished because they are unable to obtain sufficient food by any means. Chronic malnutrition results from a continuously inadequate diet, reducing physical capacity, lowering productivity, stunting growth and inhibiting learning. Over time, chronic malnutrition kills, blinds and debilitates. Yet enough food is produced worldwide to provide adequate food for all. The current global population of some 6 billion people have 15 per cent more food available per capita than had the world's 3 billion people some four decades ago. After fifty years of substantial economic growth, steady progress in agricultural productivity, remarkable increases in per capita food availability, and numerous international and national efforts to address hunger, food security remains a formidable global problem.

Food security implies an individual has access at all times to enough food for an active and healthy life. Food security has numerous interrelated dimensions. Availability of food and access to food are the two most common defining characteristics of food security. Availability and access to food are affected by population growth, demographic trends, economic development, government policies, income levels, health, nutrition, gender, environmental degradation, natural disasters, refugees, migration, disease and concentrated resource ownership. Nations increasingly understand that many of these problems cannot be resolved by one country or group; they transcend national borders, spreading starvation, instability and environmental degradation throughout the region and around the world.

During the early 1990s, food security issues pushed their way back onto a crowded international agenda. Not since the 'world food crisis' of the early 1970s had the international community focused so much attention on the seemingly never ending race between food production and population growth.[1] Record-low levels of global food reserves in the mid 1990s, weather-related crop failures, financial and economic crisis, policy-induced declines in food production and doubts about the long-term sustainability of the

Earth's resource base to meet future global demands focused increasing attention on food security. In addition, many of yesterday's issues are back on today's agenda because of renewed concerns over declining growth rates for cereal yields, falling investment levels in agricultural research, and the persistence of large numbers of malnourished people throughout the developing world.

Moreover, economic liberalisation, privatisation efforts, government spending reductions and the globalisation of investment and manufacturing began raising new concerns about agriculture's ability to compete for resources. Stabilisation policies, structural adjustment programmes and transitions from socialist to market-oriented economies influence sectoral and regional growth patterns, modify incentive structures, shift relative factor prices and reshape economic and social institutions. These far-reaching national-level reforms in economic, financial and political systems alter agriculture's capacity to attract or retain land, water, labour and investment.

Regional and multilateral trade agreements as well as international Conventions on biological diversity, forestry, wetlands, fisheries and climate change have important implications for food production, consumption and trade, further complicating food security policy choices. Because food security is fundamental to national security and economic growth, agriculture gradually began to play a more dominant role in the policy debates about how to restructure domestic economies, reorganise public sector activities, and expand regional and global trade and environmental agreements.

This chapter reviews food security issues in developing countries. The following section explores the evolving nature, characteristics and conceptual issues associated with food security, focusing on the various policy approaches used to address hunger and how those policies have changed over time. The third section discusses how food security is measured, providing an overview of regional experiences. The fourth section examines the relationship between food security, economic development and poverty. The fifth section assesses the topical issue of environmental sustainability. The sixth section attempts to explain why the too often ignored relationship between gender and food security is so crucial to a successful reduction in food insecurity. The final section provides some concluding remarks.

Food security: a question of supply or access?

Throughout the 1970s, the food security debate focused primarily on the collective ability of the world's nations to produce enough food to feed a rapidly expanding population. Most studies during this period tended to define food as cereals (Reutlinger 1977a; Valdés and Siamwalla 1981; Konandreas *et al.* 1978). Record low levels of cereal stocks and high cereal prices in the early 1970s raised fears about the long-term prospects of the world food system. The 1974 World Food Conference convened to address this growing perception that the world was moving irrevocably toward food shortages and to suggest mechanisms to protect food supplies from major crop failures.

The solutions that emerged focused on enhancing production possibilities, establishing national-level self-sufficiency targets, coordinating world food stocks and implementing import stabilisation policies (UN 1975; S. Maxwell 1994). For the most part, developing countries tended to pursue food self-sufficiency goals through agricultural policies and programmes that would increase domestic food production to meet national level targets. Even today, some countries still equate food security with food self-sufficiency, even though widespread evidence demonstrates that hunger coexists with abundant food supplies at regional, national and international levels.

Sen (1981) initiated the shift in thinking that helped broaden food security analysis from this narrow focus on national and global food supplies to include an access dimension faced by millions of households and individuals. Empirical evidence demonstrated that, while availability of food supplies is important, access to food by individuals is the greater constraint (Sen 1981; Ravallion 1987; Drèze and Sen 1989, 1990; Ravallion 1997). Access to food depends on an individual's access to resources, technology, markets, social networks and food transfer programmes. The opportunities to produce or obtain food by any of these means were described by Sen as entitlements.

Sen provided the theoretical basis for entitlements to food by demon-strating its relevance in famine situations (S. Maxwell 1994; Devereux 1993), pointing out that during the Ethiopian famine of 1972–4, food output, supplies and consumption at the national level were normal, yet 50 to 200 thousand people starved to death. Most died because they could not afford to buy food. These findings drew attention to the need for policy-oriented growth strategies aimed at providing an economic environment conducive to broad-based development, poverty reduction and access to food. Strategies to complement existing projects aimed at increasing food production and meeting national-level food self-sufficiency targets.

During the 1980s, researchers further enriched the food security debate by focusing attention on important distinctions between the household and individual as an appropriate unit of analysis. A key contribution emerging from this debate is that access to food by individuals is linked to their control over household income and household resources (S. Maxwell 1994; Evans 1991; Reutlinger 1985; Sahn 1989; Sen and Sengupta 1983). The policy implications can be enormous. For instance, research found that non-wage household income in urban Brazil has a much more positive effect on child health if it is controlled by mothers (Thomas 1991). Food security research in Kenya and Malawi found that: (a) child nutritional status is influenced by the interaction of income and gender of household head rather than just one or the other, and (b) household food security is influenced by total house-hold income, and the proportion of income controlled by women has a positive and significant influence on household caloric intake (Kennedy and Peters 1992).

The importance of nutritional security as a fundamental component of food security also began to emerge during the 1980s. Earlier approaches to food security that relied on target consumption levels (e.g. 80 per cent of the World Health Organisation's average required daily calorie intake) were shown to be inadequate for several reasons (S. Maxwell 1994). First, individual nutritional requirements vary a great deal depending on age, job, size and health (Payne and Lipton 1994). Second, behavioural characteristics are important influences on nutritional status including breast-feeding, sanitation habits and the use of local foods (World Bank 1995). Third, research suggested that micronutrient deficiencies, infections, diseases, intestinal parasites and environmental factors contributed to malnutrition as much as calorie deficiencies (Strauss and Thomas 1998; Del Rosso 1992; Tomkins and Watson 1989). Fourth, nutritional status has important effects on the quality of household labour resources (Kennedy and Bouis 1993).

During the 1990s, the food security literature expanded greatly to address market-oriented economic growth, agricultural development, poverty reduction, demographic trends, rising incomes, changing food consumption patterns, gender issues and the environment. In particular, market-oriented economic growth became *sine qua non* for reducing poverty and improving food security. Broad development lessons suggested the need for a greater emphasis on markets, removing anti-agricultural policy bias, and emphasising trade to promote growth, improve welfare and provide greater access to food (Stamoulis 1995). Specific development experiences, however, point to important caveats. First, the manner in which development strategies achieve economic growth and the number of people who participate and benefit are as important as the increased economic growth itself. Second, economic growth alone is insufficient to eliminate hunger. Third, as D. Maxwell and Wiebe (1998) point out, a complete definition of food security needs to incorporate three dimensions of access to food: (1) sufficient food to meet every individual's needs; (2) individuals must have the ability to generate sufficient food without sacrificing their endowments (Wiebe 1994); and (3) societies must be able to protect individuals from shocks, i.e. loss of job, disasters, financial crisis, etc.

Addressing these caveats became increasingly daunting for policymakers as countries opened their domestic markets to world market price signals as part of their overall policy reforms and market liberalisation. In particular, concerns rose that deregulated markets would affect food prices. The evidence shows that for more than fifty years, food supplies have been sufficient to ensure that international food prices increased less than other prices. Actions taken by governments, the private sector, and international agencies critically influence the short- to medium-term prospects (Anderson 1995).

Price fluctuations in world markets will persist because world production fluctuations are the dominant cause of price instability and those fluctuations are in part weather-determined. Price stabilisation strategies that looked to government interventions to vary the world's publicly held grain stocks will be less significant in the future with the implementation of the Uruguay Round agreement, involving as it does reductions in price support programmes in developed countries and hence cuts in world food surpluses. Any resulting increase in world price instability, if fully transmitted to domestic markets, would upset food-deficit developing countries. However, government stockholders were not aiming to stabilise international food prices (and, even if they were, they were not necessarily successful). Government programmes did crowd out private stockholders who could have contributed to the stabilising of international food prices. Therefore, the fear in food-deficit low-income countries of increased food insecurity following implementation of the Uruguay Round is not well founded (Anderson 1997; Johnson 1998).

Projections by FAO, IFPRI, the World Bank and others indicate that if governments pursue appropriate macroeconomic and sectoral policies and expand investment in agriculture, agricultural productivity will increase, global grain production will keep up with demand, and real cereal prices will continue the downward trend of the last fifty years (Alexandratos 1995; Islam 1995; Pinstrup-Anderson *et al.* 1997; Rosegrant and Ringler 1997; World Bank 1992c; Johnson 1998; Anderson *et al.* 1996).

In low-income countries where people spend a high proportion of their income on food, even small food price increases can be detrimental to the well-being of the urban and rural poor. Many of the poorest people in low-income countries also depend on agriculture – directly or indirectly – for their livelihoods, and rising crop prices may actually increase their real incomes and food intake.

Measuring progress in food security

The two most common measures of food security are: (1) whether adequate food supplies are available, and (2) whether individuals have sufficient access to those food supplies.[2] Food availability is measured in calories available per person per day at the country, regional and global levels. Both the mean and the variance of available supplies matter. The total quantity of foodstuffs produced in a country is added to the quantity imported and adjusted for changes in stocks, seed, wastage, livestock feed and non-food usages. In the mid 1990s, about 50 per cent of the world's cereal production was used for direct human consumption, and 37 per cent was used for feed (Alexandratos 1995).

In the developing countries as a group, progress in per capita food supplies has been nothing short of remarkable, increasing from 1,960 calories in the early 1960s to more than 2,600 calories by 1995/97 (Table 5.1). This 34 per cent gain per person is particularly impressive given that it took place during a period in which developing country population more than

Table 5.1 Per capita food supplies for direct human consumption

	Calories per day					
	1961/63	*1969/71*	*1979/81*	*1989/91*	*1995/97*	*2010*
Developing countries	1,960	2,130	2,320	2,510	2,626	2,730
East Asia	1,750	2,050	2,360	2,525	2,676	3,060
South Asia	2,030	2,060	2,080	2,314	2,423	2,450
Africa, sub-Saharan	2,100	2,140	2,080	2,114	2,190	2,170
Near East/North Africa	2,220	2,380	2,840	2,875	3,021	3,120
Latin America/Caribbean	2,360	2,510	2,720	2,692	2,791	2,950
Developed countries	3,020	3,180	3,270	3,301	3,223	3,470
World	2,300	2,440	2,580	2,699	2,761	2,870

Source: FAOSTAT, FAO, Rome and Alexandratos 1995.

doubled from 2.1 billion people to 4.6 billion. Between 1961/63 and 1995/97, per capita food supplies increased by more than 70 per cent in China and Indonesia; by more than 50 per cent in Pakistan and the Republic of Korea; and by more than 30 per cent in Brazil, Burkina Faso, the Dominican Republic, Ecuador, El Salvador, Jamaica, Mauritania and the Philippines.

Food supply gains resulted from a combination of stable domestic food production and strengthened import capacity. A considerable part of this gain is due to the rapid growth of food imports from the developed countries. Net cereal imports by the developing countries more than tripled during the 1970s, contributing to one-fifth of the increase in their food supplies (Alexandratos 1995).

Regions and countries did not share equally in these gains. Data in Table 5.1 show wide regional differences during the past thirty years. Table 5.2 presents per capita food supply data for selected countries by region, illustrating the significant gains made in a number of East Asian countries in particular.

Sub-Saharan Africa is the only region to stagnate, with essentially no increase in per capita food supplies since the early 1970s. The regions is generally characterised by high rates of population growth and urbanisation with declining or stagnating incomes and food production. Nor is the medium-term outlook for sub-Saharan Africa promising. Studies suggest that, at present trends, aggregate cereal demand and supply balances for African countries require a three-fold increase in cereal imports.

Some sub-Saharan African countries have made notable progress. For instance, the food production index has increased by more than 30 per cent between 1990 and 1998 in Angola, Burkina Faso, Ghana and Nigeria. Nevertheless, agriculture growth has been disappointing given its important role as the primary source of food, a principal means of livelihood and a major source of foreign exchange to finance food imports. Among the reasons for the generally poor performance are (Badiane and Delgado 1995): (a) chronic civil and social strife displacing large numbers of people; (b) severe droughts

Table 5.2 Per capita food supplies

	Calories per day			Percentage change
	1979–81	*1989–91*	*1995–97*	*1979/81 to 1995/97*
Sub-Saharan Africa				
Liberia	2,524	2,124	2,042	−19
Burundi	2,025	1,911	1,687	−17
Madagascar	2,418	2,157	2,019	−17
Central Africa Rep.	2,321	1,915	1,978	−15
Somalia	1,826	1,715	1,573	−14
Tanzania	2,277	2,216	2,000	−12
Congo DR	2,074	2,106	1,823	−12
Angola	2,147	1,798	1,900	−12
Rwanda	2,286	1,950	2,052	−10
Zambia	2,180	2,065	1,958	−10
Malawi	2,279	1,977	2,068	−9
Côte d'Ivoire	2,828	2,554	2,575	−9
Cameroon	2,346	2,168	2,144	−9
Kenya	2,146	1,916	1,977	−8
Mozambique	1,922	1,782	1,782	−7
Zimbabwe	2,230	2,146	2,095	−6
Niger	2,168	2,041	2,051	−5
Congo Rep.	2,221	2,188	2,133	−4
Sierra Leone	2,109	2,020	2,047	−3
Namibia	2,206	2,214	2,141	−3
Guinea	2,270	2,056	2,250	−1
Lesotho	2,248	2,222	2,236	−1
Swaziland	2,467	2,653	2,479	1
Uganda	2,214	2,302	2,168	2
Senegal	2,349	2,293	2,403	2
Gabon	2,416	2,447	2,527	5
Botswana	2,124	2,320	2,228	5
Sudan	2,252	2,155	2,379	6
Togo	2,186	2,292	2,336	7
Mauritius	2,669	2,838	2,923	10
Chad	1,648	1,740	1,959	19
Benin	2,046	2,297	2,466	21
Mauritania	2,123	2,557	2,616	23
Mali	1,758	2,157	2,208	26
Gambia	1,805	2,442	2,304	28
Burkina Faso	1,694	2,087	2,181	29
Nigeria	2,002	2,419	2,750	37
Ghana	1,743	2,075	2,617	50

Table 5.2   (continued)

	Calories per day			Percentage change
	1979–81	*1989–91*	*1995–97*	*1979/81 to 1995/97*
Asia				
Korea DPR	2,378	2,502	1,980	−17
Mongolia	2,168	2,203	1,920	−11
Laos	2,079	2,088	2,056	−1
Sri Lanka	2,314	2,201	2,288	−1
Philippines	2,229	2,395	2,363	6
Papua New Guinea	2,101	2,164	2,230	6
Thailand	2,193	2,235	2,351	8
Malaysia	2,724	2,758	2,938	8
Bangladesh	1,914	2,068	2,082	9
Pakistan	2,159	2,396	2,461	14
Vietnam	2,099	2,198	2,471	18
India	2,077	2,335	2,466	19
Cambodia	1,716	1,936	2,045	19
Nepal	1,905	2,371	2,315	22
China	2,315	2,653	2,834	22
Myanmar	2,318	2,625	2,853	23
Indonesia	2,176	2,617	2,900	33
Latin America and Caribbean				
Cuba	2,927	3,081	2,417	−17
Venezuela	2,759	2,390	2,388	−13
Haiti	2,042	1,769	1,837	−10
Nicaragua	2,270	2,238	2,181	−4
Uruguay	2,857	2,552	2,796	−2
Jamaica	2,647	2,594	2,595	−2
Mexico	3,114	3,080	3,108	0
Dominican Rep.	2,270	2,259	2,282	1
Paraguay	2,545	2,454	2,570	1
Guatemala	2,289	2,418	2,336	2
Bolivia	2,133	2,162	2,195	3
Costa Rica	2,587	2,716	2,686	4
Chile	2,665	2,540	2,774	4
Panama	2,271	2,346	2,425	7
Brazil	2,667	2,772	2,933	10
El Salvador	2,297	2,446	2,547	11
Peru	2,130	2,029	2,363	11
Honduras	2,117	2,302	2,366	12
Ecuador	2,359	2,499	2,660	13
Colombia	2,293	2,411	2,591	13

Source: FAOSTAT 1999.

during the 1980s and early 1990s; (c) the long-term consequences of the Cold War era on agriculture and rural development policy; and (d) the overall mismanagement of natural resources.

Per capita food supplies in the Latin America and Caribbean (LAC) region progressed steadily until the 1980s. LAC is the most urbanised and the most resource-rich of the developing country regions. LAC has 8 per cent of the world's population, 23 per cent of the arable land, more than 45 per cent of the forests and 30 per cent of its fresh water. The region also includes countries with some of the most concentrated land ownership patterns and income inequalities in the world. Agricultural production is dominated by large commercial farms. This lack of access to land is one important reason why about 75 per cent of the region's populations live in urban areas, as the landless rural poor are forced to migrate to cities in search of income-generating opportunities.

With 60 per cent of the world's population, Asia's overall performance was sufficiently strong to pull up the global average. South Asia recorded little progress until the 1980s, however. Asia's food supply gains have resulted primarily from increased domestic food production. Despite East Asia's rapid industrialisation, grain self-sufficiency decreased only marginally, from 98 per cent to 96 per cent, over the two-decade period from 1970 to 1990.[3] During the same twenty-year period, the ratio of food imports to total imports in Asia declined from 15 per cent to 5 per cent. Anderson *et al.* (1996), using an integrated economy-wide model, conclude that the food security provided by high levels of cereal self-sufficiency in the Asia region is unlikely to be threatened.[4]

Ever increasing food supplies are forecast over the next few decades (Table 5.1). FAO forecasts that food supplies will increase by 10 per cent per person in the developing countries during the twenty-year period from 1990 until 2010: food supplies will be more than 3,000 calories for East Asia, 2,450 calories for South Asia, 2,950 for Latin America and only 2,170 for sub-Saharan Africa (FAO 1996b). FAO, IFPRI and the World Bank all project substantial global increases in cereal production and consumption through 2010 (see Table 5.3).[5] All the developing regions are expected to rely on industrial country cereal exports (Australia, Canada, France and the United States). For the developing countries, the forecasts project cereal production growth rates of 1.8 to 2.1 per cent, with population growth rates of 1.7 per cent.

Attempts to understand how some countries have succeeded in increasing food supplies while others have failed is difficult given the wide range of experiences. In many countries, productivity growth contributed greatly to food security through cereal yield increases, particularly in rice and wheat. The combined effect of agricultural reforms and improved technologies helped to increase Asia's average rice yield level from 2 tonnes per hectare in 1966 to more than 3 tonnes per hectare in the 1980s (Agcaoili and Rosegrant 1995). This sustained technological performance in cereal production greatly

Table 5.3   Comparison of results of global cereals projections to 2010
(million tons, rice milled)

	Sub-Saharan Africa	Latin America and Caribbean	South Asia	East Asia	Rest of the world
Production					
Actual 1989/91	54.7	97.0	202.8	431.4	940.6
Projected to 2010					
Alexandratos	110.0	159.0	292.0	638.0	1,135.0
Agcaoili and Rosegrant	86.0	152.0	297.0	579.0	1,291.0
Mitchell and Ingco	83.0	144.0	282.0	626.0	1,176.0
Total use					
Actual 1989/91	64.7	111.4	203.3	459.1	891.3
Projected to 2010					
Alexandratos	129.0	185.0	302.0	673.0	1,045.0
Agcaoili and Rosegrant	118.0	165.0	307.0	616.0	1,200.0
Mitchell and Ingco	96.0	172.0	312.0	691.0	1,037.0
Net trade					
Actual 1989/91	−8.5	−11.3	−3.2	−27.4	54.1
Alexandratos	−19.0	−26.0	−10.0	−35.0	90.0
Agcaoili and Rosegrant	−32.0	−13.0	−10.0	−37.0	94.0
Mitchell and Ingco	−14.0	−28.0	−31.0	−59.0	132.0

Source: Islam 1995.

enhanced the region's food supplies. Cereal availability for human consumption in 1990 reached 201 kg per capita in East Asia and 156 kg in South Asia, compared with an average of 164 kg for the world (Alexandratos 1995).

To date, world food production has increased continuously because cropped area has expanded and productivity per unit area has increased. Table 5.4 presents country examples of the arable land available per person compared with per capita food supplies. No apparent relationship exists between a country's ability to provide available food supplies and its arable land supply. For many countries, technological change accounted for much of the food productivity growth over the last three decades, including genetic improvements to major crops and livestock and the adoption of improved farming techniques (including irrigation, fertiliser use, herbicides designed to kill weeds without harming the crops, and mechanised cultivation and harvesting methods).

The combination of these techniques with cultivars of higher yield potential is estimated to be responsible for more than half of the gains in farm yield (Oram 1995). In densely populated countries, however, there is little scope for further expansion of agricultural area. A study on the upper limits of the natural resource base for food production shows that the Asian region has the least leeway in the world for increasing food production without new technologies (Penning de Vries *et al.* 1995).

Table 5.4   Relationship between arable land per person and calories/per capita/day

Calories/capita/day (95/97 average)	Arable land per person (ha)		
	0.1 ha or less	Between 0.1 and 0.3 ha	More than 0.3 ha
Less than 2,200	Korea DPR Bangledesh Liberia Tanzania	Zimbabwe Laos Kenya Congo DR Nigeria	Chad Zambia Afghanistan Mongolia Cameroon
2,200–2,800	Sri Lanka Philippines Vietnam Colombia	Senegal Pakistan India Honduras	Cuba Togo Sudan Brazil
Greater than 2,800	China Malaysia Indonesia Mauritius	Myanmar Mexico	Argentina Uruguay

Source: Author's calculations based on FAO data.

After three decades of fairly steady growth in agricultural productivity, growth rates of food production have begun to lag. Warning signs include declining growth of arable and irrigated areas; increasing competition for resources between agriculture and other sectors; declining use of inputs such as fertiliser and pesticides due to environmental and health concerns; falling world food prices which discourage investment in agriculture, and neglect of agricultural research at national levels. For instance, rice yields in Indonesia have dropped from 5.2 per cent in the 1971–83 period, to 3.1 per cent in 1984–90, to less than 3 per cent today. In China, rice yield growth rates have slowed from more than 4 per cent a year in the late 1970s to about 1.6 per cent a year during the 1980s (Pinstrup-Anderson 1994).

These trends indicate that it would be imprudent to assume that yields will rise as in the past, unless actions are taken to raise research investment levels and improve the application of technology to natural resource management and to genetic improvements in key crops such as rice. The ability to maintain a stream of technical innovations will be a major determinant of food supply growth (Pardey *et al.* 1996).

Despite the overall success in food production at the global level and in every region except Africa, access to food and the lack of essential nutrients remain serious problems. In the world's poorest regions and countries, one-third of deaths among children are due to malnutrition (Del Rosso 1992). About one-half the deaths of children worldwide are associated with malnutrition, some six million deaths each year (WHO 1997). The total number of undernourished in developing countries is around 790 million (FAO 1999). An additional 34 million are in industrial and transition countries. The majority of undernourished live in Asia, accounting for almost two-thirds (526 million). India has more undernourished than all of sub-Saharan Africa. Nevertheless, undernutrition is especially severe in most of Africa. Of the 340 million people living in 26 African countries, 44 per cent are chronically undernourished. Only six other countries in the world have such high rates (Afghanistan, Bangladesh, Haiti, Korea DPR, Mongolia, and Yemen).

The vast majority are chronically malnourished because they either do not produce enough food or cannot afford to buy enough food. Table 5.5 provides data on the proportion of population undernourished for selected countries by region. The countries are ranked by percentage improvement in undernutrition between 1979/81 and 1995/97. The data indicates that in sub-Saharan Africa, undernutrition is less concentrated than in the Asian and Latin American and Caribbean regions. In Africa, two countries (Congo DR and Mozambique) account for 25 per cent of the undernourished population. In Asia, China and India account for 70 per cent and in Latin America, Brazil, Haiti, Mexico, and Peru account for 60 per cent.

Attempts to find factors contributing to success in increasing food security rarely reveal a set of common traits. No two countries are alike. One of the most common characteristics explaining success in decreasing the proportion of the population undernourished and in raising per capita food supplies is strong economic growth rates. Table 5.6 presents a series of variables for ten of the most successful countries, illustrating GDP growth rates greater than 4 per cent for all of these countries except Ecuador and Nigeria. Even in those two countries, GDP growth outpaced population growth. In contrast, most countries with significant increases in the proportion of undernourished had negative or very low GDP growth rates (Table 5.7). Bostwana and Uganda are notable exceptions. Table 5.8 provides food security related data for ten of the world's most populated developing countries, showing important gains in all countries (except Mexico) during the 1980s, with further gains in all countries except Bangladesh, Mexico and the Philippines during the 1990s.

The chronic malnutrition in these countries is inextricably linked to poverty. Poverty begets hunger, predictably and monotonously. The malnourished have little or no access to land, jobs, income or social support from their family, community or society. Food-insecure households include small and marginal farm families, landless agricultural workers, fishing villagers and forest dwellers. In many of these rural households, malnutrition is the primary cause of death among children. Evidence from South Asia further suggests that rural females, especially girls under 5 years old, are disproportionately vulnerable to food insecurity and nutritional risks within houscholds (Bardhan 1982; Dasgupta 1987; Muhavi and Preston 1991). In many African countries, a large proportion of the food-insecure are war victims (Christiaensen 1994).

Table 5.5 Undernourished population by region and country

	Population 1997 (000's)	Percentage of population undernourished			Percentage improvement in under-nourished	Numbers of under-nourished (000's)
		1979–81	1990–92	1995–97	1979/81 to 1995/97	1997
Sub-Saharan Africa						
Madagascar	14,620	18	34	39	−117	5,701.8
Côte d'voire	14,064	7	14	15	−114	2,109.6
Central Africa Rep.	3,420	22	45	42	−91	1,436.4
Liberia	2,402	22	49	42	−91	1,008.8
Tanzania	31,417	23	30	40	−74	12,566.8
Burundi	6,362	38	44	63	−66	4,008.1
Kenya	28,446	25	47	41	−64	11,662.9
Cameroon	13,924	20	30	32	−60	4,455.7
Rwanda	5,962	24	40	37	−54	2,205.9
Zambia	8,585	30	39	45	−50	3,863.3
Congo DR	47,987	37	36	55	−49	26,392.9
Angola	11,715	29	50	43	−48	5,037.5
Malawi	10,067	26	45	37	−42	3,724.8
Somalia	8,821	55	70	73	−33	6,439.3
Zimbabwe	11,215	30	40	39	−30	4,373.9
Niger	9,764	32	41	39	−22	3,808.0
Namibia	1,622	25	26	30	−20	486.6
Congo Rep.	2,709	29	32	34	−17	921.1
Mozambique	18,443	54	66	63	−17	11,619.1
Lesotho	2,016	26	31	28	−8	564.5
Sierra Leone	4,420	40	44	43	−8	1,900.6
Guinea	7,325	30	37	31	−3	2,270.8
Swaziland	925	14	9	14	0	129.5
Uganda	20,000	31	23	28	10	5,600.0
Senegal	8,772	19	19	17	11	1,491.2
Botswana	1,541	28	19	25	11	385.3
Sudan	27,718	24	31	20	17	5,543.6
Togo	4,284	31	29	23	26	985.3
Chad	7,086	69	58	46	33	3,259.6
Gabon	1,137	13	11	8	38	91.0
Mauritius	1,133	10	6	6	40	68.0
Mali	10,436	59	30	29	51	3,026.4
Burkina Faso	11,001	64	32	30	53	3,300.3
Gambia	1,189	57	17	25	56	297.3
Benin	5,629	36	21	15	58	844.4
Mauritania	2,461	35	15	13	63	319.9
Nigeria	103,898	40	13	8	80	8,311.8
Ghana	18,656	61	29	11	82	2,052.2

Table 5.5 (continued)

	Population 1997 (000's)	Percentage of population undernourished			Percentage improvement in under-nourished	Numbers of under-nourished (000's)
		1979–81	1990–92	1995–97	1979/81 to 1995/97	1997
Asia						
Korea DPR	22,981	19	16	48	−153	11,030.9
Mongolia	2,537	27	34	48	−78	1,217.8
Sri Lanka	18,274	22	29	25	−14	4,568.5
Laos	5,032	32	31	33	−3	1,660.6
Bangladesh	122,650	42	34	37	12	45,380.5
Thailand	59,736	28	27	24	14	14,336.6
Philippines	71,430	27	21	22	19	15,714.6
Papua New Guinea	4,499	31	27	24	23	1,079.8
Pakistan	144,047	31	20	19	39	27,368.9
India	966,192	38	26	22	42	212,562.2
Vietnam	76,387	33	28	19	42	14,513.5
Cambodia	10,478	62	41	33	47	3,457.7
Malaysia	20,983	4	3	2	50	419.7
Nepal	22,316	46	21	21	54	4,686.4
China	1,244,202	30	17	13	57	161,746.3
Myanmar	43,936	19	9	7	63	3,075.5
Indonesia	203,380	26	10	6	77	12,202.8
Latin America and Caribbean						
Cuba	11,068	3	3	19	−533	2,102.9
Venezuela	22,77	4	11	15	−275	3,416.6
Jamaica	2,516	8	12	11	−38	276.8
Uruguay	3,265	3	7	4	−33	130.6
Haiti	7,810	47	63	61	−30	4,770.2
Mexico	94,281	5	5	6	−20	5,656.9
Nicaragua	4,679	26	29	31	−19	1,450.5
Dominican Rep.	8,097	25	28	26	−4	2,105.2
Guatemala	10,519	17	14	17	0	1,788.2
Paraguay	5,088	13	18	13	0	661.4
Bolivia	7,774	26	25	23	12	1,788.0
Costa Rica	3,748	8	6	7	13	262.4
Panama	2,722	22	18	17	23	462.7
Chile	14,625	7	8	5	29	731.1
Peru	24,367	28	40	19	32	4,629.7
Honduras	5,981	31	23	21	32	1,256.0
Brazil	163,700	15	13	10	33	16,370.0
El Salvador	5,911	17	12	10	41	591.1
Colombia	40,043	22	17	12	45	4,805.2
Ecuador	11,937	12	8	5	58	596.9

Source: FAO 1999.

Table 5.6 Food security related data in ten of the most improved countries

	Calories per capita per day	Percentage of population undernourished	Population (000s)	Arable land per person (ha)	Average annual GDP growth		Percentage improvement in daily availability of calories		Percentage improvement in proportion of population undernourished	
	1995/97	1995/97	1997	1997	1980–90	1990–97	1979/81 to 1989/91	1989/91 to 1995/97	1979/81 to 1989/91	1989/91 to 1995/97
Ghana	2,617	11	18,656	0.15	3.0	4.2	19	26	52	62
Peru	2,363	19	24,367	0.15	–0.3	6.2	–5	16	–43	53
Uruguay	2,796	4	3,265	0.39	0.4	4.0	–11	10	–133	43
Indonesia	2,900	6	203,380	0.09	6.1	7.5	20	11	62	40
Nigeria	2,750	8	103,898	0.27	1.6	2.8	21	14	68	38
Ecuador	2,660	5	11,937	0.13	2.0	3.1	6	6	33	38
Chile	2,774	5	14,625	0.14	4.2	8.3	–5	9	–14	38
Sudan	2,379	20	27,718	0.60	0.4	7.7	–4	10	–29	35
Malaysia	2,938	2	20,983	0.09	5.3	8.6	1	7	25	33
Vietnam	2,471	19	76,387	0.07	4.6	8.6	5	12	15	32

Source: Author's calculations based on FAOSTAT 1999, Rome: FAO and World Bank Development Indicators 1999.

Table 5.7 Food security related data in twelve of the least improved countries

	Calories per capita per day	Percentage of population undernourished	Population (000s)	Arable land per person (ha)	Average annual GDP growth		Percentage improvement in daily availability of calories		Percentage improvement in proportion of population undernourished	
	1995/97	1995/97	1997	1997	1980–90	1990–97	1979/81 to 1989/91	1989/91 to 1995/97	1979/81 to 1989/91	1989/91 to 1995/97
Cuba	2,417	19	11,068	0.33	–	–	5	–22	0	–533
Korea DPR	1,980	48	22,981	0.07	–	–	5	21	16	200
Congo DR	1,823	55	47,987	0.14	1.6	–6.0	2	–13	3	–53
Gambia	2,304	24	1,189	0.16	3.6	2.2	35	–6	70	–47
Burundi	1,687	63	6,362	0.12	4.4	–3.6	–6	–12	–16	–43
Mongolia	1,920	48	2,537	0.52	5.4	–0.6	2	–13	–26	–41
Venezuela	2,388	15	22,777	0.12	1.1	2.2	–13	0	–175	–36
Tanzania	2,000	40	31,417	0.10	–	2.7	–3	–10	–30	–33
Botswana	2,228	25	1,541	0.22	10.3	4.5	9	–4	32	–32
Uganda	2,168	28	20,000	0.25	2.9	7.4	8	–6	26	–22
Guatemala	2,336	17	10,519	0.13	0.8	4.1	6	–3	18	–21
Mexico	3,108	6	94,281	0.27	0.7	2.2	–1	1	0	–20

Source: Author's calculations based on FAOSTAT 1999, Rome: FAO and World Bank Development Indicators 1999.

Table 5.8 Food security related data in ten of the most populated countries

	Calories per capita per day	Percentage of population undernourished	Population (000s)	Arable land per person (ha)	Average annual GDP growth		Percentage improvement in daily availability of calories		Percentage improvement in proportion of population undernourished	
	1995/97	1995/97	1997	1997	1980–90	1990–97	1979/81 to 1989/91	1989/91 to 1995/97	1979/81 to 1989/91	1989/91 to 1995/97
China	2,834	13	1,244,202	0.10	10.2	11.6	15	7	43	24
India	2,466	22	966,192	0.17	5.8	6.0	12	6	32	15
Indonesia	2,900	6	203,380	0.09	6.1	7.5	20	11	62	40
Brazil	2,933	10	163,700	0.33	2.7	3.4	4	6	13	23
Pakistan	2,461	19	144,047	0.15	6.3	4.2	11	3	35	5
Bangladesh	2,082	37	122,650	0.06	4.3	4.7	8	1	19	−9
Nigeria	2,750	8	103,898	0.27	1.6	2.8	21	14	68	38
Mexico	3,108	6	94,281	0.27	0.7	2.2	−1	1	0	−20
Vietnam	2,471	19	76,387	0.07	4.6	8.6	5	12	15	32
Philippines	2,363	22	71,430	0.07	1.0	3.3	7	−1	22	−5

Source: Author's calculations based on FAOSTAT 1999, Rome: FAO and World Bank Development Indicators 1999.

Food security, poverty and agricultural growth

The vast majority of the poor live in rural areas (Lipton and Ravallion 1995; World Bank 1990; Bidani and Ravallion 1993; Datt 1994; and World Bank 1992a). In East Asia, nearly 90 per cent of the poor live in rural areas (Johansen 1993). In Mexico, Central America and the Andean countries of South America, more than 60 per cent of the poor live in rural areas under much worse conditions than those in urban areas (Valdés and López 1999). Ironically, hunger is concentrated in regions where the majority of the population produce food, but where available food supplies are among the lowest in the world. A comparative study of seven Asian countries documents how much more the rural poor depend on agriculture for jobs, income and food relative to the rural non-poor (Quibria and Srinivasan 1991).

A general consensus emerged during the 1990s that policymakers tended to ignore or underestimate the poverty reduction potential of their agricultural sectors. The evidence suggests that periods of high agricultural growth rates are associated with falling rural poverty and increasing food security (Binswanger and von Braun 1991; Timmer 1992; Bell and Rich 1994; Johnson 1993). Strong agricultural growth leads to: (1) lower food prices (for urban consumers and rural net-food buyers); (2) increased income-generating opportunities for food producers and jobs for rural workers (thus reducing rural–urban migration, with positive consequences for real urban wage rates); and (3) positive intersectoral spillover effects including migration, trade and enhanced productivity (Lipton and Ravallion 1995; Timmer 1992). For example, in both China and Indonesia, rapid agricultural growth substantially reduced rural poverty, improved food security in both rural and urban sectors, and provided a significant demand-side stimulus for non-agricultural goods and services.

Improving access to food and nutrition increases learning capacity and school performance and leads to longer school attendance, fewer school and work days lost to sickness, and also leads to higher earnings, longer work lives and a more productive work force. These are essential to economic growth. And economic growth is essential for increasing incomes, reducing poverty and improving food security. The manner in which development strategies achieve growth, however, and the number of people who participate in and benefit from it are as important as the growth itself.

Economic growth is fundamental to achieving a sustainable balance between food production and food needs. In the past fifty years of development, some of the most impressive improvements in food security have been gained by those countries managing their economies to achieve broad-based economic benefits (Binswanger and Deininger 1997; Stamoulis 1995). The manner in which governments control economic policies determines whether or not households prosper, poverty declines and food security increases. The incentives provided by government policies are among the most powerful measures national governments can use to influence how economic, social, institutional and natural resources are managed.

National governments can use policies to affect agricultural sector performance through their impact on growth, equity, stability and sustainability; to affect poverty by influencing incomes, prices, trade and institutional structures; and to affect food security by modifying food prices, rural employment, allocation of productive resources, wages and incomes among both agricultural and non-farm rural producers.

By ignoring the poverty reduction potential of their agricultural sectors, policymakers allow macropolicies to inhibit rural sector growth through direct and indirect taxation of food producers, traders and exporters (Krueger *et al.* 1991; Bautista and Valdés 1993). In contrast, a non-discriminatory policy environment for agriculture and unskilled labour is more likely to promote a sustainable growth pattern that is essential for improving food security.

Agricultural sectors are growing relatively slowly, a trend of declining agricultural comparative advantage in the process of industrialisation experienced by structural changes in developing countries worldwide. The share of agricultural output in total production in developing countries as a group has declined from 26 per cent in the early 1960s to 13 per cent in 1997. For the same period, agriculture's share of GDP fell from 40 to 18 per cent in East Asia; 43 per cent to 25 per cent in South Asia, 17 per cent to 8 per cent for Latin America and the Caribbean and 28 per cent to 18 per cent for sub-Saharan Africa.

Within the existing production possibilities, many developing countries are exploring the scope for increasing agricultural output at relatively low cost through agricultural policy reforms. This is highlighted by the experience of China's institutional and market reforms (Findlay 1996). Significant potential grain output increases appear to be possible by closing the gap between current actual farm performance and best practice (Huang and Kalirajan 1996; Lin and Shen 1994).

Structural characteristics of the world's population are also changing in ways that affect food security. United Nations projections suggest that world population will increase by about 3.5 billion by 2020 to reach a total of 7.5 billion (United Nations 1999). While the population growth rate will fall, the greatest absolute number of the additional people will live in Asia, where population will increase by more than 1.5 billion by 2020. China's population will expand to around 1.5 billion people, and India to more than 1.3 billion. In addition, between 1995 and 2020, developing country urban populations are expected to double, increasing from 1.7 billion to 3.4 billion (United Nations 1998).

Thirty years ago, 80 per cent of the population in developing countries lived in rural areas. In the early 1970s, only one city in sub-Saharan Africa had more than half a million inhabitants; by 1990, 10 per cent of the region's population lived in cities of more than one million people, and by 2000, nearly 40 per cent of the population live in urban areas. In the next thirty years, the number of people living in cities in developing countries will quadruple from one billion to four billion individuals. This imposing shift towards a more urban world calls for a different set of institutions, markets, infrastructure and food policies. These structural changes also modify farm labour supplies and pose important challenges for food security.

This demographic transformation profoundly affects food consumption. As countries urbanise, consumer diets and behaviours change dramatically. Urban dwellers consume less grain and more meat, dairy products and fish than their rural counterparts, even after accounting for differences in income and prices (Huang and Bouis 1996). Direct per capita consumption of cereal as food has declined over the past three decades in the rapidly growing economies. In those countries with continued economic growth, changing food demand structure will be reflected in reduced direct demand for food grains but increased indirect demand for feed grains.

Delgado *et al.* (1999) outline seven livestock-related implications of rising incomes, increased urbanisation and population growth in developing countries:

1   rapid worldwide increases in consumption and production of livestock products;
2   increasing share of developing countries in total livestock production and consumption;
3   an ongoing change in the status of livestock production from small-scale local activities to global activities;
4   increased substitution of meat and dairy products for grains in diets;
5   rapid rise in the use of cereal-based feeds;
6   greater emphasis on grazing resources and more intensive production closer to cities; and
7   the emergence of rapid technological change in livestock production and processing in industrial systems.

Food security and sustainable development

Within several years of publication of the Brundtland Report in 1987 (WCED 1987), sustainable development had become a dominant feature of development thinking. By the time delegates met in 1992 for the United Nations Conference on Environment and Development (UNCED), the international community's guiding principles on sustainable development implied that agriculture should widen its focus from expanding production and increasing yields to include sustainable management of ecological processes, environmental services and social goods.

Despite a message of harmony, however, the concept of agricultural sustainability raises tension between market-driven economic growth strategies, social pressures for a more equitable distribution of economic opportunities and the need to maintain environmental productivity, ecological services and biodiversity to fulfil future economic and social aspirations. Often, this tension is expressed in emotional debates over how food security and agricultural activities conflict with environmental objectives in both developed and developing countries and whether poverty in the developing countries or high consumption levels in the industrial countries contribute more to environmental degradation (Mink 1993).

International Conventions on biodiversity, forestry and climate change, however important, may have negative implications for the world's food supply, at least in the short term. For example, the climate change Convention raises the possibility of establishing carbon taxes and would result in higher energy costs, new input mixes and changing technologies. The combination would imply higher production costs for food producers and higher prices for consumers. Furthermore, since transformation of forest land into agricultural land accounts for the majority of deforestation over the past ten years, international agreements that constrain forest conversion will alter future food production possibilities.

Increasing resource scarcity and environmental degradation also affect food security. UNCED represents an important expression of the international community's recognition of these matters. In many parts of the developing world, expanding populations and shortages of fertile land, water and forests are already contributing to expelling farmers from agriculture and creating thereby a class of 'environmental refugees' (Homer-Dixon *et al.* 1993)

Contemporary development also includes concepts of inter-generational equity and justice. For the first time in human history, the world community is collectively attempting to understand how today's actions may affect the planet's ecosystems one hundred years into the new millennium. Incorporating this broad range of values into sustainable food production is appealing and necessary, but difficult in practice. The question frequently posed is: how can resources be used today to greatly enhance food security but in such a way that their capacity to generate production for future generations at the same level is not diminished?

Population pressure, institutional constraints (e.g. property rights and concentrated ownership), market failures and government policies are all blamed for inducing food production patterns and practices that result in soil, water and wind erosion, nutrient mining, waterlogging, salinisation, forest destruction, sedimentation and marine pollution. Resource degradation contributes to rural poverty, urban migration and erratic food production. This deterioration in the production potential of natural resources is a major concern for future food security (Anderson 1992; Rosegrant and Ringler 1997; Stringer 1997).

Agricultural and food production practices misuse and degrade land, soil and water resources in a variety of ways. Clearing steep forested hillsides causes water and wind erosion; applying pesticides and chemical fertilisers adds toxic materials; burning vegetation cover destroys organic layers; and extensive use of farm machinery and livestock grazing compact soils. An estimated 15 per cent of the world's soils (1,965 million ha) are considered to be moderately to extremely degraded: 1,094 million ha due to water erosion, 548 million ha due to wind erosion, and the remainder due to a combination of salinisation, nutrient decline and physical compaction (UNEP 1991). In Asia, an estimated 453 million ha are considered to be moderately to extremely degraded: 315 million ha due to water erosion, 90 million ha due to wind erosion, 41 million ha due to chemical degradation and 6 million ha due to physical degradation.

Standardised surveys conducted by the Global Assessment of Human-induced Soil Degradation document considerable damage to 1.96 billion ha or 15 per cent of the world's soils (UNEP 1991). Water erosion accounts for 55 per cent of the damage followed by wind erosion (28 per cent), nutrient decline (7 per cent), salinisation (4 per cent), and physical compaction (3 per cent).

Soils suffering from severe to extreme degradation means that their original biotic functions are damaged and reclamation is at worst impossible and at least difficult or costly. Yield reduction in food crops due to these various forms of soil erosion can be significant. In Africa, yield reduction caused by past erosion is estimated at 9 per cent (FAO 1996c).

This process of resource degradation contributes to rural poverty, urban migration and erratic food production. As previously noted, the majority of the rural poor live and work in ecologically fragile, economically marginal and environmentally degraded areas. Protecting environmentally vulnerable areas and making them more productive requires long-term investments. Poor and subsistence producers in fragile areas lack the capital necessary to invest in natural resource protection; they tend to have high rates of time preference; and, normally, are unable even to avoid the impacts of environmental degradation on their existing production base. This deterioration in the production potential of natural resources is a major concern for Asia's future food security.

Poverty often induces food producers to degrade natural resources and environmental services even though they depend heavily on a sustained resource base for survival. At the same time, government programmes and policies aimed at alleviating poverty often contribute to environmental degradation by directly encouraging or unintentionally subsidising environmental degradation (Bromley *et al.* 1980; Barnes and Olivares 1988; Dasgupta and Maler 1990; Leach and Mearns 1991; Vosti *et al.* 1992; Mink 1993).

For example, clearing of forested hillsides by poor and landless families is one of the major causes of deforestation and watershed degradation, yet government policies exacerbate the problem, producing intense and lasting impacts on forest resources. Numerous studies document how taxation policy, terms of forest concessions, administered prices, controlled transportation of forest goods, land and tree tenure insecurity, tariff and non-tariff barriers to international trade, investment incentives, agricultural sector strategies and macroeconomic policies have affected negatively the economic motivations, management and conservation of forests (Contreras-Hermosilla 1993; Barbier *et al.* 1993; Panayotu 1993; Repetto 1986; World Bank 1992b).[6] The fundamental problem for policymakers remains how to address the under-lying causes, including poverty, hunger, access to land, and the lack of jobs and income-generating opportunities.

Resource degradation presents a direct threat to food security. For poor rural communities at the margin of subsistence, resource degradation means greater food production instability as the frequency of poor harvests increases. In most developing countries, population pressure and poverty appear to be linked to much of the land and water degradation, overgrazing, deforestation and fuelwood scarcity; evidence suggests that much of the responsibility lies with inappropriate government policies (Panayotou 1993; Pearce and Warford 1993).

Price subsidies (e.g. fertiliser, pesticides, credit and water) encourage excessive use of inputs by farmers; poorly defined or enforced property rights and restrictions on the length of land leases encourage excessive intensity of cultivation. Correcting these distortions through policy reform alleviate these pressures on the food-producing resource base. A recent study of long-term trends in the quality of soil in China and Indonesia is heartening, for it finds no evidence of net deterioration during the past half-century or more (Linhert 1996, 1999). Evidently in those cases at least, farmers have been investing enough back into the soil over that period to at least offset the gross damage done by poor farming practices or policies.

In recent years, increasing international concern has focused on water degradation and food security linkages.[7] The principal concern is that growing water scarcity and misuse of freshwater pose serious threats to long-term food security and sustainable development. Competition among agriculture, industry and cities for limited water supplies is already constraining development efforts in many countries (Gleick 1998; Bhatia and Falkenmark 1992; Homer-Dixon *et al.* 1993; UNCED 1992). As populations expand and economies grow, the competition for limited supplies will intensify; so will conflicts among water users.

Throughout the world, food depends increasingly on irrigation, so food security is closely linked with water security. Some 40 per cent of the world's food comes from the irrigated 17 per cent of the total cultivated land; around one-fifth the total value of fish production comes from freshwater aquaculture; and current global livestock drinking water requirements are 60 billion litres per day (forecasts estimate an increase of 0.4 billion litres per year). The majority of the incremental production comes from irrigation as farmers struggle to maintain crop yield growth to keep production in line with population and incomes.

Irrigation's contribution to food security in China, Pakistan, Egypt, Morocco and India is widely recognised (Stringer *et al.* 1993). In India, 55 per cent of agricultural output is from irrigated land. Moreover, average farm incomes increased from 80 to 100 per cent as a result of irrigation, while yields doubled over prior rainfed conditions and incremental labour days used per ha increased from 50 to 100 per cent. In Mexico, one-half the value of agriculture production and two-thirds the value of agricultural exports is from the one-third of the arable land that is irrigated.

Irrigation provides opportunities to increase and stabilise incomes and food production, while gains in productivity lower food prices and raise farm earnings. Irrigation offers more reliability, higher yields and a more diversified choice of cropping patterns; it also makes other yield-increasing innovations more attractive for investment and provides opportunities for growing high-value crops.

Even though water shortages are occurring throughout the world, misuse is widespread. Numerous studies document how small communities and large cities, farmers and industries, developing countries and industrial economies are all mismanaging water resources (Repetto 1986; World Bank 1992b; Gleick 1998; Postel 1992). Surface water quality is deteriorating in key basins from urban and industrial wastes. Groundwater is being polluted from surface sources and irreversibly damaged by saltwater intrusion. Overexploited aquifers are losing their capacity to hold water and lands are subsiding. Cities are unable to provide adequate drinking water supply and sanitation facilities. Waterlogging and salinisation are diminishing the productivity of irrigated lands. Decreasing water flows are reducing hydroelectric power generation, pollution assimilation and fish and wildlife habitat. The very ecosystems responsible for producing water and maintaining our hydrological cycles and its many related services are insufficiently monitored and poorly understood (Gleick 1993; Dasgupta and Maler 1990).

In the mid-1980s, Repetto estimated that average subsidies to irrigation in six Asian countries covered 90 per cent of the total operating and maintenance costs (Repetto 1986). Case studies indicate that irrigation fees are on the average less than 8 per cent of the benefits derived from irrigation. Despite these huge investments and growing subsidies, irrigation performance indicators are falling short of expectations for yield increases, area irrigated and technical efficiency in water use. As much as 60 per cent of the water diverted or pumped for irrigation is wasted (Stringer *et al.* 1993). Although some losses are inevitable, in too many cases this excess water seeps back into the ground, causing waterlogging and salinity. As much as one-quarter of all irrigated land in developing countries may suffer from varying degrees of salinisation (FAO 1993). Moreover, stagnant water and poor irrigation drainage significantly escalate the incidence of water-related diseases, resulting in human suffering and increased health costs.

The dilemma facing policymakers is that irrigated agriculture is expected to produce much more in the future while using less water than it uses today. At present, 2.4 billion people depend on irrigated agriculture for jobs, food and income – some 55 per cent of all wheat and rice output is irrigated. Over the next thirty years, an estimated 80 per cent of the additional food supplies required to feed the world will depend on irrigation (IIMI 1992).

Improving resource management requires recognising how agricultural land, water and forest resources are linked to the national economy. Equally important is understanding how alternative economic policy instruments influence resource use across different economic sectors; between local, regional and national levels; and among households, food producers and firms.

Gender and food security

Policymakers have only recently begun to recognise that meeting world future food needs depends more than ever on the capabilities and resources of women. Women produce more than half the food grown in developing countries. Women farmers in sub-Saharan Africa produce more than three-quarters of the region's basic food, manage some two-thirds of marketing and at least one-half of the activities required for storing food and raising animals (Gittinger 1990; Saito 1994). In addition, they are now cultivating crops and taking on tasks traditionally undertaken by men and are increasingly making decisions on the daily management of farms and households. Women account for more than two-thirds of food production in Asia and some 45 per cent in Latin America and the Caribbean (FAO 2000). In Southeast Asia, women provide up to 90 per cent of labour for rice cultivation and much of the labour for food storage, handling and marketing, and they predominate in small businesses that process food throughout the developing world. They also are responsible for the feeding, nutrition and health of hundreds of millions of families.

With few exceptions, women must fulfil these multiple jobs with little or no access to productivity-enhancing resources and services such as credit, education, training, technical assistance, marketing networks and health care. A study on credit use in five African countries found that women received less than 10 per cent of the credit awarded to male smallholders and only 15 per cent of the world's agricultural extension agents are women (FAO 2000). Women compose the poorest segment of rural populations and make up more than 70 per cent of all people living in absolute poverty (World Bank 1990).

Women could more effectively improve food access, availability and stability if development policies recognised and responded to their needs and capabilities. This requires: ensuring equal access to and control of productive resources; increased participation in decision-making and policy formulation at all levels; greater opportunities for income and employment; and reductions in time and other constraints on productivity. A World Bank study estimates that the rate of return on investments in women's education is of the order of 12 per cent in terms of increased productivity (Saito 1994). The study concludes that farm-specific yields would increase from 7 per cent to 22 per cent. Increasing women's primary schooling alone would increase agricultural output by 24 per cent.

The recent expansion of women's roles in food production and provision makes this issue even more pressing. Land scarcity, deterioration of agricultural incomes, armed conflict and diseases reduce male labour in many rural areas, increasing the number of *de facto* or *de jure* female-headed households. As a result, women are taking on new agricultural and income-earning responsibilities in addition to their traditional workload.

The assumption of these new roles bears many hidden costs for women, for their families and for the economy in general. For example, in sub-Saharan Africa, the steady migration of males to cities and other areas to look for wages or a job in the informal sector places women at the focal point of responsibility for farm work. Raising agricultural productivity and output and improving household food security demands a greater emphasis on women farmers, including policy reforms to improve women's access to land and credit, their ability to contract labour, and their willingness to adopt technology and utilise technical assistance.

Most governments have signed various international agreements, treaties and Conventions since the 1970s, pledging to pay greater attention to the needs of women, particularly rural women, and to focus more efforts and resources on raising their productivity. Despite these commitments, however, the pace of change has been slow and many development efforts are still not reaching significant numbers of women as intended (Snyder *et al.* 1996). The neglect of women and the resulting losses in potential productivity gains and in opportunities for economic growth are most obvious in the agricultural sector, where women are taking on greater responsibility for food production without a commensurate increase in agricultural inputs, resources and support services.

The reasons behind the failure to reorient development benefits towards women in agriculture are well documented (Snyder *et al.* 1996). Critics point to the continued exclusion of women from the design, planning, appraisal, implementation, management, monitoring and evaluation of rural development activities. They also cite inadequate research that continues to ignore or underestimate women's contributions to farm activities. Other reasons for poor results range from lack of female leadership and appropriate resources in recipient governments to gender biases inside donor agencies.

Summary

Throughout the developing world, the heightened role of food security is pressuring governments to modify sectoral policies to accommodate new demands for safeguarding the opportunities of future generations by protecting the earth's natural systems. The food-insecure compose heterogeneous groups, characterised by location, occupational patterns, asset ownership, race, ethnicity, age and gender. Programmes to improve food security need to be tailored to the need and circumstances of each group.

Successful development experiences suggest that significant, complement-ary improvements in food security, poverty reduction and sustainable develop-ment can be made when policymakers:

1   seek policy portfolios suited to broad-based growth and build in flexibil-ity to adjust this portfolio over time in response to new developments;
2   remove unfair market privileges, input subsidies and price incentives which decrease competition in output, input and credit markets, raise costs to consumers and taxpayers, and encourage overuse and misuse of resources;
3   ensure that equity and gender play a central role in decisions about appropriate responses to food security and sustainability concerns;
4   focus public sector actions on those rural development services under-provided by the private sector; and
5   revitalise public and private investments in agricultural research to encourage new technologies for sustainable development.

Targeted interventions to accelerate the hunger reduction process are becoming an important component in the growth-based food security strategy to deal with the wide range of shocks faced by households, including loss of job, crop failures, seasonal food shortages, economic crisis or recession, natural or human-caused disasters, etc. Two approaches to direct interventions are used: the growth-mediated security policy and the support-led security policy (Drèze and Sen 1989). In the first approach, as the benefits of economic growth accumulate, they are targeted to low-income groups through public work programmes, food subsidies and job training projects. In the second, investments in income transfer programmes, health care and education are initiated even before the proceeds from economic growth are captured. The data in Table 5.9, comparing the returns in lifelong wages from alternative interventions, emphasise the importance of matching specific food and nutrition policy variables to cost effectiveness programmes. Indeed, only the generalised food subsidy programme shows a loss, with every $1.00 spent on generalised food subsidies returning $0.90 in lifelong wages.

Development lessons suggest the best role for the public sector is to provide a conducive policy environment and basic rural infrastructure, including roads, irrigation, safe drinking water, sanitation and electrification to take full advantage of their direct effects on food security through productivity gains, lower transaction costs and employment creation; and their indirect effects on agricultural growth through the strengthening of linkages between public and private investment.

Successful development records indicate these public investments and policy attention should concentrate on resource-poor, high-poverty rural areas where food security depends on increasing production and resilience through diversification of production systems and of economic activities. For example, growth strategies should promote diversified farming systems and diversified economic activities.

Table 5.9 Returns to nutrition investments

Programme	Returns to programme dollar in lifelong wages and decreased disability*
Food supplements	1.4
Nutrition education	32.3
Nutrition as part of primary health care	2.6
Food subsidies	0.9
School feeding	2.8
Iron pills supplementation for pregnant women	24.7
Iron fortification of flour	84.1
Iodine supplementation for reproductive age women	13.8
Iodised salt	28.0
Vitamin A supplementation for all children under 5	50.0
Vitamin A fortification of sugar	16.0

Source: McGuire 1996 cited on World Bank's web page, www.worldbank.org/html/extdr/hnp/
nutrition/tnan.htm.
*For each dollar spent on a programme, this much is returned in increased lifelong wages and
decreased disability discounted to the present.

In resource-poor rural areas, important food security activities for the public sector include: providing educational, technological and financial support to encourage mixed farming systems that mitigate environmental consequences by integrating livestock, tree crops, and annual crops; establishing training programmes on soil fertility and organic matter management, moisture conservation, erosion control and nutrient recycling; encouraging diversity in research and extension efforts to accommodate site-specific differences in resource-poor and fragile areas and involve farmers in the process; establishing secure property rights for both private and common property resources including forests, pastures and watersheds; and providing nutrition-related extension services to increase food availability through home gardens, urban agriculture, food processing and preservation.

In high-potential agricultural areas with fertile soils and favourable climates, environmentally friendly intensification and specialisation require competitive markets, good management practices and timely information. Policy reforms alone can often lower costs and improve environmental incentives for small-scale processors, transporters and traders. Other low-cost measures include adjustments in extension programmes and information systems to incorporate environmental production approaches such as integrated pest management, integrated plant nutrition systems and rural energy use. In specific cases, funds must be allocated to rehabilitate, conserve and monitor resource use.

As the supply of high-potential agricultural land dwindles in developing countries, per capita food production gains rely increasingly on expanding output per unit of land. Over time, the extensive land margin shrinks and the costs of further expansion become too high relative to intensification. To compensate for this shrinking crop land base in both absolute terms and relative to population size, countries are turning to land-saving technologies to underpin their advances in food productivity growth. The development, use and appropriateness of land-saving technologies depend on a number of factors including: large amounts of private and public sector investments in human capital and physical infrastructure; a national and global system of research in biological, physical and social sciences; institutions to develop and extend new technologies; and well-developed local, domestic and international markets for both factor and product markets.

Notes

1   Among the recent international development agencies focusing on how global trends are influencing food security are the World Bank's Conference on Overcoming Global Hunger (1993), the ongoing initiative by the International Food Policy Research Institute, 2020 Vision for Food, Agriculture and the Environment (1995–6), the International Fund for Agricultural Development sponsored Conference on Hunger and Poverty (1995), and the United Nations Food and Agricultural Organisation's World Food Summit (1996).
2   Food security is a necessary but not sufficient condition for nutritional security. Micronutrient deficiencies, infectious diseases, intestinal parasites, and environmental factors can contribute to malnutrition even for people with access to adequate food supplies.
3   Self-sufficiency in other food commodities in East Asia also increased: pulses increased from 106 to 109 per cent, and vegetable oils from 132 to 146 per cent, from the early 1970s to the early 1990s.
4   The study's conclusion includes the importance of continued technical progress in agriculture; an excessive emphasis by existing studies on grains relative to meat, livestock products and processed foods in East Asian economies (especially China); and the importance for agriculture to be part of any regional free trade agreement in APEC – excluding agriculture would reduce potential global welfare gains by nearly half (Anderson *et al.* 1996).
5   See the Appendix to Part II in Islam (1995) for a comparison of these three major food supply, demand and trade studies. For a detailed analysis of each study see Mitchell and Ingco (1993) for the World Bank; Alexandratos (1995) for FAO and Agcaoili and Rosegrant (1995) for IFPRI.
6   See FAO (1994) and Contreras-Hermosilla (1993) for Asian examples.
7   For example, in January 1992, the UN System sponsored the International Conference on Water and the Environment (ICWE) in Dublin. The ICWE called for innovative approaches to the assessment, development and management of freshwater resources. In addition, the ICWE provided policy guidance for the UN Conference on Environment and Development (UNCED) in Rio de Janeiro in June 1992. UNCED highlighted the need for water sector reforms throughout the world. In 1993, the World Bank issued a comprehensive policy paper defining its new objectives for the water sector. FAO recently established an International Action Programme on Water and Sustainable Agricultural Development. Likewise, UNDP, WHO, UNICEF, WMO, UNESCO and UNEP and the regional development banks have developed water sector strategies papers. The

1990 Montreal meeting, NGOs Working Together, focused attention on drinking water supply and sanitation. The Canadian International Development Agency, the French Ministry of Cooperation, the German Agency of Technical Cooperation, the Overseas Development Administration (UK) and the US Agency for International Development have developed water resources strategies for foreign assistance.

References

Agcaoili, M. and M. Rosegrant (1995) 'Global and regional food supply, demand and trade prospects to 2010', in N. Islam (ed.) *Population and Food in the Early Twenty-First Century: Meeting Future Food Demands of an Increasing Population*, Washington, DC: IFPRI.

Alexandratos, N. (1995) *World Agriculture Towards 2010, An FAO Study*, New York: John Wiley and Sons.

Anderson, K. (1992) 'Agricultural policies, land use and the environment', the 14th Denman Lecture, Cambridge: Grant for the University of Cambridge (CIES Reprint no. 16), University of Adelaide.

—— (1995) 'Agricultural competitiveness after the Uruguay round', *Review of Marketing and Agricultural Economics*, vol. 63, no. 3, pp. 351–62.

—— (1997) 'Agricultural policy reform under the Uruguay round: impact on Asian-Pacific developing countries', *Journal of the Asia Pacific Economy*, vol. 2, no. 3, pp. 303–31.

Anderson, K., B. Dimaranan, T. Hertel and W. Martin (1996) 'Asia-Pacific food markets and trade in 2005: a global, economy-wide perspective', *Australian Journal of Agricultural and Resource Economics*, vol. 41, no. 1, pp. 19–41.

Badiane O., and C.L. Delgado (1995) *A 2020 Vision for Food, Agriculture, and the Environment in Sub-Saharan Africa*, Washington, DC: IFPRI.

Barbier, E., J. Burgess, J. Bishop, B. Aylward and C. Bann (1993) 'The economic linkages between the international trade in tropical timber and the sustainable management of tropical forests', Yokohama: International Timber Trade Organisation.

Bardhan, P.K. (1982) 'Little girls and death in India', *Economic and Political Weekly*, vol. 17, no. 36, pp. 1448–50.

Barnes, D.F. and J. Olivares (1988) 'Sustainable resource management in agriculture and rural development projects: a review of bank policies, procedures and results', *Environment Department Working Paper no. 5*, Washington, DC: World Bank.

Bautista, R. and A. Valdés (1993) *The Bias against Agriculture: Trade and Macroeconomic Policies in Developing Countries*, San Francisco: ICS Press.

Bell, C. and R. Rich (1994) 'Rural poverty and agricultural performance in post-independence India', *Oxford Bulletin of Economics and Statistics*, vol. 56, no. 2, pp. 111–33.

Bhatia, R. and M. Falkenmark (1992) 'Water resource policies and the urban poor: innovative approaches and policy imperatives', background paper for the International Conference on Water and Development, Dublin, Ireland.

Bidani, B. and M. Ravallion (1993) 'A new regional poverty profile for Indonesia', *Bulletin of Indonesian Economic Studies*, vol. 29, no. 3, pp. 37–68.

Binswanger, H.P. and K. Deininger (1997) 'Explaining agricultural and agrarian policies in developing countries', *Journal of Economic Literature*, vol. 35, no. 4, pp. 1956–2005.

Binswanger, H.P and P. Landell-Mills (1995) 'The World Bank's strategy for reducing poverty and hunger', *Environmentally Sustainable Development Studies and Monographs Series no. 4,* Washington, DC: World Bank.

Binswanger, H.P and J. von Braun (1991) 'Technological change and commercialization in agriculture: the effect on the poor', *World Bank Research Observer,* vol. 6, no. 1, pp. 57–80.

Bromley, D., D. Taylor and D. Parker (1980) 'Water reform and economic development: institutional aspects of water management in the developing countries', *Economic Development and Cultural Change,* vol. 28, no. 2, pp. 365–87.

Christiaensen, L. (1994) *Food Security: From Concept to Action,* Brussels: Belgian Administration for Development Cooperation.

Contreras-Hermosilla, Arnoldo. (1993) 'Forestry policies in India', Paper prepared for the South Asia Region Seminar on Forestry Management and Sustainable Development, Kandy, Sri Lanka, 4–9 October 1993.

Dasgupta, P. (1987) 'Selective discrimination against female children in rural Punjab, India', Population and Development Review, vol. 13, no. 1, pp. 77–100.

Dasgupta, P. and I. Maler (1990) *The Environment and Emerging Development Issues,* Helsinki: World Institute for Development Economics Research.

Datt, G. (1994) *Poverty in India, 1951–91,* Poverty and Human Resources Division, Washington, DC: World Bank.

Del Rosso, J. (1992) *Investing in Nutrition with World Bank Assistance,* Washington, DC: World Bank.

Delgado, C., M. Rosegrant, H. Steinfeld, S. Ehui and C. Courbois (1999) 'Livestock to 2020: the next food revolution', 2020 Vision for Food, Agriculture, and the Environment Discussion Paper 28, Washington, DC: IFPRI.

Devereux, S. (1993) *Theories of Famine,* New York: Harvester Wheatsheaf.

Drèze, J. and A. Sen. (1989) *Hunger and Public Action,* Oxford: Oxford University Press.

—— (1990) *The Political Economy of Hunger,* vols 1–3, Oxford: Oxford University Press.

Evans, A. (1991) *Gender Issues in Rural Household Economics,* IDS Bulletin, vol. 22, no. 1.

FAO (Food and Agriculture Organization of the United Nations) (1990) *An International Action Programme on Water and Sustainable Agricultural Development,* Rome: FAO.

—— (1994) *Forest Development and Policy Dilemmas,* Rome: FAO.

—— (1996a) *Food Security Situation and Issues in Asia and the Pacific,* Twenty-third FAO Regional Conference for Asia and the Pacific, Apia, Samoa, 14–18 May.

—— (1996b) *Food Agriculture and Food Security, The Global Dimension,* WFS96/Tech/1, Rome: FAO.

—— (1996c) *Food Production and Environmental Impact,* World Food Summit Technical Background Documents, No. 11, Rome: FAO.

—— (1999) *The State of Food Insecurity,* Rome: FAO.

—— (2000) http://www.fao.org/Gender/en/agrib4-e.htm .

Findlay, C. (1996) 'Grain output growth potential in China', paper presented at the International Workshop on Output Growth Potential, Market Development and Internationalisation in China's Grain Sector, 4–5 October, Beijing.

Gittinger, J. (1990) *Household Food Security and the Role of Women,* World Bank Discussion Paper No. 96, Washington, DC: World Bank

Gleick, P. (1993) *Water in Crisis,* New York: Oxford University Press.

—— (1998) *The World's Water 1998-99: The Biennial Report on Freshwater Resources*, Washington, DC: Island Press.

Homer-Dixon, T., J.H. Boutwell and G.W. Rathjens (1993) 'Environmental change and violent conflict', *Scientific American*, February.

Huang, J. and H. Bouis (1996) *Structural Changes in the Demand for Food in Asia*, Food, Agriculture, and the Environment Discussion Paper, no. 11, Washington, DC: IFPR.

Huang, Y. and K.P. Kalirajan (1996) 'Potential of China's grain production: evidence from the household data', paper presented at the International Workshop on Output Growth Potential, Market Development and Internationalisation in China's Grain Sector, 4–5 October, Beijing.

IIMI (International Irrigation Management Institute) (1992) *Developing Environmentally Sound and Lasting Improvements in Irrigation Management: The Role of International Research*, Colombo, Sri Lanka: IIMI.

Islam, N. (1995) *Population and Food in the Early Twenty-First Century: Meeting Future Food Demands of an Increasing Population*, Washington, DC: IFPRI.

Johansen, F. (1993) *Poverty Reduction in East Asia: The Silent Revolution*, World Bank Discussion Papers 202, Washington, DC: World Bank

Johnson, D.G. (1973) *World Agriculture in Disarray*, London: Macmillan Press Ltd.

—— (1993) 'The role of agriculture in economic development revisited', *Journal of Agricultural Economics*, vol. 8, pp. 421–34.

—— (1998) 'Food security and world trade prospects', *American Journal of Agricultural Economics*, vol. 80, no. 5, pp. 941–7.

Kennedy, E. and H. Bouis (1992) *Linkages Between Agriculture and Nutrition: Implications for Policy and Research*, Washington, DC: IFPRI.

Kennedy, E. and P. Peters (1992) 'Household food security and child nutrition: the interaction of income and gender of household head', *World Development*, vol. 20, no. 8, pp. 1077–9.

Konandreas, P., B. Huddleston and V. Ramangkura (1978) *Food Security: An Insurance Approach*, Research Report No. 4, Washington, DC: IFPRI.

Krueger, A.O., M. Schiff and A. Valdes (1991) 'Agricultural incentives in developing countries: measuring the effects of sectoral and economy wide policies', *World Bank Economic Review*, vol. 2, pp. 255–71.

Leach, M. and R. Mearns (1991) 'Environmental change, development challenge', *IDS Bulletin*, vol. 22, no. 4, p. 15.

Lin, J. and M. Shen (1994) 'Rice production constraints in China: implication for biotechnology initiative', paper presented to the International Workshop on Rice Research Prioritisation in Asia, Los Banos: International Rice Research Institute.

Linhert, P.H. (1996) 'Soil degradation and agricultural change in China and Indonesia', CIES Seminar Paper 96-14, Adelaide: CIES.

—— (1999) 'The bad earth? China's soils and agricultural development since 1930s', *Economic Development and Cultural Change*, vol. 47, no. 4, pp. 701-36.

Lipton, M. and M. Ravallion (1995) 'Poverty and policy', in J. Behrman and T.N. Srinivasan (eds) *Handbook of Development Economics Vol IIIB*, Amsterdam: Elsevier Science BV.

Maxwell, D. and K. Wiebe (1998) *Land Tenure and Food Security: A Review of Concepts, Evidence, and Methods*, Land Tenure Center Research Paper no. 129, Madison: LTC.

Maxwell, S. (1994) 'Food security: a post-modern perspective', Institute of Development Studies, Working Paper No. 9, University of Sussex.

Mink, S. (1993) *Poverty, Population and the Environment*, World Bank Discussion Paper 189, Washington, DC: World Bank.

Mitchell, D.O. and M.D. Ingco (1993) *The World Food Outlook*, Washington, DC: World Bank.

Muhavi, D.K. and S.H. Preston (1991) 'Effects of family composition on mortality differentials by sex among children in Matlab Thana, Bangladesh', *Population and Development Review*, vol. 17, no. 3.

Oram, P. (1995) *The Potential of Technology to Meet World Food Needs In 2020*, Washington, DC: IFPRI.

Panayotou, T. (1993) *Green Markets: The Economics of Sustainable Development*, San Francisco: ICS Press.

Pardy, P.G., J.M. Alston, J.E. Christian and S. Fan (1996) *Summary of a Productivity Partnership: The Benefits from US Participation in the CGIR*, Discussion Paper, Environment and Production Technology Division, Washington, DC: IFPRI

Payne, A. and M. Lipton (1994) *How Third World Households Adapt to Dietary Energy Stress: The Evidence and the Issues*, IFPRI Food Policy Review, Washington, DC: IFPRI.

Pearce, D. and J. Warford (1993) *World Without End, Economics, Environment and Sustainable Development*, New York: Oxford University Press.

Penning de Vries, F., H. Van Keulen, R. Rabbinge and J.C. Luyten (1995) *Biophysical Limits to Global Food Production*, Washington, DC: IFPRI.

Pinstrup-Anderson, P. (1994) *World Food Trends and Future Food Security*, Food Policy Statement, no. 18, Washington, DC: IFPRI.

Pinstrup-Anderson, P., P.R. Pandya-Lorch, and M.W. Rosegrant (1997) *The World Food Situation: Recent Developments, Emerging Issues, and Long-Term Prospects*, Washington, DC: IFPRI.

Postel, S. (1992) *Last Oasis: Facing Water Scarcity*, New York: W.W. Norton & Company.

Quibria, M.G. and T.N. Srinivasan (1991) *Rural Poverty in Asia: Priority Issues and Policy Options*, Manila: Asian Development Bank.

Ravallion, M. (1987) *Markets and Famines*, Oxford: Oxford University Press.

—— (1997) 'Famines and economics', *Journal of Economic Literature*, vol. 35, September, pp. 1205-42.

Repetto, R. (1986) *Skimming the Water: Rent-Seeking and the Performance of Public Irrigation Systems*, World Resources Institute Research Report no. 4, December.

Reutlinger, S. (1977a) *Food Insecurity: Magnitudes and Remedies*, World Bank Working Paper no. 267, Washington, DC: World Bank.

—— (1977b) 'Malnutrition: a poverty or a food problem?', *World Development,* vol. 5, no. 8, pp. 715-24.

—— (1985) 'Food security and poverty in LDCs', *Finance and Development*, vol. 22, no. 4, Washington, DC: IMF.

Rosegrant, M. and C. Ringler (1997) 'Environmental and resource policies: implications for global food markets', paper presented at the 41st Annual Conference of the Australian Agricultural and Resource Economics Society, 20–24 January, 1997, Pan Pacific Hotel Gold Coast.

Sahn, D.E. (1989) 'A conceptual framework for examining the seasonal aspects of household food security', in D.E. Sahn (ed.) *Seasonal Variability in Third World*

Agriculture: The Consequences for Food Security, Baltimore: Johns Hopkins University Press.

Saito, K.A. (1994) *Raising the Productivity of Women Farmers in Sub-Saharan Africa*, World Bank Discussion Paper, no. 230, Africa Technical Department Series, Washington, DC: World Bank.

Schuh, G.E. (1974) 'The exchange rate and U.S. agriculture', *American Journal of Agricultural Economics*, vol. 56, no. 1.

Sen, A. (1981) *Poverty and Famines: An Essay on Entitlement and Deprivation*, Oxford: Clarendon Press.

—— (1990) 'Food, economics, and entitlements', in J. Drèze and A. Sen (eds) *The Political Economy of Hunger*, vol. 1, Oxford: Oxford University Press.

Sen, A. and S. Sengupta (1983) 'Malnutrition of rural children and the sex bias', *Economic and Political Weekly*, vol. 18, pp. 855–64.

Snyder, M., F. Berry, and P. Mavima (1996) 'Gender policy in development assistance: improving implementation results', *World Development,* vol. 24, no. 9, pp. 1481–94.

Stamoulis, K. (1995) 'Agricultural development in the economy-wide context: approaches to policies and strategies', in N. Alexandratos (ed.) *World Agriculture Towards 2010, An FAO Study*, New York: John Wiley and Sons.

Strauss J. and D. Thomas (1998) 'Health, nutrition and economic development', *Journal of Economic Literature*, vol. 36, June, pp. 766–817.

Stringer, R. (1997) *The Environment, Economics and Water Policies*, CIES Policy Discussion Paper 97/02, Adelaide: CIES.

Stringer, R., R.A. Young and I. Carruthers (1993) 'Water policies and agriculture', in *The State of Food And Agriculture*, Rome: FAO.

Thomas, D. (1991) *Gender Differences in Household Resource Allocation*, Population and Human Resources Department, Living Standards Measurement Study, Working Paper, no. 79, Washington, DC: World Bank.

Timmer, P. (1992) 'Agriculture and economic development revisited', *Agricultural Systems*, no. 40, pp. 21-58.

Tomkins, A. and F. Watson (1989) *Malnutrition and Infection*, Administrative Committee on Coordination Subcommittee on Nutrition, Nutrition Policy Discussion Paper, no. 5, New York: United Nations.

Umale, D.L. (1993) *Irrigation Induced Salinity: A Growing Problem for Development and the Environment*, World Bank Technical Paper, no. 215, Washington, DC: World Bank.

UNCED (United Nations Conference on Environment and Development) (1992) *Agenda 21*, Chapter 18, 'The protection of the quality and supply of freshwater', New York: United Nations.

UNEP (United Nations Environment Programme) (1991) UNEP/ISRIC *Global Assessment of Human-induced Land Degradation* (GLASOD), Wageningen, the Netherlands and Nairobi, Kenya: UNEP.

United Nations (1975) *Report of the World Food Conference*, New York, 5–16 November, New York: United Nations.

—— (1998) *World Urbanization Prospects: The 1996 Revision*, New York: United Nations.

—— (1999) *World Population Prospects: The 1996 Revision*, New York: United Nations.

Valdés, A. and A. Siamwalla (1981) 'Chapter 1: Introduction', in A. Valdés (ed.) *Food Security for Developing Countries*, Boulder: Westview Press.

Valdés, A. and R. López (1999) 'Fighting rural poverty in latin america: new evidence and policy', paper presented at the American Agricultural Economics Association Meetings, Nashville, Tennessee, 8–11 August.

Vosti, S.A., T. Reardon and W. von Urff (1992) *Agricultural Sustainabilty, Growth and Poverty Alleviation: Issues and Policies*, Washington, DC: IFPRI.

Wiebe, K. (1994) 'Household food security and cautious commercialization in Kenya', PhD Dissertation, University of Wisconsin, Madison: University of Wisconsin.

WCED (World Commission on Environment and Development) (1987) *Our Common Future*, London: Oxford University Press.

WHO (World Health Organisation) (1997) *Global Database on Child Growth and Malnutrition*, Geneva: WHO.

World Bank (1986) *World Bank Development Report*, New York: Oxford University Press.

—— (1990) *World Bank Development Report*, New York: Oxford University Press.

—— (1992a) *China: Strategies for Reducing Poverty in the 1990s*, Washington, DC: World Bank.

—— (1992b) 'Development and the environment', *World Development Report*, Washington, DC: World Bank.

—— (1992c) 'Price prospects for major primary commodities', Washington, DC: World Bank.

—— (1995) *Poverty and Hunger: Issues and Options for Food Security in Developing Countries*, Washington, DC: World Bank.

6 External debt, government expenditure, investment and growth

G.S. Gupta

Introduction

The full employment theory of the classical school has been proved wrong by the real life experiences of the world since the Great Depression. Though the Keynesian theory of the possibility of both full as well as below full employment equilibrium has the limitations of ignoring the role of expectations and policy lags, among others, its prescription of enlarging the effective (aggregate) demand to remove unemployment is still valid. For a developing economy, a relatively easy way to expand aggregate demand would be through an increase in government expenditure financed through raising external debt. Thus, external debt, to the extent it is sustainable, could be a way to alleviate the problem of unemployment and to push up growth.

Demand could be pushed up through attracting foreign direct investment as well. However, this requires the presence/creation of incentives for such investments. Further, though foreign investments do create employment in the host country, their profits go to the foreign investors. If the return on investment exceeds the cost of borrowing (which is often true), foreign direct investments become inferior to external borrowings (foreign portfolio investment). Also, from the investors' point of view, direct investments are more risky than lending, particularly if it is in a developing external economy. However, external debt has one disadvantage over foreign direct investment, as the former has fixed obligations for its servicing, while the latter is to be serviced if and only when it yields profit. Grants from abroad are also a source of foreign funds but they depend on the donor countries and they are associated with the social stigma of 'mercy'.

External debt : dimension and distribution

Borrowing and lending externally has prevailed for over a century and the debt crisis of the 1980s was not the first one to be experienced. However, instead of going into its history, here we concentrate on the debt and the associated crisis which was triggered by the OPEC (Organisation of Petroleum

Exporting Countries) decision to raise the crude oil price significantly from $2.59 to $11.65 a barrel in 1974 and again in 1978 and thereafter to take it to $32 a barrel by 1981. This led to the transfer of many billions of dollars from the oil-importing countries to the oil exporters. The oil importers became suddenly poor and oil exporters were flooded with money. These petro dollars were recycled in the forms of lendings and borrowings through banks, which led to the growth of external debt.

Debt trends

The World Bank publishes data on external debt and related variables of developing countries (numbering 136) on a regular basis. These reveal that the total of such debt increased from $603 billion in 1980 to $2,171 billion in 1997 (see Table 6.1). This marks an annual growth rate of 7.8 per cent, which is greater than the economic growth rate achieved by this group of countries during the corresponding period. An intra-period analysis of the data indicates that the growth rate was much higher (8.5 per cent) during 1980 through 1995 than between 1995 and 1997 (3.1 per cent). The debt service (interest plus amortization) increased from $91 billion in 1980 to $269 billion in 1997, indicating an annual growth rate of 6.6 per cent. Debt service as a proportion to debt outstanding stands at around 12 per cent on average, which is quite low, indicating the softness of external debt.

A careful examination of the various debt indicators during approximately the last two decades (see Table 6.1) reveals that between 1980 and 1997 the ratio of:

(a) the debt to GNP has increased from 21 per cent to 35 per cent;
(b) the debt to exports (of goods and services, including workers' remittances) has increased from 85 per cent to 134 per cent;
(c) debt service to exports has gone up from 13 per cent to 17 per cent;
(d) international reserves to debt fell from 6.8 per cent to 6.4 per cent; and
(e) concessional debt to total debt went up from 18 per cent to 20 per cent.

The first four of the above five ratios indicate the ability of the borrowers to service the debt and each one of them has moved in the unfavourable direction over time. Thus, the debt burden is up not only in terms of the absolute burden but also in terms of the ability to service the same. The last ratio, the share of the concessional debt to total debt, has shown an upward trend, which is a welcome change, but it still accounts for only a small fraction (one-fifth) and the trend is rather small. There is no rule of thumb to ascertain the debt sustainability. However, an analysis of the debt to GNP ratio, debt to exports ratio and debt service to exports over time for the developing countries' group as a whole suggests a fairly comfortable position. Debt servicing has remained a small fraction of exports and the debt to GNP ratio at about one-third. The debt crisis could have been caused

Table 6.1 External debt and debt indicators of developing countries
(US$billions/per cent)

	No. of countries	End of year						Annual growth rate
		1980	1985*	1990	1995	1996	1997	1980–96/97
A Debt of all countries								
($ billion)	136	603	991	1,444	2,043	2,095	2,171	7.8
1 Total debt		(21)	(35)	(35)	(39)	(36)	(35)	
2 Total debt service	136	91	134	160	230	262	269	6.6
B Debt indicators of all								
countries (per cent)	136							
3 Total debt/exports	136	85	183	162	149	137	134	2.7
4 Total debt service/		13	25	18	17	17	17	1.6
exports								
5 Int'l reserves/total	136	6.8	14.7	7.9	6.9	6.4	6.4	-0.3
debt								
6 Concessional debt/	136	18	15	21	21	20	20	0.6
total debt								
C Debt of region								
($ billion)	136							
7 East Asia and		65	166	239	447	447	512	12.9
Pacific (EAP)	16	(16)	(29)	(37)	(36)	(34)	(32)	
8 Europe and Central		76	158	221	354	370	389	10.1
Asia (ECA)	28	(9)	(20)	(17)	(36)	(34)	(32)	
9 Latin America and		257	390	475	637	656	678	5.9
Caribbean (LAC)	27	(36)	(61)	(46)	(39)	(37)	(38)	
10 Middle East and		84	–	182	216	212	217	5.7
North Africa (MENA)	10	(18)		(38)	(35)	(31)	(29)	
11 South Asia (SA)	7	38	68	130	157	152	154	8.6
		(17)	(25)	(34)	(31)	(27)	(26)	
12 Sub-Saharan Africa		84	–	196	231	227	223	5.9
(SSA)	48	(34)	–	(75)	(82)	(78)	(71)	
D Debt by income and								
indebtedness ($ billion)	136							
13 Severely indebted and	36	57	122	210	241	233	–	8.2
low income		(31)	(38)	(139)	(111)	(94)	–	
14 Severely indebted and	12	185	392	414	557	589	–	7.5
middle income		(34)	(58)	(48)	(39)	(38)	–	
15 Moderately indebted	13	43	109	138	166	161	–	8.6
and low income		(19)	(30)	(36)	(38)	(34)	–	
16 Moderately indebted	16	184	193	363	565	577	–	7.4
and middle income		(34)	(24)	(46)	(51)	(47)	–	
17 Other developing	59	134	175	318	515	536	–	9.1
countries		(10)	(22)	(17)	(25)	(23)	–	

Source: World Bank : *Global Development Finance* (1998) and earlier issues of *World Debt Tables*.

Notes: (a) Numbers in parentheses are per cent of GNP. (b) *1985 data are not quite comparable with other years. (c) – data not available.

not by the solvency constraint but by the liquidity trouble, for the proportion of foreign exchange reserves to external debt stood only at around 7 per cent during 1990s, whereas it was around 15 per cent in 1985.

Debt by region

The 136 developing countries have been classified according to the six regions. The data on the distribution of their debt over time by this classific-ation are included in Table 6.1 above. The Latin America and Caribbean region has been owing the most while the South Asia region the least. The debt of these two regions has increased at the annual rate of about 5.9 per cent and 8.6 per cent, respectively, during the seventeen years of this analysis. The region with the second largest debt is East Asia and Pacific, whose debt has grown at the annual rate of 12.9 per cent, which is the highest rate among all the six regions. This happens to be the region which has attained perhaps the highest rate of economic growth during the period of this analysis. This gives some credibility to the theory of 'debt-led growth'. The region with the lowest growth rate in debt happens to be the Middle East and North Africa, where the growth rates have been relatively small.

In terms of the external debt relative to GNP, sub-Saharan Africa tops the list, with a debt ratio of over 70 per cent in four out of the five years for which data are reported here. Latin America and the Caribbean take the second position with the ratio hovering around 40 per cent in five out of the six years. In other regions, the debt ratio has generally been in the thirtieth percentile. Europe and Central Asia, and South Asia have been the regions with the lowest proportion of debt to GNP.

Debt by income and indebtedness[1]

Of the 136 developing economies, 36 have been classified as the severely indebted low-income countries, 12 as severely indebted middle-income, 13 as moderately indebted low-income, 16 as moderately indebted middle-income, and the remaining 59 as the other (less indebted) developing countries. As expected, the group of middle-income countries owes the most in terms of the debt size. However, the group of the severely indebted, low-income countries does not always have the highest debt to GNP ratio, and this may be true even for the combined group of all the low-income countries. In particular, the middle-income countries' debt proportions have been higher than the poor countries in the 1980s. This observation is significant in view of the debt crisis of the 1980s, which is analysed later in this chapter.

The debt to GNP ratio has varied between the low of 10 per cent in 1980 for 'other' developing countries and 139 per cent in 1990 for the severely indebted low-income countries. While all the other groups have a debt ratio of less than 50 per cent in all but one case, the severely indebted low-income countries group has this ratio close to or in excess of 100 per cent all through the 1990s. The only comfort one finds here is that the ratio of this group has witnessed a declining trend since 1990, whereas it had experienced an upward trend during the 1980s. The debt ratio has a declining trend also for the severely indebted middle-income group and this is so since 1985.

Debt by country

Global Development Finance provides data on external debt of the 138 countries that report public and publicly guaranteed debt under the Debtor Reporting System (DRS). The *World Development Report* gives detailed data on many economic variables of 130 countries. The two lists of countries, though somewhat overlapping, are partly distinct. Since we wish to analyse external debt in relation to some variables which measure economic growth, we have selected all the countries which are included in both the lists and whose population is no less than 15 million in 1998. This sampling procedure has reduced the number of countries to 44, whose data on select variables are provided in Table 6.2.

Of these 44 selected countries, 18 fall in the group of severely indebted, 13 moderately indebted and 13 less indebted. In terms of the income group, 18 belong to the low-income category and the rest to the middle-income group. By region, their classification is as follows:

East Asia and Pacific (EAP)	6
Europe and Central Asia (ECA)	8
Latin America and Caribbean (LAC)	8
Middle East and North Africa (MENA)	7
South Asia (SA)	5
Sub-Saharan Africa (SSA)	10
	44

Thus, the sample of 44 large developing countries is quite representative in terms of their various groupings.

The extent of debt could be analysed in terms of its absolute size and the sustainability of debt in terms of the debt to GNP ratio. The countries whose external debt in 1997 exceeded $100 billion include Brazil, China, Indonesia, Mexico and the Russian Federation. Of these five countries, China alone belongs to the poor country group, but it is the country with the highest population in the world. Even the other four countries have a relatively large population. Ten out of these 44 countries have the debt to GNP ratio in excess of 100 per cent. This group consists of Congo, Ethiopia, Ghana, Madagascar, Mozambique, Nigeria, Syria, Tanzania, Vietnam and Yemen. Eight of these are poor economies and barring Nigeria and Vietnam all have a relatively small population. Thus, in general, the large middle-income countries have a high external debt and the small poor countries have a high external debt to GNP ratio.

Table 6.2 External debt, government expenditure, investment and growth of large developing countries (US$ billion/per cent)

Country	Country group			External debt (US$ billion)			Central govt. total expenditure as % of GDP		Gross investment as % of GDP		Growth rate (% of annual average)	
	Region	Income	Indebtedness	1980	1990	1996	1980	1996	1980	1998	1980–90	1990–98
1 Algeria	MENA	Middle	Severe	19.4 (47)	27.9 (47)	33.2 (77)	–	29.7	39	27	2.7	1.2
2 Argentina	LAC	Middle	Severe	27.1 (36)	62.2 (46)	93.8 (32)	18.2	14.0	25	22	–0.4	5.3
3 Bangladesh	SA	Low	Moderate	4.23 (33)	12.8 (58)	16.1 (51)	–	7.4	22	21	4.3	4.8
4 Brazil	LAC	Middle	Severe	71.5 (32)	120.0 (28)	179.0 (25)	20.2	33.8	23	21	2.7	3.3
5 Chile	LAC	Low	Moderate	12.1 (46)	19.2 (67)	27.4 (38)	28.0	21.0	21	27	4.2	7.9
6 China	EAP	Low	Less	4.50 (2)	55.3 (16)	128.8 (16)	–	8.0	35	39	10.2	11.1
7 Colombia	LAC	Low	Moderate	6.94 (21)	17.2 (45)	28.9 (35)	13.4	–	19	18	3.6	4.2
8 Congo Demo. Rep.	SSA	Low	Severe	4.77 (33)	10.3 (120)	12.8 (212)	12.4	8.3	36	35	3.3	1.0
9 Egypt, Arab Rep.	MENA	Middle	Less	19.1 (89)	32.9 (79)	31.4 (46)	50.3	34.3	28	19	5.4	4.2
10 Ethiopia	SSA	Low	Severe	0.82 (150)	8.63 (127)	10.1 (169)	19.9	–	13	20	1.1	4.9

11 Ghana	SSA	Low	Severe	1.40 (32)	3.87 (67)	6.20 (100)	10.9	—	6	23	3.0	4.2
12 India	SA	Low	Moderate	20.6 (12)	83.7 (29)	89.8 (26)	13.3	15.8	20	23	5.8	6.1
13 Indonesia	EAP	Middle	Severe	20.9 (28)	69.9 (64)	129.0 (60)	22.1	14.6	24	31	6.1	5.8
14 Iran, Isl. Rep.	MENA	Middle	Less	4.50 (5)	9.02 (8)	21.2 (15)	35.7	23.2	30	—	1.7	4.0
15 Jamaica	LAC	Middle	Severe	1.91 (78)	4.67 (123)	4.04 (94)	41.5		16	34	2.0	0.1
16 Kazakhstan	ECA	Middle	Less	—	—	2.92 (14)	—	—	—	36	—	-6.9
17 Kenya	SSA	Low	Moderate	3.38 (48)	7.06 (87)	6.89 (77)	25.3	28.9	29	18	4.2	2.2
18 Madagascar	SSA	Low	Severe	1.24 (31)	3.72 (127)	4.18 (105)	—	17.3	15	13	1.1	1.3
19 Malaysia	EAP	Middle	Moderate	6.61 (28)	15.3 (38)	39.8 (42)	28.5	21.9	30	32	5.3	7.7
20 Mexico	LAC	Middle	Moderate	57.4 (31)	104.4 (41)	157.1 (49)	15.7	15.5	27	26	0.7	2.5
21 Morocco	MENA	Middle	Moderate	9.25 (51)	23.7 (95)	21.8 (61)	33.1	33.3	24	22	4.2	2.1
22 Mozambique	SSA	Low	Severe	—	4.68 (360)	5.84 (379)	—	—	6	21	-0.1	5.7
23 Myanmar	EAP	Low	Severe	1.50 (—)	4.70 (—)	5.18 (—)	15.8	10.1	21	13	0.6	6.3
24 Nepal	SA	Low	Less	0.21 (10)	1.64 (44)	2.41 (53)	14.3	17.5	18	21	4.6	4.8

Table 6.2 (continued)

Country	Region	Income	Indebted-ness	External debt (US$ billion)			Central govt. total expenditure as % of GDP		Gross investment as % of GDP		Growth rate (% of annual average)	
				1980	1990	1996	1980	1996	1980	1998	1980–90	1990–98
25 Nigeria	SSA	Low	Severe	8.92 (14)	33.4 (131)	31.4 (101)	–	–	21	20	1.6	2.6
26 Pakistan	SA	Low	Moderate	9.93 (42)	20.7 (50)	29.9 (46)	17.5	23.8	18	17	6.3	4.1
27 Peru	LAC	Middle	Severe	9.39 (48)	20.1 (63)	29.2 (49)	19.5	16.5	29	25	–0.3	5.9
28 Philippines	EAP	Middle	Moderate	17.4 (54)	30.6 (69)	41.2 (47)	13.4	18.5	29	25	1.0	3.3
29 Poland	ECA	Middle	Less	43.1 (55)	49.4 (89)	40.9 (31)	–	42.2	26	24	1.8	4.5
30 Romania	ECA	Middle	Less	9.76 (14)	1.14 (3)	8.29 (24)	44.8	31.4	40	20	0.5	–0.6
31 Russian Fed.	ECA	Middle	Less	–	59.8 (10)	124.8 (29)	–	24.7	–	20	–	–7.0
32 Saudi Arabia	MENA	Middle	Less	–	–	–	–	–	22	20	0.0	1.6
33 South Africa	SSA	Middle	Less	–	–	23.6 (19)	21.1	34.7	28	16	1.2	1.6
34 Sri Lanka	SA	Low	Less	1.84 (46)	5.87 (74)	8.00 (58)	41.4	27.7	34	24	4	5.3

35 Syrian Arab Rep.	MENA	Middle	Severe	3.55 (27)	17.1 (148)	21.4 (131)	48.2	23.8	28	29	1.5	5.9
36 Tanzania	SSA	Middle	Severe	2.45 (145)	6.41 (160)	7.41 (130)	–	–	–	16	–	2.9
37 Thailand	EAP	Middle	Moderate	8.30 (26)	28.1 (33)	90.8 (50)	18.8	16.5	29	35	7.6	7.4
38 Turkey	ECA	Middle	Moderate	19.1 (27)	49.4 (33)	79.8 (43)	21.3	26.9	18	25	5.4	4.1
39 Uganda	SSA	Low	Severe	0.69 (56)	2.58 (61)	3.67 (61)	6.2	–	6	15	3.2	7.4
40 Ukraine	ECA	Middle	Less	–	–	9.34 (22)	–	–	–	20	–	–13.1
41 Uzbekistan	ECA	Middle	Less	–	–	2.32 (10)	–	–	–	23	–	–1.9
42 Venezuela	LAC	Middle	Moderate	29.3 (42)	33.2 (70)	35.3 (54)	18.7	16.9	26	16	1.1	2
43 Vietnam	EAP	Low	Severe	–	23.5 (115)	26.8 (115)	–	–	–	29	4.6	8.6
44 Yemen, Rep.	MENA	Low	Severe	1.68 (130)	6.35 (135)	6.36 (120)	–	32.8	–	22	–	3.8

Sources: a World Bank: *Global Development Finance*, 1998 and earlier issues.
b World Bank: *World Development Report*, 1999–2000.

Notes: a Numbers in parentheses are per cent of GNP.
b Not available.

Looking at the trend in external debt across the developing economies, we notice a general increase. Of the 44 countries, the debt has increased over time for 38 countries and this includes all the countries which have either high debts or high debt to GNP ratio. However, when we look at the debt to GNP ratio, we find a mixed trend. It reveals an upward trend for ten countries and either a falling or fluctuating trend for the remaining 34 countries. Five of these ten countries belong to the group of either the high debt or high debt to GNP ratio of the previous paragraph. These are Congo, Ghana, Mozambique, Mexico and the Russian Federation. These countries appear to have the most serious debt problem. The first three are small in population, poor in per capita income and belong to sub-Saharan Africa. The last two are relatively large and with middle income. Russia could be in trouble due to the fall out of the erstwhile USSR, and the problem of Mexico is well known.

Debt crisis and resolution

Most of the external debt of all the developing countries is sovereign or guaranteed by the corresponding government. All independent nations are sovereign and they cannot be challenged in any court of law for not servicing their external debt obligations either as per the agreed time schedule or even otherwise in terms of the amounts due. However, default in debt servicing of either kind certainly affects adversely the country's global reputation as well as the internal functioning of the defaulting country. Besides, the creditor nations may impose sanctions against the defaulting countries in terms of the seizure of the latters' assets in their countries (if any), trade restrictions, future borrowings, etc. These lead to an increase in the 'country risk' for defaulting nations, which worsens the future borrowing prospects, *inter alia*. Thus, the debt-servicing time schedule is to be adhered to as much as possible, despite some economists' suggestions that debtor nations should default.

The post-Bretton Woods period of about three decades passed away rather well in terms of the international transactions and finance, including the external debt. The 1974 and 1978 oil price hikes by OPEC led to a phenomenal increase in external borrowings/lendings, which resulted in the appearance of the debt crisis of Mexico in 1982. The crisis soon spread to several other countries in Latin America and Africa. A group of 15 countries was identified as the severely indebted nations, which needed some salvation. The factors which have been argued to have triggered this crisis include:

(a) heavy borrowings by oil importing countries to finance increasing oil import bills;
(b) lending rush due to the flood of petro dollars with banks from oil export-ing nations without ensuring proper project appraisal;
(c) capital flight out of the debtor nations.

The International Monetary Fund (IMF), World Bank and the United States, among other developed countries, resorted to deliberations among themselves as well as with the countries faced with the debt crisis. The solutions suggested/implemented, the plans worked out, and the groups formed for the purpose are known as

- Baker Plan
- Brady Plan
- Toronto terms
- Enhanced Toronto terms
- Houston terms
- Naples terms
- Paris club
- London club/terms
- IMF conditionalities

These involved country-by-country rescheduling of debt servicing, debt reduction/forgiveness, new loans to complete/continue the running of viable projects and thence to improve the repayment prospects, debt to equity swaps, etc. The IMF conditionalities of austere economic surveillance were imposed on the countries who availed themselves of these concessions/benefits. Thus, the defaulting nations were forced to pursue policies that would sharply cut their current account deficits, such as a reduction in fiscal deficits, devaluation and opening of their economies. In consequence, while the objective of the reduction in the current account deficit may have been achieved, some of these countries experienced a fall in their per capita incomes, increase in unemployment and an acceleration in the rate of inflation. The 1980s have been described as a 'lost decade' for many Latin American countries.

The debt crisis has to be the joint responsibility of both the debtor as well as the creditor countries. Accordingly, while dealing with this issue, debtors have suffered through the imposition of certain macro-economic sanctions and disciplines on them, and the creditors have suffered by way of debt discounts and rescheduling of debt servicing.

Debt and economic performance

Economic performance of a nation is governed by many factors and external debt could be one of them. There are several channels through which this relationship takes place. These include debt overhang/crowding out, access to international financial markets and the level of uncertainty in the debtor country. All these theories argue for a negative relationship between external debt, and each of investment and economic growth. External debt does provide a source of funds for investment and thereby induces growth but its existence hampers them subsequently.

Table 6.2 includes data on central government expenditure as well as gross investment, both as proportions to GDP, and on the economic growth rates of the 44 large countries for two periods. To see the bi-variate relationship between external debt and each one of the other pertinent variables, the various correlation coefficients (Pearsonian) have been computed, and the same are reported in Table 6.3.

As the results in the table above would reveal, none of the correlation coefficients is highly significant. The highest significance level of 6.8 per cent is for the positive correlation between debt 1996 and investment to GDP ratio 1998. The other significant coefficients at the level of 20 per cent or below are the positive correlations between the debt to GNP ratio of 1980 and 1990 (average) and the average growth rate during 1980–90, and between the same two variables during the second period, i.e. 1990 and 1996 (average) and the average during 1990–98.

In terms of the signs of the correlation coefficients, all four correlations are positive between the debt and the growth rate variables. Though correl-

Table 6.3 Variables and correlation coefficients

Variables		Correlation coefficient	Significance level
A	*B*		
1 External debt, average of 1980 and 1990	Growth rate during 1980–90	0.0904	0.589
2 External debt to GNP ratio, average of 1980 and 1990	Growth rate during 1980–90	0.2211	0.182
3 External debt, average of 1990 and 1996	Growth rate 1990–8	0.1580	0.306
4 External debt to GNP ratio, average of 1990 and 1996	Growth rate 1990–8	0.1968	0.200
5 External debt 1980	Govt. expenditure to GDP 1980	−0.1309	0.499
6 External debt 1996	Govt. expenditure to GDP 1996	−0.1367	0.463
7 External debt to GNP 1980	Govt. expenditure to GDP 1980	0.1610	0.404
8 External debt to GNP 1996	Govt. expenditure to GDP 1996	−0.1146	0.539
9 External debt 1980	Investment to GDP 1980	0.1743	0.302
10 External debt 1996	Investment to GDP 1998	0.2805	0.068
11 External debt to GNP 1980	Investment to GDP 1980	−0.1303	0.442
12 External debt to GNP 1996	Investment to GDP 1998	0.0418	0.790

ations are devoid of causation, they do suggest a positive relationship between external debt and economic growth, and this thus supports the theory of debt-led growth. Between debt and government expenditure, three out of the four correlations are negative, and thus they argue that external debt may be crowding out government expenditure, The three out of the four correlation coefficients between the different measures of debt and gross investment are positive, which negates the hypothesis of a negative relationship between these two variables.

Although debt sustainability has no unique testing procedure, the debt to GNP ratio does throw some light on it. The average values of this ratio for the 44 countries in Table 6.2 for 1980, 1990 and 1996 come to 35.7, 67.3 and 66.3 per cent, respectively. Thus the ratio, while almost doubled during the decade of the 1980s, has remained nearly at the same level during the first six years of the 1990s. The Latin American debt crisis of the 1980s thus did not arrest the increasing trend of the debt to GNP ratio. This only suggests that, in general, the debt sustainability could not be an issue for the debt crisis. An examination of the country-wise data suggests that the countries which had significantly been above the average debt to GNP ratio in at least two of the three years for which the data are given in Table 6.2 include Congo, Ethiopia, Jamaica, Madagascar, Morocco, Mozambique, Nigeria, Syria, Tanzania, Vietnam and Yemen. By this yardstick, these could be the countries in the region of external debt trap. The countries whose debt to GNP ratio was rather low relative to the average include China, Colombia, India, Iran, Kazakhstan, Malaysia, Mexico, Nepal, Romania, Russia, South Africa, Thailand, Turkey, Ukraine and Uzbekistan. Surprisingly the latter list has countries like Mexico, Russia and some South-East Asian countries which have recently suffered a financial crisis. This only underlines the inadequacy of the debt to GNP ratio as data on which to judge the matter and/or to suggest that the default could arise not just for the inability to service but also due to the lack of the willingness to service the debt.

Conclusions

Both the external debt as well as the debt service of the 136 developing countries have grown at the rate higher than the economic growth rate achieved by the group of these countries during the last two decades. If debt leads to a smoothening of the consumption of both the borrowers as well as the lenders, and enhances the productivity of capital through its proper allocation and diffusion of technology, then the growth in external debt is good. However, if the debt is used for building up the defence services and/or for unproductive uses (like financing consumption or revenue expenditures), and particularly if it is raised when there is already idle capacity in the economy, it is an unwarranted economic activity. This chapter could not go into such details due to the paucity of the necessary data.

External debt has grown both in absolute size as well as in relation to the ability and liquidity to service the same in the last two decades. However, the ratios are still quite comfortable for the group of all the developing countries as a whole. In terms of the regional groupings, while the Latin American and Caribbean region owes the most, sub-Saharan Africa tops the list in terms of the debt to GNP ratio. The analysis of developing countries by income and indebtedness has indicated that the middle-income countries not only owe the most, they also have the highest debt to GNP ratio. The country-wise analysis of the 44 large developing countries has found that the countries which have suffered the debt crisis are not necessarily the ones which had the most unfavourable indices of debt sustainability.

External debt and economic growth are found to have had a positive correlation. Even debt and investment have witnessed a generally positive correlation. The chapter thus suggests that the capital-poor countries could aspire to grow faster than otherwise through external debt if they are able to use both the domestic capital and the borrowed funds productively.

Note

1   For the classification of countries on this basis, see World Bank, *Global Development Finance*, 1998, vol. I, pp. 65–6.

References

Claessens, Stijn *et al.* (1996) *Analytical Aspects of the Debt Problems of Heavily Indebted Poor Countries*, Policy Research Working Paper, no. 1618, Washington, DC: World Bank.

Dooley, M.P. and K.M. Kletzer (1994) 'Capital flight, external debt and domestic policies', *Federal Reserve Bank of San Francisco Economic Review*, no. 3, pp. 29–37.

Eichengreen, B. and P.H. Lindbert (1989) *The International Debt Crisis in Historical Perspective*, Cambridge and London: MIT Press.

Grossman, H.I. and J.B. Van Huyak (1988) 'Sovereign debt as a contigent crisis, excusable default, repudiation and reputation', *American Economic Review*, vol. 78, no. 5, pp. 1088–97.

Klein, T.M. (1994) *External Debt Management, An Introduction*, Washington, DC: World Bank.

Krugman, Paul (1985) 'International debt strategy in an uncertain world', in Gordon Smith and J.T. Cuddington (eds) *International Debt and Developing Countries*, Washington, DC: World Bank.

Organisation for Economic Cooperation and Development (1992) *Financing and External Debt of Developing* Countries, 1992 Survey, Paris: OECD.

Sachs, J. and S.M. Collins (eds) (1989) *Developing Country Debt and Economic Performance*, vol. 1–3, NBER and Chicago: University of Chicago Press.

7 The pure theory of international trade, globalization, growth and sustainable development
Agenda for the future

M. R. Aggarwal

Introduction: the historical perspective

The pure theory of international trade, as expounded by classical, neo-classical, and modern economists, seeks to provide an explanation of the factors, originating both from demand and supply side which tend to influence the observed pattern of trade flows and specialization among nations, and their welfare implications measured in terms of Pareto optimality, for each of the trading partners and for the world as a whole. The principle of comparative advantage was developed by Torrens (1808) and used by Ricardo (1817) to explain the pattern of trade and the benefits flowing from free trade and competition. Ricardo argues that trade between countries arises because of the relative differences in the pre-trade prices of the goods, on the assumption that the relative production costs of goods and hence relative prices (P_X/P_Y) in a closed economy, under competitive equilibrium conditions in both commodity and factor markets and a simple production function with the single input and constant returns, are entirely determined by relative labour inputs (L_X/L_Y), i.e.:

$$\left(\frac{P_x}{P_y}\right) = \left(\frac{L_x}{L_y}\right)$$

and the differences in the pre-trade domestic price ratios of the goods and the comparative advantage and disadvantage, in costs between countries will be mainly due to differences in relative labour productivity. The theory assumes, among other things, immobility of the factors of production internationally, with negligible transport costs, and unchanged technology, factor inputs and demand patterns.

Ricardo in doing so made a substantial advance from Adam Smith's position: whereas Smith (1937) argues that trade between two countries is beneficial if each has an absolute advantage over the other in the production of a good, Ricardo's 'Constant Cost' model shows that substantial gains are also possible in cases where one of the countries has an absolute advantage over the other in the production of both the goods, measured in terms of differences in relative labour productivity between nations. This can be expressed algebraically as $a_1/b_1 > a_2/b_2 > 1$ where a_1 and a_2 are the output factor ratios for country 1 and b and b are for country 2. The overall welfare implications of the classical model, assuming equilibrium world price ratio lying between the pre-trade cost-ratios of the trading partners, are the maximization of global trade, real output, and resource efficiency through exchange and specialization with free trade; and benefits to all the partners which may or may not be equally distributed due to differences in elasticity of each other's demand.

J.S. Mill introduced in a satisfactory way 'demand conditions' and made Ricardian analysis a full general equilibrium analysis. Eyebrows were raised by theorists, notably J.S. Mill (1937) and J.E. Cairnes (1874), by way of violent criticism about several of the restrictive assumptions on which Ricardo's doctrine was based, particularly labour theory of value as an analytical tool and straight line transformation frontier, but despite their criticism they could not cast much doubt on the practical relevance of the theory and in fact the principle stood very well against these attacks by absorbing successfully many of these criticisms and relaxing several of the assumptions.

Haberler (1950), the main architect of the neo-classical theory and with leanings towards classical tradition, successfully couched Ricardo's doctrine in terms of 'opportunity' rather than 'real costs', and a social indifference map, thus liberating the classical theory from the labour theory of value, while recognizing the existence of many factors and varying returns to scale and introducing concavity to the original production possibility curve. Intellectually it must be regarded as a remarkable achievement as it lifted the theory out of the real cost strait-jacket in which it had been entrenched for so many generations but it could not explain the causes of the cost differentials in the production of trading partners. Most of the subsequent formal developments of the theory by Learner (1953), Leontief (1953) and Meade (1952) were built on the foundations laid by his analysis.

Swedish economists Heckscher (1919) and Ohlin (1933), unlike Smith, Ricardo and Mill, laboured hard to provide root causes of the relative differences in labour productivity. The standard Heckscher–Ohlin (H–O) model, which was refined by Samuelson (1939), and later on by Learner (1980) by assuming two-country, two factors of production, with fixed quantities at any point of time (endowment ratio), constant returns to scale (strong factor intensity assumption), and by postulating functional relation between relative factor endowments, factor price ratios and commodity prices, concludes that trade mainly arises due to factor intensity differences in the production functions of two goods, coupled with the observed differences in relative factor endowments of the countries. It follows then

$$\left(\frac{L}{K_A}\right) > \left(\frac{L}{K_B}\right) = \left(\frac{P_L}{P_{K_A}}\right) < \left(\frac{P_L}{P_{K_B}}\right)$$

where L, K and P_L and P_K refer to amount of labour, capital and factor rentals respectively. In other words, the theorem asserts that a country will export that commodity which is produced with the relatively large amounts of its relatively abundant factor. The propositions, however, may not lead to the same results, as 'relative abundance/scarcity' was defined in more than one way. Whereas the physical definition rests on differences in relative factor endowments, the price definition rests on differences in the ratio of autarky factor rentals. The major differences between the classical and H–O theorem lie in (a) the explicit separation between the 'positive' aspects and 'normative or welfare' aspects of trade which depend upon meta-economic criteria, and (b) assuming identical inter-country differences in the production function. Johnson (1954) has synthesized various attempts to elaborate the H–O model by giving more stress on 'demand factors' which Ohlin considered as 'mere curiousity', but the basic formulation of the model in fact more or less remains the same. Further, Heckscher stated that under specifiable conditions, free trade equalizes pre-trade differences in factor rentals, although Ohlin was of the view that due to restrictive assumptions, full factor price equalization may not occur. Stolper and Samuelson (1941), Uzawa (1959) and Samuelson (1939) again set forth the Ricardo–Viner pure rent model with which they attempt to vindicate Ohlin's partial equalization hypothesis. Also, it should be noted that though the terms 'factor prices' and 'factor rentals' are used interchangeably, they do not convey the same meaning, as the prices of the factors means the rentals for the services of the productive factor and not the factor prices. The generalization of the H–O theory by Vanek and later on by Learner was disappointing for, instead of explaining trade flows in actual goods, it shows abstract amounts of factors of production embodied in the trade flows.

The findings of empirical studies since the late 1940s on Ricardian and H–O theorem, under both 'static' and dynamic conditions, have immensely shaken many widely accepted views about the causes of the operation and structure of trade. MacDougall (1951) by using multiple regression analysis and later on Stern (1975), Kravis (1970) and Bela Balassa (1963) carried out empirical tests by comparing productivity of labour in manufacturing industries in the USA which do lend, in fact, a powerful support to the Ricardian model of trade. However, results remain quite inconclusive as Bhagwati (1969), using MacDougall's data as a sample for 25 industrial products with and without 'log', was not able to find any systematic and significant correlation between relative labour costs and export prices, thus refuting the Ricardian hypothesis. Leontief's evidence (1953), widely known as the Leontief paradox, based on input–output technique and US 1947 data, though inconclusive had enormous impact on the pure theory of trade and generated a considerable amount of rethinking among economists about the proximate determinants of exports in the 1950s and 1960s. Studies made by Bhardwaj for India (1962), Tatemoto and Ichimura (1959) for Japan, and Wahl (1961) for Canada, and Ellsworth and Clark (1975) coupled with Arrow, Minhas Chenery and Solow's study using CES production function (1963) as to the existence of reversibility remain inconclusive in supporting or rejecting the H–O theorem. And in fact some of the studies did suggest that a relatively capital-rich country may not always export relatively capital intensive goods and vice versa.

The modern theories

The basic developments in the area of trade from classical to neo-classical are intellectually commendable, provided the restrictive assumptions on which these theories are based are well recognized. Modern theorists, notably Linder (1961), Kravis (1970), Posner (1961), Vernon (1979) and Hufbauer (1966), partly criticized these attempts for not taking into account the dynamic influences and tried to provide alternative explanations of the observed pattern of trade, which cannot be labelled as complete. Linder's thesis is that a large volume of trade in manufactures of a country, with each of her trading partners among the industrialized countries having identical factor endowments, can be explained, given the operation of the economies of scale in the home market in the exportable product, and similarly in the general economic conditions, through the similarity in 'demand patterns'. The theory however lacks precision and rigour as the concept of 'representative' demand used in the analysis and omission of some of the trading countries are not exactly formulated. The technology gap theory, propounded by Posner (1961), sets out to explain the flow of manufactured goods in the advanced countries in terms of innovation and imitation even within identical overall factor endowments and demand conditions, but failed to explain its exact definition, the reasons for its existence. The commodity composition and direction of trade, according to Raymond Vernon's 'product cycle model' (1966) could be predicted due to the interaction of the various stages of development through which an exportable product is likely to pass in its life cycle. This means a country, before it can export a good, must first of all develop an internal market, reap the economies of scale and continue innovating to retain its technological lead and hence its comparative advantage. This theory seems to be applicable only in the case of consumer durables, in terms of time span from innovation to eventual high consumer demand. On the basis of strong theoretical foundations Kravis reaches the conclusion that availability of scarce natural resources or 'supply elasticities' and domestic agricultural support programmes between trading partners is the fundamental cause of trade, which are mildly supported by Bhagwati. Trade tends to be confined to goods which are not available at home – in the absolute sense. Findlay, however, says that this theory is only true in a very special case, while there are as many countries as there are commodities and each country has only one input. According to Grubel and Lloyd (1975), inter-industry trade is quite compatible with the H–O model but the products of intra-industry are exchanged between the trading partners in the industrialized countries on a large scale, in the manufactured goods. Models with imperfectly, instead of perfectly competitive markets are indeed needed to explain such a trade. The level of intra-industry trade of industry can be measured by the following index given by Balassa (1968):

$$B_j = \left(\frac{X_j - M_j}{X_j + M_j} \right) \times 100$$

where X_j and M_j are the values of the exports of good j by a country, and matching imports of good j respectively. Here $0 \le B_j \le 100$.

Thus, when B_j tends towards zero, trade comprises either exports or imports only, indicating that inter-industry trade is taking place. When B_j tends towards 100, exports are matched by imports, and the proportion of exchange which is an intra-industry type tends towards its maximum.

Empirical studies of various cost functions in some of the industrialized countries have found widespread evidence of increasing returns to scale in some of the cases, due to economies of scale which in turn can generate mutually beneficial trade, even with identical factor endowments and zero opportunities for new product developments.

One may, from the above review, conclude that there does not exist any simple explanation or theory for the observed pattern of trade between different countries at any given point of time. It is true, more than ever before, for international trade has become in recent times a highly complex phenomenon, and the global trading system is in disarray, with the lowest international cooperation since World War II, and in fact under such situations it is quite unreasonable to expect any one explanation to account fully for the observed pattern of trade flows. At the present juncture, what is needed is a broad theory which may merge most of the possible explanatory factors into a 'composite variable', which makes theoretical sense and stands very well in empirical investigation. However, on the whole, it can be said with certainty that the neo-classical factor proportion theory which has evolved over time comes out at the top as compared to other theories in terms of sound theoretical framework, empirical testing, explanatory power and its use in understanding the crucial factors responsible for predicting the observed patterns in trade and production flows, and influencing policy decisions.

From the foregoing, it is clear that the pure theory of international trade establishes the superiority of free trade among nations over trade with restrictions/managed trade, i.e. of competition both in factor and goods market, the invisible hand over interference. Indeed, the theory fundamentally is an extension of the theory of optimization.

Globalization, role of state and development

Under the Structural Adjustment Programme (SAP), most of the developing areas in the various regions of the world, including India, have taken, during the 1980s and 1990s, numerous measures in the different sectors of their economies (both internal and external) to integrate with the rest of the world in order to reap the gains from global free trade based on exchange and specialization.

In some quarters, it is thought that under the current process of reforms, the 'state' will have no role to play as an economic actor, which is a totally mistaken view. The role of state under perfect competition, markets, information and absence of externalities, ignoring the problem of income distribution, no doubt is minimal but it had and continues to play a significant role where 'imperfections' exist in the market. In India and elsewhere what actually has happened during the last four decades is that the state has attempted to do much of what it cannot or should not do and it has done too little where it should have actually done more. Irrational policy intervention by the state in the different sectors has created serious distortions which in turn have reduced the overall economic and social rates of growth. The role of the state has to be redefined. It now must provide public services and goods, educational and infrastructural facilities, specify clearly the rules of the game for active players, both in the private and public sectors, provide adequate investment in human capital development, create a stable macro-economic environment, as these cannot be left to market forces. This is in fact clear from the development experience of newly industrialized countries (NIC).

The export-led growth strategy based on transnational private foreign investment, without doubt, paid rich dividends in the newly industrialized countries. The high degree of openness measured in terms of ratio of exports and imports to national income and rates of growth in exports which are found to be statistically significant and positively correlated with the changes in real income coupled with consistent and sound macro-economic fiscal, monetary and exchange rates, which besides minimizing numerous rigidities and distortions in the product and commodity markets (getting the prices right), discouraging rent-seeking behaviour, helped them to exploit existing comparative advantages – all of them actively interplayed for economic transformation and expansion. In other words, favourable external environment, 'getting the prices right' and 'getting polices right' worked in a mutually reinforcing manner for their remarkable economic performance.

However, an in-depth examination of the various policies pursued by the NICs in the past reveal that the state played an active but selective interventionist role through budget discipline, managing exchange rates, devising institutional frameworks marked by strong government discipline over the private sector, and the complete commitment of the government to exports that has helped minimize the resource costs. This means that 'getting prices right', will not be enough to accelerate the process of economic growth in developing areas but has to be supplemented effectively by other well-targeted protectionist polices in the different sectors.

The global economic climate remained quite growth-conducive in the 1970s to some of the countries in Asia and Latin America which had high rates of growth of real per capita product. However, it seems it will become less favourable and more shaky in the near future due to global payments and imbalances particularly of the USA, secular decline of developed countries from lending resulting in an overall shortage of liquidity and high cost of capital, a slow-down in the worldwide aggregate real income and output due to past disinflationary policies. All this may further lead to a tightening of the availability of capital and increased protectionism, a general shift from tariffs to non-tariff barriers, i.e. state participation in trade, para tariffs, specific limitations on trade flows and technical and legal regulations, and their expected unilateral intensification due to the fear of direct and indirect displacement in the import competing sectors having relatively low productivity of labour (Tables 7.1 and 7.2). Practically, we may, if this trend continues, pass into what Friedman (1977) calls an 'era of managed trade' from an 'era of free trade'. In fact, a more or less similar situation may emerge on the international scene, if appropriate economic measures are not taken by the super economic powers, as was witnessed after World War I when trade dependency ratios increased despite a rising wave of protectionism. The South including India may become to a large extent the victim of the deterioration in the world economy. Admittedly, there will be phasing out, within the next ten years (2005), of the import quotas on textiles and clothing in place under MFA, under the final Treaty of Uruguay Round of GATT negotiated at Marrakesh by 115 countries in April 1994. At present there are 134 members out of which 80 per cent are developing, least developed and transition economies. At the time of the birth of GATT, there were 23 member countries, of which 11 were from developing areas. And out of the 30 countries which are negotiating to join, all belong to under-developed countries and transition economies. However, the fact remains that free trade at the global level will work as an engine of economic growth only if all forms of non-tariff barriers are reduced progressively by the North, and the WTO must devise effective dispute settlement procedures for cutting such abuses, keeping in view the larger interests of the relatively less developed areas.

However, there is a clear need for addressing the unfinished business of the Tokyo and Uruguay Rounds, *inter alia*, tariff peaks and tariff escalation in food, textiles, clothing, footwear and leather industries, the postponement until 2005 of any meaningful removal of restraints in developing countries' exports of textile and clothing, embryonic liberalization of trade in agri-culture, abuse of anti-dumping procedures, the problem of rules of origin and technical standards and environmental barriers, so that the poor, the weak and vulnerable are able to partake of the benefits of global trade.

Table 7.1 Quantum of tariffs and non-tariff barriers (before and after the Uruguay Round), 1988–1995 (percentages)

Sector	USA			EU			Japan			Canada		
	1988	1993	Uruguay Round	1988	1993	Uruguay Round	1988	1993	Uruguay Round	1988	1993	Uruguay Round
Raw material	6.0	4.8	3.1	16.4	1.8	7.7	8.9	7.6	4.9	5.2	3.7	1.6
Agriculture, forestry and fishing	5.4	3.5	2.7	18.0	21.1	95	11.1	10.4	7.0	6.4	4.4	2.3
Mining and quarrying	2.3	2.3	2.3	0.0	3.7	4.2	3.5	0.4	0.4	0.4	0.7	0.7
Manufacturing	8.1	6.7	3.7	16.8	20.3	9.2	11.9	10.7	6.9	6.5	2.1	0.2
Semi-finished manufacturing goods	33.3	32.2	11.1	34.0	29.4	3.1	27.6	27.1	26.7	15.3	13.1	0.8
Finished manufacturing goods	22.0	21.8	7.9	23.7	24.2	4.2	5.3	3.7	2.3	8.7	8.9	2.0
All products	24.1	23.6	8.5	25.9	25.2	4.3	13.7	12.6	11.1	10.3	9.5	1.6

Source: Michael Daly and Hirocki Kuwaharan, 'The impact of the Uruguay Round on tariffs and non-tariff barriers to trade', *The World Economy*, vol 111, no. 2, 1998.

Table 7.2 Quantum of tariffs (before and after the Uruguay Round), 1988–1995 (percentages)

Sector	USA			EU			Japan			Canada		
	1988	1993	Uruguay Round	1988	1993	Uruguay Round	1988	1993	Uruguay Round	1988	1993	Uruguay Round
Raw material	3.2	3.3	2.5	6.0	6.0	8.4	3.8	3.8	3.8	3.4	3.3	3.4
Agriculture, forestry and fishing	3.8	4.1	3.2	8.5	8.5	9.3	5.1	5.1	4.0	3.6	3.5	3.5
Mining and quarrying	1.0	1.0	0.3	0.8	0.8	0.3	0.5	0.3	0.3	2.7	2.8	0.7
Manufacturing	2.3	2.3	1.8	5.2	5.4	9.2	3.4	3.4	2.7	2.5	2.4	4.2
Semi-finished manufacturing goods	7.0	7.0	3.8	7.3	7.3	4.4	6.6	6.8	4.8	9.9	9.4	4.0
Finished manufacturing goods	6.3	6.6	4.3	7.8	8.1	8.0	7.8	7.8	5.2	9.8	9.6	5.8
All products	6.2	6.4	4.0	7.5	7.6	6.1	6.9	7.0	4.8	9.1	8.9	5.0

Source: Michael Daly and Hirocki Kuwaharan, 'The impact of the Uruguay Round on tariffs and non-tariff barriers to trade' in Quad, The World Economy, vol 111, no. 2, 1998.

The rate of growth of an economy, in terms of Solow and Swan's neo-classical growth model and Harrod and Domar's growth model, given the capital–output ratio, will be largely influenced by the ratio of savings to real income (S/Y) which in turn will determine the required amount of investment in order to realize planned rates of economic growth on the assumption that savings will be productively used. And obviously, a decrease in the required level of investible resources due to either external or internal factors would lead to a fall in the rate of growth. But the adverse impact of a lower volume of investment could be mitigated by achieving a greater 'efficiency' in the use of scarce investment resources, partly through a reduction in the capital–output ratio. Output and exports of manufactures and semi-manufactures produced efficiently would find easy and ready markets in the highly competitive markets of the West where the South is simply a price taker. In fact, increasing efficiency in the use of resources in various sectors of the economy, combined with productivity, should become the centre of broad economic policy and management in the South. What it actually means is that market-oriented friendly policies will act as an engine of economic growth with greater force, through the deepening of structural reforms at the 'internal level'. Some of the possible interrelated measures, i.e. a balance between increase in productivity and increase in real wage rate, maintaining realistic and competitive exchange rates and price stability, which could be taken without much effort, would go a long way in meeting the desired objectives.

One of the most pervasive and characteristic features of the 1980s has been the remarkable renaissance of 'regionalism', through the formation of trade blocks in Europe, North America and South and South-East Asia. The USA, within four decades after World War II, remained firmly committed to multilaterism but was opposed to regionalism. However, negotiations for forming a Canada–USA free trade agreement were initiated in 1983 and the process was completed in 1988. Later on, NAFTA, comprising the USA, Canada and Mexico and APEC (1989), a loose grouping of 18 Pacific Rim countries including the USA, Japan and China, came into existence in order to promote free trade among themselves. In 1994, the APEC members committed themselves to form a FTA by 2010 for the higher-income countries. The USA also aimed to form a FTA embracing 34 democracies in the Western Hemisphere (except Cuba) by 2005. The EC was enlarged from 9 members to 12 in 1986 and 15 in 1994. Now the group is having a common currency, the Euro. The world in fact is witnessing a paradoxical situation. As the pace of globalization is gaining momentum, the urge among the countries all over the world to club together at regional level is becoming stronger (Tables 7.3, 7.4 and 7.5). According to the WTO, it has been notified of almost 180 regional trade arrangements. India is not a member of any of these groups except SAPTA, where the volume of intra-regional trade is virtually negligible. In fact under SAPTA, all the members have practically agreed to disagree on all major issues during the last decade. It would be very difficult for the developing areas under these circumstances to increase their

Table 7.3 Regional free trade arrangements, share of world trade, 1994

Group	% share
EU	22.8
Euro Med	2.3
NAFTA	7.9
Mercosur	0.3
FTAA	2.6*
AFFTA	1.3
Australia – New Zealand	0.1
APEC	23.7
Total	61.0

Source: C. Fred Bregsten, *Foreign Affairs,* May/June 1996.

Note: *Excluding sub-regions.

Table 7.4 Economic regional arrangements (1987–1990) by number of arrangements

	1987	1988	1989	1990
By sectoral composition				
Steel	38	52	50	39
Agricultual and food products	20	55	51	59
Automobiles and transport equipment	14	17	20	23
Textiles and clothing	28	72	66	51
Electronic and Clothing	11	19	28	37
Footwear	8	14	18	21
Other	15	32	56	54
Total	134	261	289	284
By protected markets				
European Community	69	137	173	n.a
United States	48	62	69	n.a
Japan	6	14	14	n.a
Other industrial countries	11	47	32	n.a
Eastern Europe	–	1	1	n.a
Total	135	260	288	
By restrained exporters				
Japan	25	34	70	n.a
Eastern Europe	20	45	41	n.a
Korea	24	25	38	n.a
Other industrial countries	23	59	57	n.a
Other developing countries	42	98	83	n.a
Total	134	255	289	

Source: Harold Sander and Andras Inotai (ed.) *World Trade after the Uruguay Round, Prospects and Policy Options for 21st Century.*

Table 7.5   Growth in regional trade agreements, 1940–1990

1   Number of arrangements

Signatories over time	1940s	1950s	1960s	1970s	1980s	1990s
Western Europe	0	1	4	13	3	8
North Africa/W. Asia	0	0	1	0	0	0
Latin America	0	2	3	1	2	1
Asia/Oceana	0	1	3	3	2	3
North America	0	0	0	0	1	1
Sub-Saharan Africa	1	1	3	0	0	1
C. & E. Europe	0	0	0	0	0	21

2   Inter-regional trade agreements entering into force

Signatories over time	1940s	1950s	1960s	1970s	1980s	1990s
Western Europe and C.E. Europe	0	0	0	5	1	37
Western Europe and North Africa/W. Asia	0	0	4	21	0	3
Western Europe and Sub-Saharan Africa	0	0	1	2	0	0
Western Europe and others	0	0	1	2	2	1
Oceana and Sub-Saharan Africa	0	1	0	0	0	0
North America and Latin America	0	0	0	0	1	2
North America & N. Africa/West Asia	0	0	0	0	0	5
C.E. Europe & N. Africa/W. Asia	0	1	1	1	1	0

Source: Harold Sander and Andras Inotai (ed.) *World Trade after the Uruguay Round, Prospects and Policy Options for 21st Century.*

rates of growth of exports, hence income, in the markets of G-3 despite all their efforts to integrate with the emerging world trading system. Though the GATT has sanctioned the formation of such regional groups under its article XXIV, 'regionalism' violates the central principle of GATT of non-discrimination and certainly cannot go hand in hand with the spirit of global internationalization. In such a situation, the importance of increasing intra-regional trade in the developing areas currently is immense as it would promote their collective economic growth, besides increasing and further strengthening the sense of unity and solidarity. According to Aggarwal there exists a vast scope for expanding intra-regional trade which is extremely low in the various groupings despite so many years of regional economic cooperation. The lack of complementarity and its potential erosion through the erection of tariffs and non-tariff barriers in production structures, following the self-sufficiency policies in the basic and capital goods sectors, are the most important internal factors explaining the low level of intra-trade. This is quite in evidence from the low and declining values of the index RCAX/RCAM (take the case of SAARC) given by Balassa and Trade Intensity Index (TII), where

$$RCAX = \left(\frac{X^{K,i}}{X^i}\right) \Big/ \left(\frac{X^{K,w}}{X^w}\right)$$

$$RCAM = \left(\frac{M^{K,i}}{M^i}\right) \Big/ \left(\frac{M^{K,w}}{M^w}\right)$$

and trade intensity index of country i with country j:

$$TII = \left(\frac{X_{i,j}}{X_i}\right) \Big/ \left(\frac{M_j}{M_W - M_i}\right)$$

where $X^{K,i}$ is the export of product K by country i, X^i is the total exports of country i, $X^{K,w}$ is the world exports of product K, X^W is world exports, $M^{K,i}$ is the import of product K by country i, M^i is total imports of country i, $M^{K,w}$ is world imports of product K, and M^W is world total imports. $X_{i,j}$, X_i, M_j, M_w and M_i represent exports of country i to country j, total exports of country i to total imports of country j, total world imports, and imports of country i respectively.

There is no general agreement on the precise meaning of sustainability but it is taken to mean in some quarters improving the quality of human life while living within the carrying capacity of supporting eco-systems, i.e. assets such as the ozone layer, fertile soil and healthy wetlands which provide services people rely on to live and which we do not know how to replace. Another definition focuses on balancing social, economic and ecological goals, and aims at meeting a broad range of human needs and aspirations, including health, literacy and political freedom as well as purely material needs. Sustainable development, however, according to the Brundtland Report (1987), is an alternative design for development which by definition is environmentally benign and eco-friendly, i.e. those who reap the fruits of economic development today must not make future generations worse off by excessively degrading the earth, using its exhaustible resources and polluting its ecology and environment; it states that the resultant economic development which erodes natural capital has catastrophic consequences. This concept now has been recognized as a 'true index' of development as compared to the traditional one-dimensional measure of development – real income per capita – which has been replaced by the Physical Quality of Life (PQLI) index, based on basic human needs. This is based on recognition of the fact that pollution of the environment by various types of acids generated as a result of the speeding up of the process of industrialization and exports has altered the chemistry of the atmosphere at a rapid pace, and given rise to various social costs which are only noted after a certain time.

Bhagwati (1993) is of the view that globalization and internationalization of trade and capital through the entry of MNCs, GATT (now WTO) and NAFTA will not upset the balance between economic progress and ecology and will in fact promote growth in the long run. On the other hand, Herman E. Daly of the World Bank and followers assert that growth flowing from free trade will harm both environment and welfare. This seems to be partly true as the unrestricted operation of the MNCs may become the prime threat to environment due to (i) 'greenhouse effect' and (ii) their ability to locate their plants in developing areas in order to escape the strict environmental standards imposed by their own countries, (iii) having control of more than 70 per cent of traded goods and 80 per cent of the total world land devoted to export-oriented crops; (iv) major users of fossil fuels which release carbon dioxide in the atmosphere. The irresponsible use of heavy equipment, indiscriminate cutting of forests and widespread serial spraying and sale of domestically banned, outdated and dangerous chemicals must be blamed on MNCs having monopoly power over natural resources. Second, the developing countries in fact may be pressurized into over-exploiting their natural resources in order to meet external financial obligations which have grown exponentially, and to increase exports. And it is regrettable that no existing theory of trade and the WTO (established in January 1995) takes into account adequately the dimension of sustainable development.

The main objective of liberalization and globalization at present is to achieve infinite growth in a world of finite resources, which is neither possible nor desirable. Hence, protection of the environment must be a part of the guiding principles of the WTO as most of the developing countries have become its members. Also it immediately calls for an active role of the state, both at the national and international level, to minimize the negative impact, i.e. hidden social and environmental costs of excessive trends towards globalization. In order to achieve these objectives, a major responsibility lies on the shoulders of advanced economies to develop new, gentle and ecologically sustainable technologies, i.e. technologies which maximize the productivity of natural resources and not of labour, so that nature's infinite store-house is not exhausted. The North must set positive examples for the South showing that it is possible to reconcile economic prosperity with environmental problems. It is important to note in this connection that though it is a mistake to expect to achieve too many objectives with the help of the WTO, some beginning could be made in this direction.

The suggestions of T.N. Srinivasan (1999) in this regard, that the Trade-related Intellectual Property Rights (TRIPS) may be taken out of the WTO and handled by the World Intellectual Property Organisation (WIPO), that the Committee on Trade and Environment (CTE), whose main aim is simply to identify between trade measures and environmental concern, be wound up and that the issue of environment be tackled by UNEP, and that labour be excluded from the purview of GATT and handled by ILO, will go a long way in satisfying the aspirations of the South. He further opines that the issue of regional arrangements could be dealt with by introducing a 'sunset clause' whereby preferences available to members of the regional group against the world be extended to all the WTO members in, say, five years. Lastly, he suggests that agricultural trade could be brought under GATT very easily without changing the main structure of the WTO.

Towards some generalizations

Several broad generalizations may be derived from the foregoing analysis. The final success of the policies of globalization and market-oriented reforms, from the point of view of the South's overall economic and social growth and the revitalization of the future world trading order, will, to a great extent, depend on a marked improvement in the global macro-economic environment, making it conducive to sustainable development. The spread of recovery from the USA to the rest of the North is vital to ease the costs of the adjustment process. Success also depends on the will of the industrialized countries to reduce non-tariff barriers and overcome internal structural impediments to growth by maintaining low rates of inflation and interest and adjusting their macro-domestic policies consistently with those of other developed countries. The creation of such a global framework, of cooperation rather than confrontation, would contribute towards support of the wider interests of the South. All this needs to be coupled with a strong commitment and concerted efforts by the South to extend and deepen ongoing internal and external reforms and to increase intra-regional trade through the progressive elimination of tariff and non-tariff barriers. Thus by avoiding inappropriate trade liberalization and pursuing programmes of complementary expansion, world trade can create a favourable climate for good governance.

References

Aggarwal, M.R. (1992) 'Prospects of trade expansion in the SAARC region', *The Developing Economies*, vol. 30, March: Tokyo.

Arrow, K.H., H. Chenery, B. Minhas and R. Solow (1961) 'Capital labour subtitution and economic effeciency', *Review of Economics and Studies*.

Balassa, Bela (1963) 'An emperical demonstration of classical comparative cost', *Review of Economic Statistics*, vol. 45, pp. 231–8.

—— (1965) 'Tariff protection in industrial countries: an evaluation', *Journal of Political Economy*, vol. 1, no. 23, pp. 579–94.

—— (1968) 'Tariff protection in industrial countries and its effects on the exports of processed goods from developing countries', *Canadian Journal of Economics*, no. 1, pp. 583 94.

Bhagwati, J. (1964) 'On the equivalence of tariffs and quotas', in Walter Laqueur (ed.) *Trade Tariffs and Growth*, London: Weidenfeld and Nicholson.

—— (1971) 'The pure theory of international trade: a survey', in Walter Laqueur (ed.) *Trade, Tariffs and Growth*, London: Weidenfeld and Nicholson.

—— (1991) *The World Trading System at Risk*, Princeton: Princeton University Press.

Bhardwaj, R. (1962) 'Factor proportions and the structure of Indo-US trade', *Indian Economic Journal*, vol. 10.

Cairnes, J.E. (1874) *Some Leading Principles of Political Economy*, London: Macmillan.

Ellsworth, P.T. and Leith J. Clark. (1975) *The International Economy* (5th edition), New York: Macmillan.

Friedman, M. (1977) 'Nobel lecture: inflation and unemployment', *Journal of Political Economy*, vol. 1, no. 35, pp. 451–72.

Grubel, H.G. and H.G. Johnson (eds) (1971) *Effective Tariff Protection*, Geneva: Graduate Institute of International Studies.

Grubel, Herbert and Peter Lloyd (1975) *Intra-Industry Trade*, London: Macmillan.

Haberler, G. (1950) 'Some problems in the pure theory of international trade', *Economic Journal*, vol. 1, no. 10, pp. 223–40.

—— (1961) *A Survey of International Trade Theory*, Special Papers in International Economics, no. 1, Chapter II, Princeton: Princeton University Press.

Heckscher, F. (1919) 'The effects of foreign trade on the distribution of income', *Ekonomiske Tidskrift*, reprinted in H. Ellis and I.A. Metzler (eds) (1948) *Readings in The Theory of International Trade*, Homewood: Illinois, Irwin.

Hufbauer, Garry C. (1966) *Synthetic Materials and the Theory of International Trade*, London: Duckworth.

Hufbauer, G. and J. Chilas (1974) 'Specialisation by industrial countries: extent and consequences', in H. Gierschfed, *The International Division of Labour : Problems and Perspective*, Tubingen: J.C.B. Mohr.

Johnson, Harry (1950) 'Optimum Welfare and Maximum Revenue Tariffs', *Review of Economic Studies*, vol. 19, pp. 28–35.

—— (1954) 'Optimum tariffs and retaliation' *Review of Economic Studies*, pp. 142–3

—— (1955) 'Economic expansion and international trade', *Manchester School of Economic and Social Studies*, vol. 23, pp. 95–112.

Krause, L.B. (1959): 'U.S. imports and the tariff', *American Economic Review*, vol. 49, pp. 542–51.

Kravis, Irwin B. (1970) 'Trade as a handmaiden of growth. Similarities between the 19th and 20th centuries', *Economics Journal*, vol. 80, pp. 850–72

—— (1984) 'Comparative studies of national income and prices', *Journal of Economic Literature*.

Krueger, Anne (1974) 'The political economy of the rent seeking society,' *American Economic Review* vol. pp. 64, 291–303.

Krugman, Paul (1979) 'Increasing returns, monopolistic competition and international trade', *Journal of International Economics*, vol. 9, pp. 469–79.

Learner, Edward E. (1980) 'The Leontief paradox re-examined', *Journal of Political Economy*, vol. 88, pp. 495–503

Learner, A.P. (1953) *Essays in Economic Analysis*, London: Macmillan.

Leontief, Wassily (1953) 'Domestic production and foreign trade: the american capital position re-examined' *Economia Internationale*, vol. 7, pp. 3–32.

Linder, Staffan (1961) *An Essay on Trade and Transformation*, New York: John Wiley.

Lipsey, R.G. and K. Lancaster (1956–7) 'The general theory of second best', *Review of Economic Studies*, vol. 24, pp. 11–32.

MacDougall, G.D.A. (1951) 'British and American exports. A study suggested by the theory of comparative costs, part 1', *Economic Journal*, vol. 61, pp. 697–724.

Meade, J. (1952) *The Theory of International Economic Policy, vol. 1. The Balance of Payments*, London: Oxford University Press.

Mills, J.S. (1937) *Principles of Political Economy*, London: Longman Green.

Minhas, B.S. (1962) 'The homohypallagic production function, factor intensity, reversals and the Heckscher-Ohlin Theorem', *Journal of Political Economy*, vol. 1, no. 60, pp. 138–56

Ohlin, B. (1933) *Inter-Regional and International Trade*, Cambridge, MA: Harvard University Press.

Panchmukhi, V.R. (1993) 'The emerging international trading order', *RIS Digest*, September.

Posner, M.V. (1961) 'Technical change and international trade', *Oxford Economic Papers*, vol. 13, pp. 333–41.

Ricardo, David (1817) *The Principles of Political Economy and Taxation*, London: Dent edition 1973.

Samuelson, Paul (1939) 'The gains from international trade', *Canadian Journal of Economics and Political Science*, vol. 5, pp. 195–205.

—— (1948) 'International trade and the equalisation of factor prices', *Economic Journal*, vol. 1, no. 8, pp. 163–84.

Smith, Adam (1937) *The Wealth of Nations*, New York: Modern Library.

Sriniwasan TN (1999) WTO Symposium on Trade and Development, 17–18 March.

Stern, Robert M (1975) 'Testing trade theories', in P.B. Kenen (ed.) *International Trade and Finance*, Cambridge: Cambridge University Press, pp. 3–49.

Stolper, F. and P.A. Samuelson (1941) 'Protection and real wages', *Review of Economic Studies*.

Tatemoto, M. and S. Ichimura (1959) 'Factor proportions and the foreign trade. The case of Japan', *Review of Economics and Statistics*, 41, pp. 442–8.

Torrens, R. (1808) *The Principles and Practical Operation of Sir Robert Peels Act of 1844 Explained and Defended*, 3rd edn, London: Longman.

Uzawa, H. (1959) 'Prices of factors of production in international trade', *Econometrica*, vol. 27, pp. 448–68.

Vanek, Jaroslav (1959) ' The natural resources content of foreign trade (1870–1955) and the relative abundance of natural resources in the USA', *Review of Economics and Statistics*, pp. 146–53.

Vernon, Raymond (1979) 'The product cycle hypothesis in a new international environment', *Oxford Bulletin of Economics and Statistics*, vol. 41, pp. 255–6.

Wahl, D.F. (1961) 'Capital and labour requirements for Canada's foreign trade', *Canadian Journal of Economics and Political Science*, vol. 27, pp. 349–58.

World Bank (1993) *The East Asian Miracle Economic Growth and Policy*, Oxford: Oxford University Press.

8 Knowledge, technology transfer and multinational corporations

Shankaran Nambiar

Introduction

Technology transfer poses interesting challenges to the economist in view of the profound implications it generates. The multiplicity of issues that technology transfer impinges upon gives it, in large part, its importance. This is particularly so since the areas it affects are important to an economy. One fundamental issue that arises as a consequence of technology transfer is that of global markets. Those early commentators, Marx and Engels (1967: 81–4), accurately anticipated that with modern industry we would have the 'universal inter-dependence of nations'. They further added: 'The intellectual creations of individual nations become common property.'

Although Marx and Engels were not referring directly to technology transfer, their remarks could very well apply to technology transfer. As a matter of fact, it is increasingly realised that knowledge is the cornerstone of growth. Zysman and Cohen (1983) note that the newer technologies such as information processing form the industrial infrastructure for economies, assuming the importance that roads and bridges played during the industrial revolution. Knowledge and information are the basis for technology. While some aspects of the knowledge and information that constitute technology can be concealed, with technology transfer other aspects become 'common property'.

In Schumpeter's analysis (Schumpeter 1934) innovators and innovation are central sources of economic growth. Changes to knowledge assume the role of bringing improvements in the efficiency of firms and industries. Schumpeter's characterisation sees periodic waves of innovation in the capitalist system, where newer technologies act as the engine for replacing older, inefficient firms and industries with more efficient firms and industries.

The theme of knowledge as the stimulus for growth takes a new form in Romer's formulation of growth. Romer (1986, 1994) and Lucas (1988) argue in favour of the endogenity of growth. The new growth theorists realise that increases in output are the outcome both of physical and human capital. Knowledge in its various manifestations, as education, research and development, skills and training, influences and determines human capital, resulting ultimately in technological progress. The role of knowledge, via human capital, is quite distinct from changes in physical capital, which is exogenously determined.

This chapter examines the phenomenon of technology transfer from the viewpoint of the economics of knowledge. The first section will discuss aspects of knowledge that are useful in building a construct with which technology transfer can be analysed. The second section will introduce the role of multinational corporations (MNCs) as a site on which knowledge and learning occur. The third section will go further to examine the role of MNCs in the transfer of technology. The fourth section will list the various channels through which technology transfer can take place. The purpose of doing this is to consider in some detail, in the fifth section, the loss of information that comes about through technology transfer. Finally, some concluding remarks will be made.

Modelling knowledge

Paul David's (1993: 216) Simplest Linear Model (SLIM) perceives the generation of knowledge as taking a linear causal sequence in which,

> (1) fundamental science yields discoveries, which lead to (2) experimental findings of applied science, which leads to (3) acts of invention, which provide stimuli and basis for (4) entrepreneurial acts of innovation (commercial introduction of novel products and production methods), which incite (5) imitation and so bring about (6) diffusion of the new technology into general use.
>
> (David 1993: 216)

The SLIM model emphasises the importance of research, experimentation and reverse engineering. The foundations of knowledge generation would be absent if countries did not invest sufficiently in research and development (R&D). The trajectory taken in developed countries might follow the SLIM model quite closely, leading ultimately to Step 6, where the diffusion of technology extends to the transfer of technology. It can be argued that knowledge is generated differently in developing countries, where newly industrialising countries (NICs) learn from the diffused technology that originates from developed countries (Nambiar 1996). NICs can imitate the technology available in developed countries, and by imitation can learn to use the technology, thus acquiring the knowledge associated with technology that has been learnt through imitation.

Romer (1994: 12), by asserting that 'technological advance comes from things that people do', draws attention to the fact that technological advancement comes not just from the formal research that is conducted in laboratories but through the informal learning processes that accompany the generation of knowledge. Romer's assertion can be understood more clearly if we consider David's (1993) distinction between 'structured' and 'tacit' knowledge. Structured knowledge is knowledge that comes in codified forms and can be represented as research reports, journal articles and formulae.

Blueprints, circuit diagrams and manuals are further examples of structured knowledge. Structured knowledge must, however, be complemented with tacit knowledge. Tacit knowledge is knowledge resulting from experience and practice. It is the kind of knowledge that comes out of exposure to routines, through experience, and from learning by observation and learning by doing.

The different 'things that people do' to bring about technological advancement would include creating a technology policy, creating higher educational levels in science and technology and, most importantly, facilitating the exchange of knowledge. At one level it is necessary that those participating in the creation and extension of knowledge share in a common language of codes, conventions, symbols and assumptions. At another level, it is necessary that there be a culture that enables structured knowledge to be learnt and transmitted. In order that this be done, knowledge has to be experientially acquired, transferrred by demonstration in a contextual setting, and absorbed.

The MNC is a crucial conduit for learning and the transfer of knowledge. In this regard MNCs have an interesting role to play since their production is globally dispersed, their markets are equally spread out, and learning and the transfer of knowledge (or more specifically, technology, in this case) is just as global in nature. In spite of the extent of dispersion, the process of technology transfer is governed by economic rationality. Profit maximisation remains the central objective of MNCs with the costs of (and benefits from) the loss of knowledge being a decisive factor in determining the decision to transfer technology.

MNCs and the transfer of technology

Hymer correctly observed the growth and development of the MNC. He realised the logical necessity of such an organisation and noted the role MNCs had to play in the development of capitalism. Hymer (1972: 60) commented that:

> [t]he multinational corporation, because of its great power to plan economic activity, represents an important step forward over previous methods of organizing international exchange. It demonstrates the social nature of production on a global scale. As it eliminates the anarchy of international markets and brings about a more extensive and productive international division of labour, it releases great sources of latent energy.

With the advent of the internationalisation of capital and MNCs, the overlap between the nation-state and the territorial extent of the firm has ceased to coincide. As far as international markets are concerned, MNCs are in the best possible position to plan activity since their activities span over several geographical territories and relevant markets.

This is not to say that nation-states as atomic units have no use. It might be useful at this point to mention that Murray (1971) distinguishes six state functions: (1) guaranteeing property rights, (2) encouraging economic liberalisation, (3) providing economic ochestration, (4) ensuring the provision of inputs, (5) intervening for social consensus, and (6) managing the external relations of a capitalist system.

It is obvious that without the involvement of the state, technology cannot be developed. Murray acknowledges, for instance, the contribution of the state to R&D expenditure. In recent years, the developed countries have been making valiant efforts to promote liberalisation through international organisations such as APEC, GATT, and more recently, through the WTO.

Having mentioned that the nation-state does have its role to play in supporting the economy, it follows that by effectively performing its functions the state encourages the growth of MNCs. As mentioned previously, it is nonetheless the responsibility of MNCs to integrate their activities across geographical space. It is in recognition of this fact that a global industry is defined as one where there is 'some competitive advantage to integrating activities on a worldwide basis' (Porter 1986: 19).

In response to this definition, it is noteworthy that Kobrin (1991: 31–2) suggests three sources through which MNCs gain strategic advantages. First, MNCs can take advantage of the factors of production that are globally available, selecting resources that are cheaper. Second, centrally controlled multinational operations enable MNCs to provide

> sources of competitive advantage such as the *ability to transfer learning across markets*, increased returns to basic R&D, exploitation of ambiguous national jurisdiction, subsidization across markets, diversification in terms of adverse economic or political conditions in individual countries, and the ability to scan for new technologies or market opportunities worldwide.
>
> (Kobrin 1991: 31; italics added)

Third, it is only MNCs that are able to take advantage of the economies of scale of markets in many countries, rather than national markets which are too small to support efficient business activity.

MNCs and nation-states work in tandem to increase an economy's competitive advantage. The state provides necessary conditions such as the required institutional structure (property rights, laws), the global environment of liberal economic exchange (free markets, removal of barriers to trade and expatriation of funds), and domestic support for the growth of knowledge (funding of universities, R&D). With these necessary conditions in place, the

MNCs then utilise them so as to create their competitive advantage. Knowledge and learning are important factors in this scheme of affairs.

The globalisation of production carries with it the implication of the globalisation of knowledge. Fundamental education and research are, generally, undertaken in developed countries. This knowledge is then acquired by MNCs in the developed countries, which build upon what they have acquired for their industrial and commercial purposes. The transmission of knowledge can, subsequently, take two routes: (1) the exchange of knowledge between two MNCs, or (2) the exchange of knowledge between an MNC and its subsidiary.

MNCs can develop their strategic advantage by forming alliances with actual or potential competitors. The stronger and more confident MNCs realise that globalisation is a process that cannot be denied. It would be possible, in the short term, for a developed country to insulate itself from any technology transfer leakages; but that would, in the same stroke, act as a barrier to the inflow of knowledge. Simon (1991: 17) persuasively remarks:

> one could argue that it is counterproductive for any country, especially the United States, to spend the energy to close its borders and to try to shut off the multiplicity of technology transfer mechanisms that have proliferated over the last decade or so. After all, from the American perspective, a good argument could be made that it has in fact been the contribution of foreigners, studying and conducting research in the US in both science and engineering, that has been a primary source of American technological advance.

If MNCs are to adopt an open policy, then they would be more robust if they cooperated at least on the basis of knowledge-related joint ventures. MNCs can form alliances by trading their specialised skills. They can exchange their technological developments, or gain access to patents, licences, customer markets, raw materials and other inputs.

MNCs such as Phillips, Toshiba, Motorola and Boeing have been known to have forged inter-firm ventures where the objective of enriching their knowledge bases was, in some way, a consideration. Most significant, perhaps, have been the strategic alliances and partnerships in the informatics sector which has witnessed a large number of accords being signed between Western European countries and Japan. The United States has formed alliances with Japan, South Korea and Taiwan.

An interesting example of the exchange of knowledge is that involving Motorola of the United States and Toshiba of Japan in 1987 (Simon 1991: 19). The nature of the exchange involved Motorola transferring its microprocessor technology to Toshiba, in return for which Toshiba was supposed to pass on its memory technology to Motorola. That aspect of the exchange revolved around enhancing the respective knowledge capabilities of the two MNCs. This was supplemented by a purely commercial exchange, where

Toshiba was expected to assist Motorola in expanding its sales into the Japanese electronics market. This exchange indicates the extremely sensitive position that knowledge possesses, and the risks that MNCs must be prepared to take if they are to develop their mutual technological capabilities.

Having established the important role that MNCs have to play in the transfer of technology, we need to consider the possible processes through which technology transfer occurs. The next section provides such a foundation, so that we may draw upon this to analyse the resulting loss of information due to technology transfer and assess its economic impact.

Channels of technology transfer

One possible framework for categorising the transfer of technology is based on the different channels through which the process can take place. Enos *et al.* (1997) enumerate foreign direct investment, joint ventures, subcontracting, strategic alliances, South–South transfers and international agencies as routes through which technology can be transferred. Mansfield (1995: 146) notes that the export of goods is one important channel of technology transfer. This is made possible because the exporters will help the buyers of technology to use it efficiently, perhaps by imparting appropriate training. The export of goods makes imitation and reverse engineering possible. A second channel is through licensing agreements (i.e. patents, trademarks, and technical assistance). Joint ventures provide a third channel for technology transfer. Finally, in Mansfield's scheme, the establishment and utilisation of subsidiaries overseas lays the ground for the transfer of knowledge through training by assisting in upgrading technology and by extending technical information and capabilities.

Foreign direct investment and the export of goods are channels of technology transfer where the process of technology transfer is completely unintended. These routes have been known to provide the impetus for imitation and reverse engineering. Other routes through which technology transfer can occur, that is, through licensing agreements and the establishment of subsidiaries overseas, will result in transfer mechanisms that are predictable. In fact, the nature of production, with the advent of increasing automation and flexible production systems, has necessitated subcontracting links, which, in turn encourages technology transfer.

A study undertaken by Narayanan *et al.* (1994) confirms the huge role of knowledge in technology transfer. This study also models a possible pathway through which knowledge is transferred. Narayanan *et al.* propose a four-stage framework involving: (1) the importing and adoption of foreign technology, (2) the acquisition of operating, maintenance and repair skills, (3) innovation, and (4) the diffusion of technology. This model clearly indicates that access to technology (by the adoption of foreign technology) is the precondition for any learning to take place. Once access to technology is guaranteed, then the development and growth of knowledge can take place.

By using and implementing technical sequences, even if this be done only by instruction, workers acquire structural and tacit knowledge. At this stage the practical dimension of knowledge is cultivated since workers are able to progress beyond the ambit of technical articles, textbooks, manuals and circuit diagrams that exist outside of a practical manufacturing context. The process of knowledge acquisition is seen to deepen if it is possible to apply what has been learnt, to extend the principles and techniques that have been learnt, and to modify and innovate in order to adapt to changing situations or circumstances. The ultimate test of having fully acquired knowledge is exhibited when a firm is in a position to distribute the knowledge it now possesses to other firms.

The growth of MNCs and the proliferation of markets and production across the globe have resulted in the dispersion of knowledge. Although states, too, participate in technology transfer, MNCs have a particularly significant contribution to make. The acquisition of knowledge and its diffusion are central to the process of technology transfer. But while MNCs need to encourage technology transfer for their own profit-maximisation purposes, they are nonetheless subject to information loss.

Technology transfer and information loss

Technology transfer implies the loss of information to the firm that originally was in possession of a bundle of knowledge. Whether it be information that is acquired through reverse engineering, imitation or subcontracting, the knowledge that is gained by the follower firm is information lost for the firm that was the technology leader. In the case of information that is lost as a consequence of goods that a firm exports – goods that a firm in the importing country can disassemble and thereby gain valuable knowledge – there is little that can be done. To perfectly conceal such knowledge it would be necessary to protect the commodity from falling into the hands of any potential competitor, an impracticable solution.

In the case of knowledge that an MNC willingly transfers as technology, as in franchising or in the case of information that is predictably lost in subcontracting, the MNC has some measure of control. Yet, if a firm decides to enter into a relationship that entails technology transfer it is because the firm that transfers knowledge finds that its marginal benefit is at least equal to the additional cost incurred from transferring an additional unit of knowledge (Narayanan 1992). If in spite of the cost to a firm due to the information lost the firm still decides to support the growth of ancilliary firms, it is because of factors such as the high cost of importing raw materials, the objective of keeping inventory levels low and the need to get a quick supply of inputs from ancilliary firms (Rasiah 1989, 1994).

Nevertheless, technology transfer often does not result in any loss of dominance to an MNC because the ancilliary firms that supply the MNCs with their requirements do not have the requisite capital or expertise to duplicate the entire range of operations that an MNC typically possesses.

Understanding the nature of information loss in technology transfer is made clearer if it is recognised that there is, at one end of the spectrum, a subset of information that an MNC would possess which is fairly obvious, routine and non-exclusive (Nambiar 1997b). This variety of information is sought out by technology followers; it is information that can be costlessly acquired by most firms. Firms would make no effort to protect the safety of such information, and little will be done to protect the loss of information from this subset. It would, in fact, be cost-ineffective to attempt to control or monitor information loss arising from this category of knowledge.

At the other end of the spectrum of knowledge exists information that is highly valued and extremely specialised. Information such as this is highly exclusive; and possession of such knowledge is what gives a firm its monopolistic advantage. This category of information requires an investment if it is to be protected. A firm would find it economically rational to commit itself to sunk costs so as to prevent any loss of information coming from this category.

There is an intermediate range of information that exists between the top band that is highly valued and the bottom band which is trivially available. The bundles of information in this subset are worthy of monitoring because although they may not be exclusive to the firm, they are still not commonplace information. This category of information a firm might be willing to trade, if sufficiently attractive, and if it helps improve the firm's overall position in the long run. The bundles of information in this subset are an example of those that MNCs transfer to ancilliary or subcontracting firms. Ancilliary firms produce inputs or components for MNCs on the basis of technology and expertise that MNCs extend to the ancilliaries from this subset of information.

Considering the fact that there are two important classes of information (that is, information that a firm cannot afford to lose at any cost, and information that a firm can afford to exchange) it has been observed that an MNC can characteristically expect to face losses through several routes (Nambiar 1997b). One source of loss is through staff mobility, when workers who have acquired tacit knowledge in various fields of expertise carry forward this expertise with them to the firm that they are joining. A second source of loss occurs when workers carry to their work places the structured knowledge that they gained while at their previous firms of employment. Finally, inadequate institutional support can encourage information loss. This happens when intellectual property rights, copyright and patent laws, and the implementation of these laws, for instance, is not effectively implemented and enforced in an economy.

Clearly, the revelation of information has crucial economic consequences for a firm. The extent of information revealed or lost will directly impinge upon a firm's profits and market share. MNCs in Malaysia were slow to transfer technology in the late seventies and eighties (Chee and Chan 1982; Fong 1988). At that stage in the development of technology transfer in Malaysia, the technology that was used in Malaysia was often of a lower order than that in the host country. No attempt was made to adapt the technology employed from the parent company to suit Malaysian conditions. If there was any transfer of expertise at all it was at the level of imparting managerial and administrative skills to Malaysians.

The issue of optimal information revelation is of relevance to MNCs now. Taking the case of technology transfer in the Malaysian electronics and electrical industry, the MNCs located in Malaysia are faced with a fresh problem. Increased production costs in the home country, intense price competition and decreasing market shares have forced MNCs to locate their firms in Malaysia (Rasiah 1989; Hill 1989). Further, improved quality requirements, quicker delivery periods, the advent of automation and improved production processes necessitate technology transfer (Salih and Young 1989; Rasiah 1989). With the increased use of automation and the introduction of flexible production systems, more subcontracting links have been established out of necessity (Rasiah 1994). The changing scenario of technology transfer makes it imperative that the level of information revelation is an important constraint that has to be taken into account in determining optimal profits.

Globalisation and the transfer of technology

We have so far discussed how technology can be transferred and the role that MNCs play in this process. In examining technology transfer we have identified knowledge, its creation and diffusion, as crucial issues. Knowledge has been acknowledged to play the crucial role in technology transfer that it does in its various forms and stages. This includes all aspects and phases of learning, where the acquisition of information is seen to be a part of the overall process of knowledge accumulation. Knowledge plays a fundamental and pervasive role in technology transfer. It would therefore be fairly accurate to describe the transfer of technology as the transfer of knowledge.

The global character of production and the matrix of relationships (between states, MNCs, R&D centres across countries and local firms) naturally makes an impact on the transfer of technology. The problem is complex because of the many agents involved, their dispersion over geo-graphical space, the division of processes (and labour) and the vast interlinkages. Globalisation has far-reaching effects, but the impact of globalisation is felt more sharply (1) in the sphere of production, (2) on capability development, and (3) on the role of nation-states in relation to MNCs. The interaction of these three factors influences the texture of technology transfer in the face of globalisation. Obviously, the nature and extent of technology transfer is determined by a multitude of factors, but a consideration of the aforementioned factors would give a broad sense of the relation between globalisation and technology transfer.

Before proceeding further it is perhaps useful to clarify what is meant by globalisation. McGrew (1992) gives a comprehensive definition when he asserts:

> Globalisation refers to the multiplicity of linkages and interconnections between the states and societies which make up the present world system. It describes the process by which events, decisions, and activities in one part of the world come to have significant consequences for individuals and communities in quite distant parts of the globe. Globalisation has two distinct phenomena: scope (or stretching) and intensity (or deepening). On the one hand, it defines a set of processes which embrace most of the globe or which operate world-wide; the concept therefore has a spatial connotation. . . . On the other hand, it also implies an intensification of the levels of interaction, interconnectedness or interdependence between the states and societies which constitute the world community. Accordingly, alongside the stretching goes a deepening of global processes.

Using McGrew's definition as a point of departure, two characteristics regarding globalisation emerge. They involve:

1 the increasing interconnectedness or interdependence between states and societies, and
2 the coordination of processes, decisions and activities although they are fragmented and globally dispersed.

The feature of interconnectedness lies at the root of the complexity of globalisation. This is because production processes are decentralised and located across the globe. In addition, the division of labour takes a global character; and markets are created and penetrated across geographical boundaries. All of this implies linkages between firms (local and MNC), states, R&D centres (private and public) and educational institutions. Given the global nature of production, division of labour and markets, it is necessary that institutions be developed so that common standards, weights, rules, engineering processes, symbols and notations are used (North 1990).

The shared institutions between states, firms and workers would make the exchange of knowledge possible. Shared institutions are a prerequisite for the exchange or transfer of knowledge, regardless of whether this knowledge pertains to technology, managerial systems or research findings. Common institutions must be supported by a common system or body of knowledge or technology, if knowledge or technology is to be transferred. For example, only if two engineers from two different countries share the same conventions, scientific symbols and notation, and manufacturing principles, would they be able to discuss, say, a circuit diagram and how the experiences resulting from its use in one country can be modified or transplanted into a factory in another country. Shared conventions and mutually accessible institutions become more and more necessary with the increasing globalisation of production.

The global dimension of production, requires, first of all, good links between production and R&D. A close interconnection between both elements facilitates innovation and improved corporate performance (Sagal 1978; Souder and Padmanabahn 1989). Howells and Wood (1993) enumerate five issues that exacerbate the need for a closer interface between production and R&D. First, the longer time span for R&D, which in turn involves larger costs, stands in conflict with shorter product life cycles. Second, the growth in external research and the increasing technical collaboration between firms, higher education institutes (HEIs) and research institutes leads, again, to increased costs, and to the problem of coordination. This issue is not simplified with globalisation. Third, the R&D-production interface comes under pressure because of the need for closer proximity with targeted markets and suppliers. Fourth, different R&D 'cultures' exist and these cultures must interlock with production. On a global basis, the problem of coordination and match between R&D cultures and production in different countries is heightened because of national preferences and priorities. The spatial and temporal problems that come with geographical distances also adds to the challenge of achieving smooth interaction between R&D cultures and the cultures peculiar to production in specific countries. Fifth is the problem of globalisation *per se*, or the problem arising simply from having to contend with differences in time and distances in space, which creates what Howells and Wood (1993: 97) term 'as "space-time" compression associated with the need to coordinate global operations and resources within increasingly tight time schedules'.

A second major way in which production is affected by globalisation is through sourcing and supplier relations. MNCs have the option of sourcing for materials and components from suppliers who are located close to the headquarters. Alternatively, MNCs can source from overseas firms which may (or may not) be associated with the MNCs' operations overseas. By decentralising or globally dispersing their sources of supply, MNCs can benefit from the best suppliers. Corporations can then take advantage of countries which have an edge in particular technologies, labour skills, competitive cost conditions or governments that offer incentives, subsidies or fiscal benefits. On the positive side, MNCs have found that the globalisation of supply linkages and subcontracting has resulted in improved product quality, lower manufacturing costs and shorter delivery times.

Globalisation has, in a manner of speaking, brought states and firms closer, bringing the focus onto production and markets rather than onto states. This spatial compression offers a conducive environment for technology transfer. Changing trends in production, particularly flexible manufacturing systems, the interrelationship between firms, R&D centres and HEIs in different countries, and overseas supply chains and subcontracting, all provide opportunities for technology transfer. Subcontractors and other suppliers have to acquaint themselves with the standards, processes, methods and other requirements as expected of them by the parent MNCs. Very often MNCs are quite willing to equip their subsidiaries with the necessary expertise, thus facilitating the transfer of technology. Also, globalisation leads to an expansion in the number and type of overseas subsidiaries. Although MNCs can take advantage of scale and scope economies by emphasising product standardisation and centralised control, to do so would detract from gains through innovativeness and adaptation to market needs (Howells and Wood 1993: 107). By encouraging innovativeness and adaptation, the parent MNCs, while monitoring the manufacturing operations of their overseas firms, transfer knowledge, generally speaking. In specific instances, the parent companies technically assist their subsidiaries with process innovations so that market needs can be promptly and effectively met. In doing this the subsidiaries gain from technology transfer.

To what extent subsidiaries are able to gain from technology transfer depends on the technological capabilities they possess. In fact, within the context of globalisation the relationship between capability development and globalisation is an interesting issue. Capability development and globalisation have a reciprocal relationship in the sense that states and firms must have the capacity to take advantage of the benefits that can accrue through globalisation. On the other hand, globalisation forces states and firms to adapt and make changes because the ramifications and forces associated with globalisation are so powerful that a country which ignores the changing global situation will be marginalised.

An abundance of natural resources is of prime importance in agriculturally related and extractive industries. Countries that rely on primary commodities in order to attract MNCs are susceptible to the fluctuations so widely associated with these industries. Small countries like Singapore and Hong Kong do not have the physical area to attract such industries, which by their nature are land-extensive. Even a country like Malaysia, which was historically dependent on primary commodities, has come to realise that more sophisticated capabilities must be developed if they are to achieve greater growth.

In engineering industries, for instance, a high level of technological capability is necessary. The greater the need for technological capability the more sophisticated the technology involved (Pavitt 1984). In addition, there must be an abundant supply of local technical and managerial skills. While these skills may not be of a very high order, they must be sufficiently high in order to absorb the transfer of technology from the parent firm. Also, with flexible manufacturing systems, the presence of a high degree of decentralisation, the segmentation of production, the use of multi-sourcing and the reliance on a developed network of suppliers, it becomes necessary to have the capabilities to foster the requisite interrelationships.

As Lall (1997: 242) comments: 'In many process industries, there is little need to depend on suppliers of components and specialized inputs. In engineering industries, however, efficiency depends on specialization and a dense network of linkages between subcontractors, suppliers and service firms.' Clearly, before the linkages can be established, the subcontractors, suppliers and service firms must have the expertise, technology and financial ability to tolerate costs and uncertainty. MNCs would be drawn to allocate their investments in economies where these preconditions are satisfied. The higher technology investments will be located in those economies which have more satisfactory preconditions. Local capabilities must be adequately developed if local firms are to attract foreign direct investment. In particular, local firms stand in a better position to enjoy technology transfer if they possess the required capabilites in the following areas:

- labour skills
- manufacturing know-how
- materials handling
- machinery maintenance
- managerial skills
- networking of subcontractors and suppliers.

Much must be done by the state if an economy is to develop a satisfactory level of technological capability. Firms can contribute to capability development; but they can do so only within the context of the overall development that is determined by the state. This in turn leads us to the role that states play under conditions of globalisation.

The pressures exerted by globalisation demand that the state makes its economy more receptive to knowledge. This implies being capable of absorbing knowledge, creating knowledge and utilising knowledge. Without denying that physical infrasture must be improved, telecommunications facilities be extended, and credit availability be accessible, there is a fundamental need to extend the knowledge base of an economy. Very broadly, this can be achieved by encouraging research and by emphasising human resource development.

Technological change must be recognised to be an endogenous factor rather than as an exogenous element that is imposed upon an economy. This perspective takes the view that economies can grow if they actively take measures to develop factors that enhance growth (Romer 1986; Lucas 1988). Romer (1994: 3) expresses this position succinctly when he notes that the new growth theory 'distinguishes itself from neoclassical growth by emphasising that economic growth is an endogenous outcome of an economic system, not the result of forces that impinge from outside'.

It has been observed that education and training have a special role to play in promoting growth (Grossman and Helpman 1994). In fact, the new growth theorists see capital as including both physical and human capital. It then stands to reason that the state has to invest in improving the quality of education and training. Only then will labour be better skilled, and so more prepared to absorb new technical capabilities. At a higher level, better qualified labour (including engineers and researchers) would be better prepared to engage in R&D and to contribute to product and process innovation. The state's role, aside from maintaining a good educational system (primary, secondary and tertiary education), would have to be extended to imparting technical and industry-specific skills training. Most developing countries concentrate on education as delivered by schools and universities, but not on imparting skills that are relevant to manufacturing needs. In terms of Lall's typology (1997: 248), the sort of education and training that we are presently discussing is useful for operational purposes (i.e. to manage and operate production facilities designed and built by foreign partners), and for duplication (i.e. to expand output without foreign assistance). It may even be adequate to ensure technological self-reliance (i.e. to adapt existing systems, technologies, or to adapt to them); but definitely inadequate to support innovation (i.e. to extend existing technologies or to generate new technological solutions without any foreign assistance).

A state has to encourage R&D if it is to promote innovation in the economy. At the level of the state, some measures towards achieving this objective can be attained by planning for a comprehensive science and technology (S&T) policy. Such a policy would include interaction between primary and secondary industries, R&D institutions and HEIs. The state's participation in planning and coordinating research programmes would also be necessary. Further, the S&T infrastructure must be strengthened and private sector involvement in S&T must be encouraged.

Government participation in the commercialisation of R&D activities is necessary to foster R&D activities. This is because the private sector has no economic incentive to finance research that is likely to benefit other firms. The private manufacturing sector will not find it rational to invest in the production of services that possess the characteristics of public goods. Such research, when conducted, will be intra-firm and so would not produce any positive externalities. If research findings are to find their way into the public domain, it is necessary for the state to fund appropriate research projects because research can consume long periods of time, carry high levels of risk, and, often, show little promise of quick and profitable returns. It is in this respect that the state must intervene, both to provide insurance and to 'market' research once commercially viable outcomes are produced.

Government policies to encourage S&T, R&D and to raise the level of education and skills training are long-term policies. The effects of these policies bear fruit over a long period of time and they help a country to make the technological leap. Broadly speaking, a country's set of knowledge capabilities has to be extended both if it is to be able to absorb the technology that it must utilise and to adapt this technology. If this foundation is not available, it goes without saying that an economy will not have the necessary preconditions in order to innovate and to generate its own body of technological capabilities without the assistance of MNCs and other foreign partners.

Within a more immediate timeframe, a country can design its industrial policy in order to attract foreign investment. Typically, developing countries have offered incentives such as tax exemptions and pioneer status to investors. They have also curtailed the development of trade unions, and so have offered the incentive of a docile labour force. In addition to good infrastructure, free trade zones and licensed manufacturing warehouses have been established by developing countries. But these measures which have had their success in the seventies and eighties were directed at industries which were labour-intensive in their production processes, and were low in value addition. However, the rapid pace of globalisation, the changing nature of technologies and the shift from low-skilled, labour-intensive production to high-skilled, capital-intensive production places a larger burden on knowledge as an input in the production function. This implies that states in developing countries have to adopt a different strategy to take advantage of globalisation.

Conclusion

With the globalisation of production processes the transfer of technology is inevitable. Interesting insights can be gained by examining technology transfer from the perspective of knowledge and information revelation. There are two immediate advantages to adopting a knowledge-based perspective in studying technology transfer. First, by changing one's vantage point to that of a knowledge-based perspective one is relieved of the undue importance that is attached to the physical aspects of technology transfer. Indeed, technology transfer cannot be confined to machines and equipment; and technology transfer cannot be carried out in the absence of knowledge. Second, knowledge has costs that are attached to it. There are costs attached to acquiring knowledge, there are costs attached to imparting knowledge; and the loss of information impacts upon profits. All of this makes the role of knowledge in the process of technology transfer worthy of examination.

This chapter has concentrated on the role of MNCs in the transfer of technology. While MNCs are an important component in the process of technology transfer they are not the only agents that facilitate the process. Governments, universities and research centres are other conduits for the transfer of technology. In fact, the transfer of technology can be expedited if a comprehensive science and technology policy is devised.

Research in the area of technology transfer must look at the interaction between the different agents that can promote technology transfer in terms of their motivation to encourage the process and the decision-making problems that they encounter in the absence of perfect information. This can be extended to include the effects of path dependence and lock-in. With the freer flow of knowledge, firms and economies can escape the less productive routines that they have committed themselves to. This is a problem which can generate an interesting line of research.

References

Chee, P.L. and P. Chan (1982) 'Factor proportions problem and the transfer of technology: a case study of MNCs in Malaysia', Discussion Paper Series no. 82–08, Council for Asian Manpower Studies, University of the Philippines.

David, P.A. (1993) 'Knowledge, property, and the system dynamics of technological change', proceedings of the World Bank Annual Conference on Development Economics 1992, The World Bank.

Enos, J., S. Lall and M. Yun (1997) 'Transfer of technology', *Asian-Pacific Economic Literature*, vol. 11, no. 1.

Fong, C.O. (1988) 'Multinational corporation in ASEAN: technology transfer and linkages with host economies', a paper presented at the 13th Annual Conference of the Federation of ASEAN Economic Associations, Penang.

Grossman, G.M. and E. Helpman (1994) 'Endogenous innovation in the theory of growth', *Journal of Economic Perspectives*, vol. 8, no. 1.

Hill, D.J. (1989) 'Future of the semiconductor industry in Malaysia: an American viewpoint', in S. Narayanan and R. Rasiah, *et al.* (eds) *Changing Dimensions of the Electronics Industry in Malaysia: The 1980s and Beyond*, Malaysian Economic Association and Malaysian Institute of Economic Research: Kuala Lumpur.

Howells, J. and M. Wood (1993) *The Globalisation of Production and Technology*, London: Belhaven Press.

Hymer, S. (1972) 'The multinational corporation and the law of uneven development', in H. Radice (ed.), *International Firms and Modern Imperialism*, Middlesex: Penguin Books.

Kobrin, S.J. (1991) 'The implications of global integration for the national control of technology', in T. Agmon and M.A. Von Glinow (eds) *Technology Transfer in International Business*, New York: Oxford University Press.

Lall, S. (1997) 'Investment, technology and international competitiveness', in J.H. Dunning and K.A. Hamdani (eds) *The New Globalism and Developing Countries*, Tokyo: United Nations University Press.

Lucas, R.E. Jr (1988) 'On the mechanics of economic development', *Journal of Monetary Economics*, vol. 22, no. 1.

McGrew, A. (1992) 'Conceptualising global politics', in A.G. McGrew and P.G. Lewis (eds) *Global Politics: Globalization and the Nation State*, Cambridge: Polity Press.

Mansfield, E. (1995) 'Technological change and the international diffusion of technology: a survey of findings', in E. Mansfield (ed.) *Innovation, Technology and the Economy*, Aldershot: Edward Elgar.

Marx, K. and F. Engels (1967) *The Communist Manifesto*, Middlesex: Penguin Books.

Murray, R. (1971) 'The internationalization of capital and the nation state', in H. Radice (ed.) *International Firms and Modern Imperialism*, Middlesex: Penguin Books.

Nambiar, S. (1996) 'Knowledge, learning and the transfer of technology: some issues and the Malaysian experience', *Borneo Review*, vol. 7, no. 1.

—— (1997a) 'Knowledge and its place in Malaysian industrialisation', in B.N.

Ghosh, Y.K. Lai and S. Narayanan (eds), *Industrialisation in Malaysia: Some Contemporary Issues*, Kuala Lumpur: Utusan Publications.

—— (1997b) 'Information and profits: the case of technology transfer in the Malaysian electronics industry', *Asian Academy of Management Journal*, vol. 2, no. 2.

—— (1998) 'State and firm in technology transfer: the case of the Malaysian electronics and electrical industry', *Asian Economies*, vol. 27, no. 3.

—— (1999) 'Fostering technology trnsfer: the case of the electronics and electrical industry in Malaysia', in B.N. Ghosh and M.S. Salleh (eds), *Political Economy of Development in Malaysia*, Kuala Lumpur: Utusan Publications.

Narayanan, S. (1992) 'MNCs and the transfer of technology to ASEAN: an exploratory framework', in B.N. Ghosh, Y.K. Lai and S. Narayanan (eds) *Industrialisation in Malaysia: Some Contemporary Issues*, Kuala Lumpur: Utusan Publications.

Narayanan, S., Y.W. Lai. and K.G. Cheah (1994) 'Evaluating technology transfer: an analytical framework and an application to the electronics and electrical sector in Malaysia', in K. Erdener and S. Mohamed (eds) *Capitalising the Potentials of Globalisation – Strategies and Dynamics of Business,* Proceedings of the Third Annual World Business Congress, Philadelphia, PA: Pennsyvania State University.

North, D. (1990) *Institutions, Institutional Change and Economic Performance*, Cambridge: Cambridge University Press.

Pavitt, K. (1984) 'Sectoral patterns of technical change: towards a taxonomy and a theory', *Research Policy*, vol. 13.

Porter, M. (ed.) (1986) *Competition in Global Industries*, Cambridge: Harvard Business School Press.

Rasiah, R. (1989) 'Technology change and the electronics industry: the impact on Penang in the 1980s', in S. Narayanan and R. Rasiah *et al.* (eds) *Changing Dimensions of the Electronics Industry in Malaysia: The 1980s and Beyond*, Kuala Lumpur: Malaysian Economic Association and Malaysian Institute of Economic Research.

—— (1994) 'Flexible production systems and local machine-tool subcontracting: electronics components transnationals in Malaysia', *Cambridge Journal of Economics*, vol.18.

Romer, P.M. (1986) 'Increasing returns and long-run growth', *Journal of Political Economy*, vol. 22, no. 1.

—— (1994) 'The origins of endogenous growth', *Journal of Economic Perspectives*, vol. 8, no. 1.

Sagal, M.W. (1978) 'Effective technology transfer – from laboratory to production', *Mechanical Engineering*, vol. 10, no. 4.

Salih, K. and M.L. Young (1989) 'Economic restructuring and the future of the semiconductor industry in Malaysia', in S. Narayanan and R. Rasiah *et al.* (eds) *Changing Dimensions of the Electronics Industry in Malaysia: The 1980s and Beyond*, Kuala Lumpur: Malaysian Economic Association and Malaysian Institute of Economic Research.

Schumpeter, J. (1934) *The Theory of Economic Development*, London: Oxford University Press.

Simon, D. (1991) 'International business and the transborder movement of technology: a dialectic perspective', in T. Agmon and M.A. Von Glinow (eds) *Technology Transfer in International Business*, New York: Oxford University Press.

Souder, W.E. and V. Padmanabahn (1989) 'Transferring new technologies from R&D to manufacturing', *Research and Technology Management*, September–October.

Zysman, J. and S.S. Cohen. (1983) 'Double or nothing: open trade and competitive industry', *Foreign Affairs*, Summer.

9 The International Monetary Fund

Functions, financial crises and future relevance

George Kadmos and Phillip Anthony O'Hara

Introduction

The purpose of this chapter is to critically evaluate the role and functioning of the International Monetary Fund (IMF) in the light of its changing organisational dynamics and the real-world operation of financial crises. The chapter commences with an examination of the purpose and role of the IMF set in an historical context. Then we look at the IMF in action during the recent financial crises in Mexico, Asia and Russia. Finally, we examine the relevance of the IMF for the future operation of capitalism. We conclude that the institutional dynamics needed in the future will centre on a global central bank, plus the critical role of monitoring and supervision, cooperation with nations and institutions, policies which negate rigid blueprints, and technical and financial assistance to nations.

Purpose and role of the IMF

The International Monetary Fund was established as a monetary institution responsible for monitoring global monetary conditions. The IMF's lending powers were designed to enable it to carry out this role. However, given its 'global' position as the only truly international monetary institution, the IMF remains a mystery to most people. Considerable confusion exists about the IMF's role and activities, and even more confusion exists over the differences between the IMF and World Bank. Not surprising, the IMF has taken a battering from various corners over its inability to carry out its role constructively and many believe that the IMF has outlived its usefulness in a modern global economy. The IMF is largely seen as a powerful and generally 'euro-centric' political institution coercing poor nations to adopt economic policies unsuited to the needs of their fragile economies.

According to the IMF (1999: 1):

> Article I [of the IMF Charter] specifies that the IMF is to promote international monetary cooperation; to facilitate the expansion of international trade, and thus contribute to high employment and real income growth; to promote exchange stability; to assist in the establishment of a

multilateral system of currency payments and in the elimination of foreign exchange restrictions; to give confidence to members by making resources temporarily available under adequate safeguards in order to minimize the disruption from adjustment of balance of payments problems; and to help reduce balance of payments disequilibria.

The IMF believes that it has no 'real' power: its influence is derived from its ability to negotiate with its members and persuade them to adopt macro-economic policies that are suited to improving their economic conditions. Strictly speaking, it is true that the IMF has no 'real' power; but it yields considerable influence over its ability to place conditions on loans to members. It is these conditions that ensure the IMF opinions carry weight in the global community. It is therefore necessary to appreciate the exact role and purpose of the IMF. Hence this section will investigate the origins of the IMF and provide a brief summary about how it lends to member countries.

Origins of the International Monetary Fund

The establishment of the International Monetary Fund is a remarkable feat considering what the fund's original members were willing to surrender in order to establish an untried and rather idealistic concept. The need for an international monetary agency became apparent during the Great Depression during the 1930s. According to Horsefield (1972: 4), the depression precipitated a mammoth collapse in commodity prices and world trade, the depth of which had not been experienced before. The gold value of world trade declined by 47.5 per cent between 1929 and 1932. No nation was immune from the contagion effects of the depression. Individual governments moved to devalue their currencies in order to restore their competitive positions.

One of the consequences of the depression was the widespread loss of confidence in paper money that had previously been backed by the gold standard. The standard had defined the value of each currency in terms of a given amount of gold. Following the depression, nations preferred to trade exclusively in gold, which raised the demand for gold far above the levels that supply could satisfy. Given that the values of international currencies were questioned, many nations abandoned the gold standard in order to protect their gold stocks. Trading between economies became difficult, especially considering that some nations remained on the gold standard while others did not. This only exacerbated the effects of the depression, destroying export markets throughout the world. Many other nations, desperate to find new export markets or keep existing ones, artificially made their goods appear cheaper by devaluing their national currencies so as to undercut the trade of other nations selling the same products.[1] These practices did little but encourage retaliation between nations that thwarted the economies overcoming the depression.[2]

The depression reinforced the need to establish an international framework that could help to smooth future economic downturns and prevent them developing into global recessions. Once victory seemed inevitable during World War II, Allied governments were concerned that the world economy would slump back into depression after the cessation of hostilities. Governments began to seriously consider ways to prevent another world depression. Both the United States and United Kingdom worked closely to steer the world's economies away from the fate that had gripped the world through the 1930s.

Harry Dexter White (1892–1948) and John Maynard Keynes (1883–1946) are generally recognised as the founding fathers of the organisation. According to Horsefield (1972: 3) both men were convinced that an economic collapse after World War II could be avoided by massive international cooperation. White in the United States and Keynes in the United Kingdom proposed similar plans for the establishment of an international monetary body. However, though the plans were 'generally' similar, each plan reflected different purposes according to the individual needs of each economy. The depression in the United States had stemmed principally from domestic developments including the burst of the speculative bubble that had influenced the United States stock market. As the depression spread globally, international economies devalued their currencies in order to maintain their competitive position. This hampered United States export programs that endeavoured to find a way out of the depression. The United States wanted to prevent the competitive devaluation that had taken place throughout the 1930s and ensure the stability of currencies. The United Kingdom, on the other hand, faced different constraints to the United States. Whereas the depression was largely a domestic phenomenon in the US, the depression hit the United Kingdom export industry heavily. The UK economy was far more reliant on international trade. Keeping her competitive position internationally was paramount to the United Kingdom. Keynes proposed a mechanism by which individual countries could adjust their exchange rates according to their individual needs.

The Bretton Woods Conference

The Bretton Woods Conference, comprising delegates from forty-four nations, took place at Bretton Woods, New Hampshire, USA in July 1944. The Conference agreed to establish two international monetary institutions: the International Monetary Fund (IMF) and the International Bank for Reconstruction and Development (IBRD). The latter organisation became what is commonly known as the World Bank. The IMF began operations in Washington, DC in May 1946. It then had thirty-nine members.[3] The Bretton Woods Conference agreed on a number of conditions with which nations had to be willing to comply if they wanted to become members. Each prospective member had to agree to establish a par value for its currency that would fix the value of the currency to the US dollar or gold.[4] The aim of this was to prevent fluctuations in national currencies, especially artificial devaluations that had caused much damage during the depression.[5] Nations also had to agree to convert each other's currencies at par value.[6] This would help to stabilise international trade and make it easier for nations to purchase goods from each other. Members also had to agree to contribute to the running of the IMF. Each 'quota' is based on the volume of international trade, national income and international reserve holdings that each nation holds. Nations were required to contribute part of their contribution in gold and the remainder in their own currency.[7] Quotas are used to finance loans made to member countries in times of economic need.[8] They also have two other important functions. One is to determine how much each member is able to borrow from the fund. The more the member contributes, the more the member is able to borrow in times of need. The second purpose of quotas is to determine the voting power of each member. Quotas have changed over time, depending on changing circumstances. The IMF uses a system of weighted voting power.[9] The allotment system is designed to recognise and protect the interests of those members who contribute the most to the IMF. The more a member contributes in the form of quotas, the larger is their voting power.[10]

The Bretton Woods agreement sought to create order by coordinating economic policy globally through adherence to a set of agreed exchange rates, by liberalising trade flows, and by providing external finance to cushion balance of payments adjustment. At the same time, the World Bank was given the task of providing longer-term finance in circumstances where a need existed but private capital failed to meet it. Early on, the principal global financing need appeared to be to support European economic reconstruction. However, after this had been achieved, largely through Marshall Aid, attention shifted to the financing needs of developing countries.

The lending arrangements of the IMF

In order to summarise the IMF's lending arrangements it is important to understand the type of nations the IMF deals with. Williamson (1982: 13) separates IMF debtor nations into two categories. The first includes all major industrial and newly industrial nations as well as the major socialist nations (prior to the break up of communism) that are able to access funds from both the IMF and from the international capital market. These nations do not need to borrow from the IMF to finance deficits and only turn to the fund during crises that undermine their creditworthiness. The second group of debtor nations include most of the poorer developing nations that have little access to international capital markets and are thus reliant on the funds from the IMF. Since the early 1970s, the IMF's clientele has increasingly come from this second group, to the point that predominantly, the IMF is now totally devoted to this group. The fund's relationship to these two groups is obviously quite different.

An important component of IMF lending is the conditions that are placed on each individual loan. Conditionality refers to the policies that debtor nations are expected to adopt when obtaining credit from the IMF. According to Williamson (1983) the IMF's original Articles of Agreement do not make specific provision for the attachment of conditions on loans. These conditions have evolved over the course of the IMF and reflect changing patterns in IMF lending. These conditions are separated into loans that are based on 'high conditionality' and those based on 'low conditionality'. The conditions are intended to ensure that the debtor nation is able to implement the necessary reforms that will prevent recourse.[11] This of course, depends on whether the crisis that brought the nations to the IMF was temporary or not. If it was temporary, then the nations may borrow on 'low conditionality' that is, the IMF may consider current policies to be suited and expects the policies to be appropriate in the long term. If the cause of the crisis is considered more long term and deep seated, then funding may only be given on 'high conditionality' and the debtor nation will be forced to change its policies in order to convince the IMF that the nation is making the right decisions to prevent further economic instability.

The IMF's current lending activities can be summarised as follows. Nations can be separated between those that can obtain commercial lines of credit and those that are unable to obtain commercial credit. The first group of nations do not generally require IMF funds, they have access to international capital markets, but they will find it expedient to use the fund now and again when it is offered on favourable terms. Many of these nations use the IMF as a lender of first resort and not a lender of last resort.[12] It is generally agreed that the fund should be seen as a lender of last resort and that nations should try to obtain credit via the international capital market before requesting funds from the IMF. The second group are highly reliant on IMF funds; they have little access to international capital markets and can only obtain funds through the IMF. The IMF places varying degrees of 'conditions' on its funds. Both 'high conditionality' loans and 'low conditionality' loans are available to the second class of nations. Increasingly, the IMF lends more on high conditionality than low conditionality. Even though they are resented in many instances, high conditionality loans give poor nations access to IMF advice and knowledge. The suitability of this knowledge can be questioned. Is the IMF in a proper position to understand the difficulty of each nation and the specific policies needed to solve the individual's economic problems?

The IMF in action: Mexican, Asian and Russian economic crises

The changes taking place in international markets during the last decade have been unprecedented during this century. In less than ten years, the global economy has witnessed a liquidity crisis in Mexico, severe recession in Asia and contagion effects from this in Russia and Latin America. In analysing the relevance of the International Monetary Fund, it is important to closely monitor its performance over the past decade in handling the changes that have swept foreign markets. This section will discuss the IMF's role in three major crises: the Mexican, Asian and Russian economic downturns.

The Mexican crisis 1994–1995

The Mexican economy has been plagued with crises over the past two and half decades. In fact the recent bout of financial crisis is the fourth to hit the vulnerable economy since 1975. If one is to analyse the Mexican crisis of 1994–5, it is imperative that it is undertaken with an understanding of the economic fortunes of the Mexican economy over several decades. From about the 1950s to the early 1970s, Mexico was a financially stable country with high growth and relatively low inflation. Mexico benefited from the sharp increase in oil prices during 1973–4, which generated significantly higher export revenue. International capital, mainly from the Middle East, flowed in via European banks, providing excellent investment opportunities.

According to Hoskins and Coons (1995) the 1976–7 crisis was caused by massive government spending on programs designed to improve Mexico's export capacity. The Mexican government implemented expansionary policies that created large fiscal deficits and generated large capital inflows, causing an overvalued currency. Instead of using the opportunity to open her markets, Mexico retained restrictive trade practices that limited import and export growth. As a result, external debt tripled from 1970 to 1976. The programs failed to lift Mexico's export performance, which increased uncertainty among investors. The US government provided over $300 million and the IMF over $960 million to the Mexican authorities to stabilise its currency.

By the early 1980s the Mexican economy was vulnerable to changing conditions and perceptions in international capital markets. Peach and Adkisson (1997) report that rising interest rates and falling oil prices hit the economy hard, resulting in a capital market revaluation of the peso. The government of the day devalued the peso by more than 40 per cent. Investors reacted to the devaluation in the same manner as they had done during the past two financial crises. The peso continued to depreciate, causing a significant debt crisis. Debt levels skyrocketed during 1982 as the economy suffered the consequences of easy credit and the restrictive trade policies of the 1970s.

Camdessus (1995) reports that throughout the 1980s the Mexican economy struggled under its crushing debt burden. Per capita GDP growth from 1981 to 1988 was −2 per cent per year. Government spending on public services such as health and education fell under the debt burden. The focus shifted to market-oriented reforms. Mexico cut government spending while refocusing on social needs, reforming the tax system, privatising state enterprises, and liberalising trade.[13] The 1988 crisis was no different to the previous two. Once again the catalyst for the crisis was the flight of foreign capital following further political unrest and devaluation. Again billions of dollars were provided by the IMF and the US government to help authorities stabilise the peso.

The Mexican government, headed by the populist President Salinas, accelerated liberal reforms during 1989 with considerable emphasis on privatisation and encouraged greater foreign investment than ever before. On top of this, Salinas deregulated the banking industry and permitted new foreign financial institutions to enter the domestic market. Carlos Salinas was determined to shape a new Mexico into the twenty-first century and as such had a profound impact on Mexico. In fact, according to Boothe (1995: 1), investment capital totalling some US$70 billion entered the country between 1986 and 1994.[14] Most of this investment flowed in from the United States, Japan, Germany and Canada. Major American and international corporations built vast franchise operations throughout the country. The signing of the North American Free Trade Agreement (NAFTA) between the United States, Mexico and Canada also increased Mexico's economic prospects. When NAFTA was passed, one of the primary arguments was that trading with Mexico would create new jobs in America. The argument prevailed despite historical and research studies indicating that NAFTA would encourage movement of manufacturing and labour-intensive jobs to Mexican nationals, at the expense of American jobs. Though Mexico's population totalled 90 million, it was never realised by those supporting NAFTA in the United States that only 10 million of the population was classified as middle class and therefore could afford to purchase American products.[15] About 200,000 people in Mexico control most of the wealth, with thirty-two families, all billionaires, controlling the vast bulk of wealth in Mexico.

The Mexican economy under Salinas enjoyed considerable success in the late 1980s to early 1990s. However, the successes did not come without a price. The government was determined to maintain a fixed exchange rate and supported the peso through international borrowing. According to Williamson (1995) the massive increase in public debt was supported by an equally large increase in private debt. Thus an over-reliance on credit, increased consumer spending, an inefficient fixed exchange rate and ballooning in short-term debt set the scene for a major financial crisis. The crisis occurred in 1995 and was the worst crisis to hit that country since the 1930s. During late 1994 higher interest rates in the United States pushed rates significantly higher in Mexico. Mortgage rates on homes soared as high as 70 per cent while credit card rates topped 10 per cent per month. Ordinary Mexican citizens who had enjoyed a steady rise in their standard of living suddenly found that their well-paid jobs were insufficient to meet their debt commitments. Fiscal and monetary policies were changed to focus on creating the conditions necessary for abating inflationary pressures and, ultimately, achieving a sustainable reduction in interest rates.

Monetary authorities were also struggling throughout 1994 to keep the Mexican currency at its fixed-rate level. By December 1994, Mexico's foreign reserves had been depleted to about US$5 billion and, according to Gil-Diaz (1997), the authorities were facing the prospect that up to US$23 billion of Tesebono liabilities (short-term debt) would not be rolled over once they matured. The Mexican government was unable to persuade anyone to lend them the capital needed to avoid a financial crisis. The government faced two prospects: to increase interest rates to the level that would stop the flight of foreign capital or to print the money it needed to survive. The first option would probably strangle investment and cause massive unemployment. The second would probably cause hyperinflation, increasing Mexico's exports in foreign markets. Either way, the prospects were bleak for the authorities. The Mexican economy experienced a severe recession in 1995. Real GDP fell by close to 7 per cent, although it hit bottom around mid-year. Domestic demand collapsed following the March 1995 stabilisation measures.[16] This, together with improved international competitiveness, brought the current account close to balance. Inflation peaked at 52 per cent in the twelve months to December.

The crisis which hit Mexico was the result of several policy mistakes that precipitated international investor panic. According to Goldman (1996), the political risk to equity holders increased substantially with the assassination of a prominent presidential candidate.[17] The central bank compensated the rise in interest rates by expanding domestic credit. Investors converted the credit into dollars, draining Mexico of its reserves of foreign exchange. In an attempt to reduce the cost of government borrowing, the central bank converted its short-term 'peso' denominated debt into short-term 'dollar' denominated debt. The policy actions taken in 1994 resulted in the government holding a considerable amount of short-term dollar denominated debt while its stock of foreign reserves had dwindled to dangerous levels. The government began to seriously consider devaluing the currency. The Mexican government's first attempt to devalue the currency on 20 December panicked investors. The peso slumped drastically, raising all 'dollar' denominated debt. The result was a severe liquidity crisis. This also contaminated domestic credit conditions, precipitating the threat of a collapse in the banking system.

The IMF rescue package designed for Mexico consisted of two components. The first, according to Camdessus (1995), involved a strong adjustment program aimed at reducing the external current account deficit from 8 per cent of GDP to 1 per cent of GDP in twelve months. The second component consisted of a large-scale international rescue package designed to stabilise the peso and encourage the return of international capital. Mexico initially negotiated an external support package amounting to about US$18 billion dollars, comprising $9 billion from the US government, $3 billion from US commercial banks and $6 billion from other foreign governments. Within a few weeks the amount had risen to the US$40 billion range, while by the end of February the rescue package had reached a final size of US$52 billion.[18] The package of external support also included $17.8 billion of credits from the International Monetary Fund, $10 billion in short-term loans from central banks via the Bank for International Settlements, and several billion dollars of loans from other governments in North and South America.[19] The disbursement schedule was subject to Mexico sticking to its programmed restraint in government spending and monetary growth. As a source of collateral the Mexican government agreed to have importers of Mexican oil products make payment through an account at the Federal Reserve Bank of New York.

Since the 1995 crisis the Mexican economy has bounced back strongly. According to an *IMF Bulletin* (1998), real GDP growth in Mexico has topped 5 per cent per year since 1996 and employment in the formal sector has risen by 14 per cent against pre-crisis levels. However, the good performance should be put in perspective. Real wages are still 20 per cent lower than in 1994 and despite four years of growth, per capita output has risen by around only 3 per cent.[20] One of the major challenges for Mexico in the future will be to create employment for the rapidly growing labour force – nearly one million people enter the labour market every year. In addition, Mexico's foreign debt appears to be more manageable, a fact highlighted by the government's recent repayment, in full and ahead of schedule, of the emergency line of credit extended by the US government at the height of the country's recent economic crisis.

Asian economic crisis 1997–1998

The crisis that swept Asia during 1997–8 was the largest economic crisis to hit that region this century. However, like the crisis in Mexico, the Asian crisis was either largely unexpected or its severity was not taken seriously. Why there appeared to be such faith in the ability of the regional economies to bounce back is astonishing considering the magnitude of the crisis. Taking the first three months of 1998 as an example, $700 billion had been wiped off Asia's main stock markets, with some nations losing 90 per cent of the value of their currency.

In Asia, the economic fundamentals had been solid for decades. Government budgets had been balanced for years, current account deficits were controllable and currencies had enjoyed considerable stability that aided the strong growth over the previous two decades. In that period Asian economies had grown enormously through intensive investment in export-led industries. The catalyst for Asian growth had been the low level of real exchange rates or relative prices between East and West adjusted for the nominal exchange rate. Massive profit and volume opportunities generated export-led growth in high price and income markets.

A combination of inadequate financial supervision, poor risk assessment and the maintenance of relatively fixed exchange rates caused the Asian crisis. These factors led banks and corporations to borrow large amounts of international capital, much of it short-term, denominated in foreign currency, and unhedged. As the recession in Japan and the economic slow-down in Europe diverted investments to Asia, much of the funds were used to finance speculative real estate or stock market acquisitions. According to Mayer (1998: 1) 'what was new in this crisis was the predominance of interbank lending as the source of trouble'. Reassured by lender of last resort facilities, domestic banks often failed to gather minimum information on how their customers intended to repay their loans. Investment in South-East Asia skyrocketed, with increasing short-run profit expectations. Of course the validation of short-run profit expectations by realised profit depends upon the level of investment activity. For decades short-run profit expectations validated the level of investment in Asia. Increased competition from other powerhouses in Asia, specifically China, have stripped Asian nations of their traditional export markets. The loss of these markets has significantly reduced Asian business profitability. This in turn reduced short-run profit expectations but did not reduce investment demand. Hence investment continued to surge ahead while profit expectations fell.

But this is only one side of the coin, and ignores the contribution made by private firms and the financial system to instability in the last few years. Economic instability in Asia has been exacerbated by what Minsky would call the *endogenous credit expansion* propelled by deregulated financial processes.[21] In Asia's case, a loose monetary policy and expansionary banking credit (much of it financed from overseas) have had an enormous influence on the region's economies.[22] Governments loosened monetary policy and encouraged investment projects to be evaluated using euphoric prospective cash flows. The general decline in risk aversion thus set off both growth in investment and exponential growth in the price level of assets.

As was the case in Mexico, short-term foreign currency-denominated debt exacerbated Asia's problems via currency attacks and accelerated investor pullout. However monetary authorities were well aware of the increase in short-term debt but little attention was paid to the danger signs that were appearing. Even though the IMF was fully aware of these massive foreign capital inflows, no action was taken to restrict such inflows because authorities perceived the funds to be diverted to favourable investment projects that would provide continued high rates of economic growth. The massive capital inflows, especially in Indonesia's case, were directed at inefficient speculated assets such as property and stock assets. In many instances, solvent firms found themselves in severe trouble due to collapsing currencies. The combination of falling property and stock prices coupled with a general slowdown led to a self-perpetuating process of corporate insolvencies and bank failures that accelerated currency depreciations. This only caused a further selling of home currencies, making firms even less profitable.[23]

Owing to its unique role in safeguarding the stability of the international financial system, the IMF played a central role during the crisis. The IMF's goal was relatively simple – to restore stability and confidence in the region and divert the crisis spreading to the rest of the world. The IMF's immediate response was to aid the three economies most affected by the crisis – Thailand, Indonesia and Korea – and avoid a contagion effect elsewhere. According to Lane (1999: 45) the IMF responded to the Asian crisis by adopting three main policy responses: the first consisted of supporting and financing large packages used to stabilise the fall in the domestic currencies,[24] the second involved persuading governments to adopt sweeping reform processes aimed squarely at the structure of each economy, and the third entailed convincing governments of the need for immediate change in macroeconomic policy to counteract the crisis itself. The IMF encouraged the governments to adopt harsh economic reforms. This included a contractionary monetary policy designed to restore confidence in the foreign exchange market, a tightening of fiscal policy to ensure that government deficits were at a minimum, structural reforms to the impediments of further economic growth, and an improvement in the financial supervision of the banking sector.

The IMF was committed to restructuring bank and financial structures in order to help re-establish investor confidence. Monetary policy was designed to check the downward spiral of exchange rates and to prevent such rates moving away from fundamental levels. The decision to allow currencies to continue to float freed governments from trying to defend indefensible pegged rates. The IMF implemented a thorough round of structural reforms aimed at the heart of the weaknesses of the financial systems. The IMF's long-term strategy of reforming Asia's financial markets had merit. Evidence does suggest that the nations with the most open financial markets in South-East Asia have been affected less by the economic crisis. Indonesia, Malaysia, Singapore and Thailand all introduced financial liberalisation policies of removing interest rate restrictions and mobilising savings in the 1970s, which were soon followed by dismantling current account and capital account controls.[25] While Malaysia and Singapore had dismantled all controls, and had taken steps to further deepen and develop their financial systems as far back as 1978, the other two with large rural economies are still in the process of complete change. Thus Singapore and Malaysia, which had gained substantially from greater openness to the rest of the world, have been affected less by the currency crisis. Indonesia and Thailand, which are still in the process of complete reform, have been hit the hardest.

With hindsight it is now clear that the initial IMF reforms in 1997 failed to restore investor confidence and the economies slipped during 1998 further and further into crisis. A large part of this failure can be attributed to the fact that external creditors were not convinced that IMF rescue packages were sufficient to restore currencies to a level that would improve their debtors' ability to service foreign-denominated short-term debts. More importantly, the IMF reform programs were aimed at improving the economy as a whole, not the ability of individuals to repay their debt.

Restoring creditor confidence was even more difficult considering that the majority of debt was held by private individuals or organisations and not by the government.

Many economists believe that monetary policies were not tightened sufficiently or for long enough in the immediate pre-devaluation phase of the emerging crises in the developing Asian economies. Had monetary policy been tightened adequately in order to defend exchange rates in the first part of 1997, it is possible that the crisis might have been moderated, if not avoided. However, the IMF did call on Indonesia to tighten monetary policy during initial negotiations between the two in 1997. In fact, Indonesia accepted the IMF's conditions in 1997 that specifically instructed that nation to tighten monetary policy. Indonesia was incapable of implementing the tight monetary policy that the IMF had wished mainly because its banking and financial systems were on the brink of collapse. Leading into 1998, Indonesia's banking system was severely weakened by a combination of bank collapses and the fall in the rupiah which compounded losses and bankruptcies. Indonesia's central bank, Bank Indonesia, found itself in the predicament of trying to provide the much-needed liquidity on one hand, while sticking to the IMF program of tight monetary policy. At least in this case, the choice was obvious. Without knowing whether banks were facing insolvency or liquidity problems, Bank Indonesia indiscriminately provided the liquidity to prop up the payment system. The end result was that Bank Indonesia had no intention, at least at this stage, of adhering to the IMF's 1997 program schedule. As such the IMF was forced to modify their 1997 agreement during the latter half of 1998, again calling for tight monetary policy. This time the economy had at least stabilised albeit slightly, and Bank Indonesia was more successful in adhering to the new agreement, especially considering the currency had appreciated away from crisis levels.

Given the situation in Indonesia, it is doubtful whether higher interest rates would have been favourable to international capital flows, considering that companies' liquidity problems were already exacerbated following the rupiah collapse. On the balance of probabilities, it would seem that international capital markets had already 'tried and convicted' the Indonesia economy. Higher interest rates would have worsened the situation for domestic economic activity and sent many more businesses to the wall. Given that the international market had abandoned Indonesia, it would seem logical that Bank Indonesia would abandon the IMF's program and satisfy domestic liquidity requirements.

The situation in Korea and Thailand was quite different to that of Indonesia. The IMF called for tight monetary policy in both countries, as it had done with Indonesia in 1997 and both countries were able to adhere to this policy. Such restrictive monetary policy prevented the currencies from collapsing to the same extent as Indonesia's, and as such, monetary authorities were much more successful in adhering to the IMF's programs. This of course reflects the differences in the severity of the crises in each country.

Thailand and Korea were not facing the banking collapses that Indonesia was facing nor did it experience the severe currency depreciation that Indonesia faced. As such, monetary authorities were far better equipped to stick to IMF programs than were monetary authorities in Indonesia.

A major lesson from the Asian crisis is the need for the IMF to be fully aware of the severity of any approaching crisis. The IMF clearly miscalcul- ated the true extent of the crisis.[26] Aghevli (1999) states that the IMF was unaware of the full extent of Thailand's problems because their currency was being heavily supported by the government's intervention in the forward market. The IMF apparently had no idea that most of that country's foreign reserve was being used to stabilise the baht until the government finally approached the IMF in mid 1997 with the news that their foreign reserves were nearly depleted.[27] Austerity policies promoted by the IMF clearly missed their mark and misrepresented the true causes of the crisis. It does appear that a significant part of the IMF mistake lay in poor forecasts. This may be partly due to the information the IMF was receiving from the countries themselves. Every time the IMF received additional information, its fiscal proposals were adjusted. This did not help to stabilise an already volatile economy. The signals sent to the market were detrimental to quick recovery. Had the IMF known the true picture, its response may have had a much faster positive influence on stabilising the economies.[28]

The programs set up by the IMF and agreed to by the authorities were meant to restore investor confidence and reverse the flight of international capital flows that had crippled the exchange rates. It is now clear that the initial IMF programs were less successful in Thailand and Korea and failed dismally in Indonesia. Market confidence was not restored and exchange rates continued to fall throughout the first half of 1998. Such currency depreciations compounded corporate debt, which weakened banking systems even further. The vicious cycle had set in. The more the currency fell, the more debt corporations accumulated; the weaker the banking and financial systems, the further the currency fell. The IMF had completely underestimated the severity of the crisis. This underestimation was not restricted to the IMF, the entire financial world had also discounted the crisis. But the fact that the IMF had done so highlights the inadequacies of the IMF at present. Its inability to correctly gauge the economy and therefore implement appropriate policy is a serious flaw.

Asia appears to be recovering – albeit slowly. Economies are approaching pre-crisis levels spurred on by an increase in domestic demand, especially private consumption. In many economies, fiscal policy has been used moderately to encourage faster recovery. Exports are also slowly increasing to take advantage of a strong economy globally. The exceptions to the rule remain Indonesia and Thailand, though both economies have stabilised significantly and trends suggest that economic activity will pick up through- out the next twelve months. It will be important that the lessons learnt during the crisis are adhered to and that recovery does not provide a false sense of security to authorities. Many reforms are still either in process or yet to be tackled. Asia can rebound again, but important challenges will need to be faced before the economies are able to be as successful in the first few decades of the new millennium as they had been during the last few decades of the previous one.

The Russian crisis 1997–1998

Following the several waves of pressure on emerging markets since 1997 that had emanated mainly from Asia, Russia became a new source of contagion during August 1998, causing global confidence to deteriorate. Prior to the Asian economic crisis, the Russian economy had stabilised after earlier problems and its stock market had risen 150 per cent for the twelve months ending June 1997. Russia has had a torrid run in moving towards a market economy. Sanders (1998) reports that GDP in Russia fell 42 per cent between 1992 and 1995, while industrial production fell 46 per cent over the same time. The Russian people have been devastated by several years of economic turmoil. Since the Soviet Union collapsed, real income has plummeted nearly 40 per cent. A quarter of the population now lives under the subsistence level while a third live under the poverty line. One-quarter of the working force is either not paid at all, or paid months in arrears.

However, by the second half of 1997 the Russian economy began to feel the effect of the Asian crisis as foreign investors withdrew from the market.[29] A decline in world oil prices and a blow-out in the Russian budget exacerbated the contagion effects from the Asian crisis.[30]

By May 1998 the situation was so severe that the economy was on the verge of collapse. In an attempt to control the exchange rate, the Russian central bank increased interest rates on government bonds to 200 per cent a year. It also supported the currency on the open market by purchasing its currency in an effort to keep the exchange rate at an acceptable level. It became obvious that the Central Bank could not support the currency forever and that it was only a matter of time until the government had to borrow even more funds to support the ruble. It was also obvious that the Russian government would be forced to negotiate yet another bailout package with the IMF.

The IMF prescription for Russia was no different to the advice it gave Mexico and Asia: fiscal and monetary contraction, liberalisation and privatisation of markets and banking sector reform. The IMF agreed in July 1997 'in principle' to a $22.5 billion dollar bailout, which included previously committed funding from the IMF as well as funds from the World Bank and the government of Japan. The IMF's objective was to provide foreign currency reserves that would enable Russia to defend the ruble long enough to implement the reforms needed to achieve long-term stability. However, by August the Russian Central Bank announced that it was incapable of supporting the currency any longer and the ruble fell 300 per cent, from 6.2 rubles per US dollar to over 20.

It is, however, now obvious that the IMF and its \$22.5 billion bailout failed to rescue Russia. Investor confidence was not strengthened, the stock market continued its decline, and interest rates on government bonds again climbed above 200 per cent. The causes for cynicism about Russia run deep. A number of interrelated difficulties have combined to cause a general breakdown of the Russian economy. The first problem relates to fiscal policy. The Russian budget deficit had been running at about 7.5 per cent of GDP for several years while the taxation system had completely broken down and is totally ineffective. The process of collecting taxes is also considered to be inefficient and corrupt. Gaidar (1999) believes that a soft budget constraint coexisting with a soft administrative constraint exacerbated the Russian crisis, whereas in the former Soviet economy, soft budget constraints existed with hard administrative constraint, ensuring a rigid control over the appointment and performance of managers. The soft budget constraint was seen as a consequence of 'a state budget process far removed from consideration of efficiency and profit'. This problem is not restricted to Russia alone: nearly all the post-communist economies have suffered the consequences of soft budget constraints and soft administrative constraints.

Gaidar (1997: 13) lists two main points of criticism of the IMF's response to the Russian economy prior to the Asian crisis. The first includes the fact that the IMF lost precious time to aid the Russian economy by taking its time to influence the Russian reform process. The IMF's packages were too little too late and 'condemned Russia to prolonged crisis and stagnation'; the second fault lay in the programs the IMF suggested in the first place. Excessive tightness and dogmatism of IMF programs that were inappropriate to Russia's needs condemned them to fail. In a 'postsocialist era, due to a special structure of the economy, inflation has a nonmonetary character, which is why ordinary stabilisation programs directed at slowing down the rates of money growth are not applicable in those conditions'.

The post-communist national economy is full of goods and services considered inferior in both quality and price compared to other international markets. Clearly a major problem is to do with government mismanagement and lack of expertise. Russia has an inadequate level of trained and experienced labour. The move from 'communism' to the 'free market' has left a wide gap in training and expertise that Russia is finding difficult to fill. As such, the Russian legal and legislative system is inappropriate for the new market economy. The end result is that the legal and political system in inept, corrupt and unwilling to solve Russia's economic problems. The IMF bailout has helped to calm the Russian financial markets and more importantly given the government crucial breathing space to implement its reform agenda. The fundamental problem with the Russian economy has less to do with bad IMF advice and more to do with domestic policy inaction. The Russian government and people themselves have shown little enthusiasm in adopting the necessary reforms that will complete transition to a market economy. The result is that Russia is caught between its old self and a haphazard attempt to conform to a market economy.

Such an economic and political structure is not conducive to market stability. The loans made by the IMF and the conditions that accompanied them could never be seriously meet.[31] The Russian government was both incapable and unwilling to carry out the necessary reforms that accompanied IMF loans.[32] On the part of the IMF, it was unable to convince the Russian government to carry out the reform process, but continued to pay the tranche payments.[33] The IMF continues to play a pivotal role in Russia's progress. But it is often criticised as being the cause of Russian economic problems. However, without the IMF most probably Russia's problems would be more severe.[34] The IMF is a critical influence pushing toward reform in Russia.

Concluding remarks on financial crises

There are striking similarities between the three crises that have been discussed to date. With respect to Mexico and Asia, the crises were largely unanticipated. Mexico and most of Asia 'appeared' to be running sound economies. Mexico has been enjoying a good run since the mid 1980s and the Asian Miracle appeared to never end in Asia. This provided ideal opportunities for investors. Once problems started investor confidence changed abruptly, leading to bouts of panic and massive outflows of foreign capital. Similarly, the sudden interruption of capital flows unleashed a deep crisis in domestic financial markets, threatening the stability of the economies.

What exacerbated the problems in both Mexico and Asia was the fact that Mexico and most of Asia operated pegged exchanged rate systems. This made it difficult for governments to defend their currencies during the crises. In both instances, stocks of foreign capital were at dangerous levels due to efforts to stabilise local currencies. Efforts to stabilise the currency via interest rate raises caused severe negative impacts on the financial systems and spilled over into the banking systems. The fact that both Mexico and most of Asia run pegged exchange rate systems encouraged investors to borrow in foreign currencies and transfer the risk from the investor to the banks. In Mexico, as in Asia, appreciation of the real exchange rate, growing short-term external debt, and the size of the external current account deficit, compounded by the weakness of the financial system, exerted strong pressure on the foreign exchange market. This resulted in drastic devaluations as it became impossible to defend currency parities indefinitely by drawing down reserves and raising interest rates, particularly in light of the weakness of domestic financial systems.

In all three cases, important information pertaining to the level of foreign reserve levels was withheld from the IMF. With respect to Asia, this was especially the case in Thailand. Investors were therefore uninformed about the true extent of the economic problems. Once investors were confronted with the problems, they behaved accordingly. The crisis in Mexico, Asia and Russia shows that the global capital market exposes and punishes economic weaknesses especially those that are unanticipated. It is also clear that the global market brings the increased risk of global contagion. It is therefore essential that governments adopt appropriate policies. However, what appears to be more important than coherent economic policy is the free transparency of financial systems. This raises the question of the ability to monitor and supervise capital markets. Economies must be open and information made available to investors. Unlike in Mexico, IMF rescue packages in both Asia and Russia included substantial structural reforms in the banking and financial sectors. These reforms were the main part of the IMF rescue packages aimed at restoring investor confidence and ensuring positive rates of economic growth in the future.

The IMF has been offering the same structural 'template' for troubled economies for over two decades. Three main instruments appear to have been used by the IMF in Mexico, Asia and Russia: tight monetary policy designed to increase local interest rates and prop up falling currencies; tight fiscal policy via increased taxation and lower government spending in order to reduce the government deficit; and liberalisation of financial markets in order to remove restrictions on foreign capital flows while placing restrictions on domestic bank lending practices. The consequences of these policies are also similar. In Mexico, Asia and Russia the IMF policies designed to stabilise the economy in the long run also helped to destabilise them in the short run. High interest rates and restrictions on credit restricted consumer demand and forced many profitable businesses to the wall. This in turn led to further unemployment, reductions in production and a further fall in investor confidence.

Relevance of the IMF for the future

The past decade has witnessed a systematic reduction in international barriers to goods, services and capital across national borders. These changes pose new challenges to the international community. Industrial and developing nations alike are now more exposed to shifts in their external positions than ever before. The crises that hit Asia and Russia have now become a familiar feature of the global economy. This raises the question of the relevance and future role of the International Monetary Fund. The IMF today is remarkably different to the one that was established in 1945, and the world economy is fundamentally different. The IMF's main functions today are somewhat different from those it was empowered to perform fifty-four years previously.

Many commentators believe that the IMF has lost its relevance and therefore should be abolished.[35] The Fund's performance during the Asian and Russian crises has given what was a very small minority increased vigour to press their case for the IMF's termination. Many others believe that the hundreds of billions of dollars that have been lent to developing nations since the Fund's inception have actually damaged their prospects and reduced their rate of growth. Instead of promoting stable economic growth, many believe that the IMF has encouraged financial profligacy and international dependency. Most of all, these critics are concerned that the IMF has supported corrupt regimes that dominate workers. Apart from this, the debt burden that these developing economies carry stifles economic growth to the point that governments are barely covering the interest payments on their loans, let alone investing in their infrastructure.[36]

Niskanen (1999: 331) argues that there are three reasons why the IMF should be abolished. First, the IMF is incapable of fulfilling the role of lender of last resort because it is unable to create high-powered money and cannot react quickly to prevent liquidity crises. The time taken once an application for funds is received is time consuming. IMF loans are only granted after lengthy negotiations between the borrowing nation and the IMF council. Therefore the IMF is incapable of preventing collateral damage caused by a crisis; it is, however, capable of mopping up the damage done once the crisis has emerged. Second, the IMF has not been effective in persuading borrowing nations to adopt the macroeconomic policies necessary to prevent further crises. For example, many of the poorer developing countries such as Mexico are requiring assistance regularly. With the number of nations that require continual assistance, it may appear that the IMF has not been successful in persuading the respective governments to turn their economies around.[37] Third, because the loan process is time consuming, borrowing nations often find themselves with IMF funds which are too little, too late. Often IMF assistance cannot ensure exchange rate stability, resulting in depreciation of domestic currencies that only serve to increase the amount owed in domestic currency to meet the obligations made in foreign currency.

Calls for the abolition of the IMF originate predominately in the major industrial nations. Without the IMF, however, poorer nations would have little access to funds. These countries are unable to obtain funds from international capital markets and are therefore reliant on the IMF. International capital markets lend little money to poor nations that are in need of massive structural changes. What is clear is that, despite the problems the IMF obviously has, its role is still important and therefore we need to improve the IMF in order for it to be relevant in the future.

Global Central Bank and a second Bretton Woods

The Mexican, Asian and Russian crises have highlighted the need to reform the International Monetary Fund. In the future, the IMF should move from being an institution that predominantly acts as a lender of last resort to being one that monitors and coordinates global macroeconomic policies with domestic governments. The relevance of the IMF hinges on its success in achieving this goal. To a large extent, this will depend on how the IMF relates to the major industrial powers. As it stands now, the IMF has little influence with these governments. The IMF must be seen to be the premier monetary institution not just by the poorer nations, but by the major industrial powers as well.

The relevance of the IMF and the role it should play in the future is obviously dictated by the environment in which it is forced to operate. Soros (1999: 56) paints the future correctly by stating that 'the essential point is that the global capitalist system is characterised by not just global free trade but more specifically by the free movement of capital'. It is therefore doubtful that the IMF, in its current role, is useful in playing an active and beneficial role in the future. Currently, the IMF performs three main functions: surveillance and analysis of member nations' economies and the international economy as a whole, lending to member nations, and offering technical assistance and training. Historically, the fund has performed the second role under its main goal of being a 'stabilisation fund'. According to Soros (1999), international capital flows are too volatile, and this can subject recipient economies to crises that are too large and frequent. At the moment there are few controls over international banking activities. At present bankers are encouraged to increase their lending, and corporations, through the taxation system, have an incentive to increase leverage ratios. Therefore a system of capital controls similar to the proposal put forth by Malaysia may be necessary. The crises in Asia that spread to Russia and then on to Latin America highlight the dangers of contagion. It is therefore important that the world finds a solution to the dangers of excess volatility and the threat of contagion.

What the world needs is a global monetary institution that is capable of regulating the new global market and preventing future crises from turning into severe depressions. The experiences both in Mexico and in Asia highlight the damage that can be done in a modern system of free capital mobility. In both cases, investor panic led to the devaluation of local currencies, destroying strong economies. Of course, the uninhibited access of foreign capital exacerbated the problems. Credit and finance were too easily accessible in many cases and there were no controls on how these funds were being used. Lack of transparency withheld information from investors. This contributed to a series of panics that caused major runs on currencies. It is clear in this global market that no one government is powerful enough to defend against a run on its currency. The global market is too big for any one player – and it will get bigger. Even the largest economic power – the United States – will not be immune to the global economy.

There appears to be strong grounds for a second Bretton Woods-type conference. It is true that since the IMF was established in 1944, the international financial system has evolved to the extent that largely restricts the IMF's capability to stabilise world markets. It is therefore time to restructure the IMF so it can carry out a more integral role in the global economy. This includes allowing the IMF to take a proactive role in preventing future crises – not just stabilising them once they have arrived. At present, the IMF's influence in preventing crises is limited. The future IMF must move away from stabilising economies after crises to an institution that endeavours to prevent crises.

The IMF therefore must be active in four areas: monitoring global trends, coordinating global macroeconomic policy between domestic governments and itself, providing appropriate assistance to economies in need (while considering domestic issues when recommending policy changes), and providing technical assistance wherever possible. Of course, the IMF can have a role in many other areas, but these activities should form the core of its operations into the next century.

Monitoring and supervision

The IMF needs to continue to monitor the international monetary system and the world economy as a whole. Its relationship with the governments of its members must be strengthened, especially the relationship with the major economic powers. The IMF will continue providing important financial and technical assistance to developing and transitional economies. The enormous growth in international capital markets has rendered the IMF ineffective in the major industrial nations, while its role in the developing and transitional economies is unclear and fragile. The recent crisis in Asia and Russia highlights the need for the IMF to be better equipped to minimise the risk of contagion. The higher the risk of contagion, the higher the risk of irrational behaviour among investors. The IMF needs to ensure that it has enough cash on hand to meet its members' borrowing needs in the event of an economic crisis.

The key to preventing another crisis, and one in which the IMF needs to be involved, is transparency. The experiences during the Asian and Russian crises show that governments are reluctant to provide a complete picture of their economic situation often until it is too late. Both Russia and Thailand withheld important information pertaining to their economies that the IMF should have known before recommending policies. This succeeded in exacerbating the effects of the crisis in Asia and Russia, which could have been avoided if the information was known sooner. Lane (1999: 47) agrees that the IMF must be better equipped to monitor the situation within domestic economies and that the IMF requires 'improvements in standards for data dissemination and steps to increase the transparency of policies that help markets to improve their pricing of risk, inhibiting the build up of imbalances, and also spur policymakers to take timely action to address vulnerabilities'.

The IMF has a role to play when monitoring moral hazard. Foreign lenders and domestic borrowers must be aware of the risks involved in behaving in ways counter to financial stability. Domestic governments must also take responsibility for the workings of their own banking systems. What was made apparent during the Asian crisis is the point that good economic management by the domestic government is not sufficient to prevent a financial crisis. As previously stated, most of the fiscal and monetary policies adopted by Asian governments were appropriate. What they lacked was sound financial supervision and good corporate practices.

Mayer (1998) highlights the need for 'some sort of registry that would call attention to any bank's or national banking system's continuing increase in short-term borrowings from financial firms'. The IMF is empowered under Article IV of its Charter to exercise 'firm surveillance over the exchange rate polices of its members'. According to the IMF's *Annual Report* (IMF 1992: 15):

> The effectiveness of Fund Surveillance has less to do with strengthening the principles of surveillance and more to do with the willingness of member countries to consider fully the views expressed by the international community – through the forum – in formulating and adopting their macroeconomic and structural policies.

IMF surveillance should concentrate on the cause of such crises and the policies required to smooth the adverse effects on both domestic and global markets. Surveillance can also provide the early warning required, ensuring that policies and measures are in place to ensure that the adverse effects are less unstable. Good surveillance should reduce the collateral damage and the rescue packages required in assisting troubled economies. Surveillance should also highlight vulnerabilities in members' economies. Such vulnerabilities can be addressed before problems occur. Inadequate economic information can add to the severity of crises facing domestic economies and prevent authorities from providing the correct policy advice to ensure an economy is in the best position to ride out the crisis.

Cooperation

Because of the globalisation of capital markets, monetary and fiscal policies can no longer be made on the basis of exclusively domestic considerations. Approximately US$1.3 trillion is traded every day in world currency markets. The sheer size of the new global market means that without joint action, individual central banks have little influence in the market. Monetary authorities will need to make some adjustment in order to enable them to function effectively in an interdependent world. Economic policy will need to be far more coordinated than ever before. The IMF stands well placed to have a significant impact in ensuring that governments closely work together in order to achieve 'global' goals in the future. At present, the IMF appears to have little influence in the major industrial economies.[38] According to Fischer (1995: 171), the IMF has evolved into a 'specialised development agency' that acts as a lender of last resort to the poorer economic nations.

The need to integrate the former 'communist' countries and shape the poorer nations in Africa and Asia has provided a new challenge for the

IMF.[39] However, its effectiveness in carrying out these challenges depends on its own relationship with the major industrial countries. The relevance of the IMF, therefore, depends on how well it deals with its richer members and if it is able to persuade them to follow global rather than domestic interests. The IMF was founded predominantly by the United States and the United Kingdom. During the first few decades, the IMF served both the interest of the major industrial powers as well as the interest of the emerging economies. The institution was created by the major economies in order to stabilise an unstable global economy. The post-war (1950s–1960s) boom in the major industrial economies can to some degree be attributed to the success of the IMF and World Bank.

The major industrial countries account for over two-thirds of world production and, therefore, their support is crucial if the appropriate changes are to be made. The problem with the international economic community, as Fischer (1995) recognises, is that the major industrial economies have shown little inclination to alter their domestic economic policies unless such change is in their 'best interest'. The IMF needs to encourage greater financial sector cooperation to promote stability and to avoid currency runs. It needs to encourage individual governments to implement stricter control on their banking systems while providing a better safety net in case of trouble. Risk control should be improved by encouraging better disclosures concerning interbank lending, while the government encourages better market discipline by exercising closer monitoring activities. Good fiscal and monetary policy must encompass improved compliance monitoring by the central banks. While individual central banks are ideally suited to monitor domestic activities, the IMF is well placed to monitor global trends.

The IMF must also encourage better cooperation between the major economies and the developing nations. Central banks from the major industrial economies are well equipped to monitor domestic lending activities. Central banks in major industrial economies have developed well laid out rules of supervision. Though domestic lending practices are well monitored, the same cannot be said for international lending practices. It is clear most foreign capital pouring into developing economies originates from the major industrial powers. Guitian (1994) believes that better supervision of foreign capital would help smaller vulnerable economies by reducing their country risk and satisfying investors that an increase in foreign capital will be put to good use. Currently there is no global central bank that monitors these flows. It is appropriate that the IMF take a larger role in this area.

Recommending appropriate policies

The IMF has encouraged rapid liberalisation irrespective of the condition of the relevant banking and financial system. Many commentators believe that the pace of change placed on some economies by the IMF causes instability rather than enhancing stability. Meyer (1999) believes that 'we have to match the pace of capital account liberalisation with careful consideration of exchange rate regimes and efforts to improve corporate governance and bank regulation and supervision'. He goes on to say that:

> The sequencing perspective also suggests that the story behind the crisis in emerging Asian economies may have less to do with the inherent instabilities of global capitalism than with a mismatch between the evolution of institutions and policies and the pace of liberalization of financial markets and the capital account, the critical entry points to global capitalism.
>
> (Meyer 1999: 152)

Taylor (1997: 146) states that IMF packages attempt to promote faster economic growth as well as economic reform by 'stabilising' the macro economy then 'adjusting' the market by implementing sweeping reforms. Many economists believe that the IMF acts too swiftly and therefore implements policies that 'overkill' the causes of the crisis being felt. Instead of stabilising the economy, many believe, IMF policies contract economies into recessions. The result is the adoption of IMF policies that end up backfiring on economies that are not 'ready' for the pace of reform.[40] For instance, Taylor believes that IMF policy is too influenced by what he calls the 'Washington consensus' which amalgamates traditional macroeconomic stabilisation policies such as market deregulation, supply-side reform and privatisation of public enterprises into one. The Washington consensus is considered to be inappropriate in all circumstances and should not be used by the IMF or World Bank as a 'template' for global restructuring.

There is considerable debate that debtor nations should have the right to decide for themselves how they wish to adjust when confronted with a permanent adverse shock.[41] If the nation fails to implement appropriate policies suited to their domestic needs, they then should be forced to accept the IMF's conditions without exception. The unwillingness of Russia to commit to any reform agenda has probably convinced the international community that the best method is to coordinate policy between domestic governments and the IMF. Although the IMF states that its policies are always agreed on beforehand, it is clear that domestic governments have little influence when much-needed IMF funds are in the balance. The IMF must recognise the independence of each economy and avoid using 'template policies' when negotiating IMF loans. The speed at which financial liberalisation is undertaken must be appropriate for the economy in question. The IMF needs to be better aware of the limitations of each economy it deals with. While the benefits of financial liberalisation are plentiful, the speed at which it takes place is crucial. Should a country be exposed to too much change it will experience structural setbacks that may not just jeopardise the economy in question, but eventually the region in which it resides. Aghevli (1999: 31) admits that most Asian economies 'liberalised short term capital inflows before foreign direct investment, when they should have done it the other way around'. The result was a 'combination of partial liberalisation and structural rigidities that meant capital was invested without regard to risk'.

Technical and financial assistance

The IMF has been extensively involved in the provision of technical assistance since its inception. The Fund currently provides assistance in a wide variety of fields including fiscal and monetary policy, balance of payments, exchange rate, trade and finance and statistical collection. The IMF assistance packages are usually provided in conjunction with financial assistance, though there are cases where the provision of technical assistance only has been considered appropriate.

The goal for the IMF is to ensure that transitional economies are able to access much-needed foreign capital without making their economy volatile to the crises that have plagued Mexico, Asia and Russia. It is therefore important that the IMF is able to provide the expertise needed to transform these economies at a pace that is commensurate with their capacity to develop sound regulatory and institutional structures. The IMF must also ensure that moral hazard problems are attended to. Financial intermediaries have little incentive to adopt safe lending practices when their actions are guaranteed by a higher institution. Though there was no direct guarantee to intermediaries in Asia, the perception was widespread that governments would bail out institutions that found themselves gravely in danger.

The IMF must continue providing the technical assistance that economies need to move from closed inefficient markets to global capitalist markets. The problems in Russia are exacerbated by the lack of trained and skilled professionals in the areas of economics and finance. Russia's successful transformation to an open market economy depends on it attaining sufficient skills and experience. The IMF should work closely with major industrial economies to ensure that all developing nations attain the necessary skills to ensure a stable market.

In addition to providing the necessary technical assistance, the IMF should be equipped to provide the necessary financial assistance during major economic crises. Soros (1999: 60) proposes a new global monetary currency (a new 'SDR') that would be used to supplement members' current assets. He proposes the establishment of an 'International Credit Insurance Corporation'. The new institution would guarantee, up to a certain limit, the loans that member states make with private financial institutions.[42] If the member state were to default on its debt payments, the IMF would pay those debts up to the limits the member state has agreed with the IMF. The IMF, acting as the global central bank, would effectively become the lender of last resort to the global economy.

Many opponents of the IMF are totally against the idea of giving the IMF more money. These economists believe that current capital markets are able to provide the funds to liquidity-constrained economies at interest rates that reflect the level of country risk. Private markets are therefore in the best position to lend money to these economies. The IMF increases moral hazard and sends a message to investors that they can invest with little fear of a total loss. Moral hazard results in excessive risk-taking because investors are shielded from losing all their money. The private market is seen on the other hand as preventing moral hazard problems from arising. Private financial institutions are less likely to accept riskier investment projects if they have lost their safety net.[43] The market would also be able to provide funds necessary quickly, and as such, prevent investors from fleeing from one market to the next. Many believe that the IMF should have allowed the private sector to sort out the problems in Asia. Private institutions could have renegotiated debt with their creditors. The role of the IMF would have been one of consultation and not involvement. However, no matter which way you look at it, the so-called 'private sector' view fails to appreciate the extent of the Asian crisis. Once many of the Asian currencies had collapsed, debtors were either insolvent or close to bankruptcy and the prospect of renegotiating any further lending would have been near impossible. If some had been successful, the terms that they would be forced to accept would not have been conducive to long-term recovery.

However, in order to work, the IMF must have power to prevent any one member falling into too much debt with private institutions. There should be a limit to the extent that any one nation can borrow. This is imperative if the new central bank is to work. The guarantee limits placed on each member state should be sufficient to pay the vast majority of that member's debts. If a member were to default on debts that were well above the guaranteed limit provided by the IMF, such guarantees might not be sufficient in preventing further crises and contagion effects. It might be possible to extend guarantees above those which were originally agreed upon, thereby allowing members to increase their debt burden, but only if the total value of world debt did not exceed the total value of guarantees. The IMF needs to be able to fend off not just a regional crisis, such as the Asian economic crisis, but also a global crisis that endangers the whole world. Unless the 'global free market' is appropriately monitored and controlled, it will always have the power to destroy international capital markets.

The future role of the IMF should be changed from 'ex-post stabilisation' to 'prevention'. This can only be achieved by allowing the IMF to have real power to carry out its role. One method would be to convene a second Bretton Woods conference. As stated previously, the key is to align the major industrial powers. There appears to be widespread contempt for the IMF in some of the major industrial powers – especially the United States. These powers must be brought back into the fold and a new agreement reached. The worst possible outcome is for the world to do nothing until a major financial crisis forces it to act. If the world adopts the necessary adjustments now, it will go a long way in preventing a major global crisis. Economic crises are as natural as booms. It is clear that the more global markets become, the greater the risk of contagion and the greater the collateral damage inflicted once a crisis does occur. Therefore, monetary authorities should act sooner rather than later.

Conclusion

The IMF has had extensive influence in the post-war world economy. This influence ranges from the resurrection of many war-torn industrial economies after World War II to the adoption of the Bretton Woods agreement on exchange rate management. During the 1960s and 1970s the IMF was prominent in the integration of the newly industrialising countries into the international economy. The IMF was also significantly involved in the transition from a fixed rate system to one of flexible exchange rates. The IMF has also been successful in preventing wider collateral damage following the debt crisis of the early 1980s and is now involved in reshaping the former communist countries into market economies.

The IMF's future is important for the stability of the financial system as a whole. In all three financial crises, in Mexico, Asia and Russia, the crux of the problem appears to be the failure of domestic governments to control large current account deficits, inefficient exchange rate systems, the bursting of speculative bubbles in the property and stock markets, the transition of previously tightly regulated markets into free market systems, and the failure of monetary authorities to provide the prudential supervision required in an open market. In all three cases, the weakness of the banking and financial sectors played a significant role in the severity of the crises. IMF efforts should be directed at ensuring that banking and financial systems are appropriate and capable of handling the changing trends.

The lessons learnt from the Mexican, Asian and Russian crises clearly show the need for a global monetary authority that is able to monitor developments while having the financial clout to implement swift remedies. The common mistake made by the IMF during the Mexican, Asian and Russian crises was that it failed to gauge the true extent of the problems being faced. This resulted either in inappropriate policy being recommended or in decisions being made too little, too late. The IMF should have more effective surveillance over countries' economic policies and practices. This includes the power to force full disclosure of relevant financial and economic data to the market. The IMF also has a role to play in encouraging better prudential supervision by central banks and encourage them to adopt acceptable 'best practice'. It is clear that the integration of financial markets must be undertaken in an orderly way and in the best interests of the integrating economy. It would appear that the IMF has paid too much attention to the speed with which many markets were reforming their economies, which aided instability within the market. Financial liberalisation must be undertaken carefully. The IMF is well placed to ensure that this is accomplished. The IMF is also well placed to promote regional and global cooperation between emerging markets and established markets.

The fixed exchange rate system has been abolished in favour of a more flexible exchange rate regime. The mobility of capital is also much freer than it was fifty years ago, while the market's ability to punish weak economies is much greater. Economies are far more integrated than they were and the consequences of a player's actions can permeate across international markets quickly. With the emergence of the global economy and the ease with which markets can be punished for the ills of their governments, severe crises are probably becoming the norm. The pulse of the global economy is investor confidence. Once this confidence is damaged, it takes an enormous effort to restore. The loss of confidence can cause investors to behave erratically. Erratic investor behaviour affects exchange rates and stock prices. In addition, weakness in one economy can increase the likelihood of problems in another. The collateral damage caused by contagion can damage world markets for a long time.

The relevance of the IMF can be summed up in four main areas: surveillance, coordination, good policy proposals and a continuous supply of technical and financial assistance. Proper IMF surveillance will play a crucial role in the prevention of future crises. The IMF must increase its monitoring of international capital markets, including assessing the risks involved in further opening capital markets. In addition to increasing surveillance, the IMF must promote greater openness between its members and itself and between the members themselves. The IMF must improve the availability of information between capital markets. The IMF is also well placed to encourage governments to improve their banking systems in order to prevent the unsupervised lending arrangements that were partially responsible for the Asian crisis.

Freer information will help to prevent small economic shocks turning into major global crises. The IMF is well placed to improve information between interbank and inter-government lending. Third, the IMF must establish sound economic policies that are suited to individual economies. All too often, the IMF has used 'template' fiscal and monetary proposals that are ill suited to the economy in question. Unless the IMF understands local conditions its efforts to stabilise economies will prove futile. The IMF should encourage economies to modernise, but they must do so in an efficient and prudential manner. This will help to maximise the benefits and minimise the risks associated with restructuring an economy. Furthermore, financial globalisation has increased the speed with which disturbances in one country can be transmitted to others. The new global economy, although a cause of improved economic conditions for many, has increased the likelihood of a major global economic crisis. The IMF's role in preventing this crisis is paramount. What is therefore needed is a second Bretton Woods conference to effectively make the IMF the new 'global central bank'. The IMF must have the power and resources to prevent a global crisis. It will only be able to accomplish this task if it has the support of the major industrial powers. Just as the United States and United Kingdom were willing to concede considerable autonomy to the IMF during its inception, the major industrial powers must show the same goodwill now and concede again in order to ensure a stable global market. It is also important that the second conference be held sooner rather than later. The worst-case scenario is for the world to do nothing until a major global crisis forces it to act.[44]

Notes

1   Under a fixed exchange rate system a government can adjust its balance of payments by trading its domestic currency for foreign currency or gold. Currency devaluation depreciates the domestic currency with respect to foreign currencies. Reciprocal to this is the appreciation of foreign currency with respect to the domestic currency. Because foreign currency is now worth more, domestic goods are cheaper in foreign stores, stimulating an increase in the demand for domestic exports.

2   Governments that devalue their currency in order to stabilise a chronic imbalance in their balance of payments often succeed in only weakening the currency's international acceptance as legal tender.

3   The IMF now has 182 members.

4   Of course, this was abandoned in 1972, when the United States removed itself from the gold standard. Most nations now have flexible exchange rates that float freely and are not fixed to any specific level.

5   Gold was also set at US$35 per ounce.

6   An agreement was also reached to set upper and lower limits within which exchange rate fluctuations were permitted in response to market conditions. At the time of the conference the IMF set this limit at 1 per cent in either direction.

7   As at January 1999, the total value of quotas is approximately SDR 212 billion (about US$300 billion).

8   Quotas are assessed every five years and can be changed according to the needs of the IMF and the economic prosperity of the member.

9   Each member has a basic allotment of 250 votes; in addition, it obtains one votes for each 100,000 SDR it contributes to the fund.

10   The United States, being the largest economy, contributes most to the IMF, about 18 per cent of the IMF's funds. It subsequently has the largest number of votes, about 18 per cent of total votes.

11   Dell (1981) states that there should exist a degree of conditionality that should vary depending on the size and 'originality' of the deficit. The author proposes that funding should be made available to other forms of deficits and not just those that originate due to export shortfalls. Nations may fall into deficit because of wars in neighbouring countries, natural disasters, protectionism in developed countries or the position of the world business cycle.

12   Williamson (1982: 18) states that India used the IMF as a lender of first resort in November 1981 when it obtained a $5 billion loan. Critics believe that India had not exhausted its credit with the commercial banks before approaching the IMF.

13 Camdessus (1995) reports that Mexico achieved good economic performances before the crisis. Inflation fell from 160 per cent in 1987 to 8 per cent in 1993. Economic growth, which had languished at zero between 1985 and 1988, increased to 3 per cent in 1993. The problem of course, is that this increase in positive economic activity paved the way for Mexico's worsening current account deficit. By 1993, Mexico's current account deficit rose to 6.5 per cent of GDP and was principally financed by short-term debt. As early as February 1994, the IMF stressed to the government the need to reduce the current account deficit in order to offer some defence against a sudden reversal of capital flows.

14 Of the some $70 billion dollars invested in Mexico, only $10 billion actually went into new factories, industry, capital creation, and job creation entities. The rest went into speculation, debt service, and into the coffers of the thirty-two wealthiest *haciendas* of Mexico. Much of it flowed into offshore banks and investment houses.

15 Eighty-five per cent of Mexican lived on an income equivalent to that of the lowest 10 per cent in the United States.

16 The Mexican economic crisis has inflicted havoc in almost all of Latin America's financial markets. Central America did not escape the consequences of the Mexican economic crisis. The region was inundated by enormous trade deficits, as well as volatility in the levels of foreign reserves. The most pressing challenges facing Central American leaders are to promote exports and narrow trade deficits, stabilise currencies, stimulate investment, and deter short-term capital flight.

17 According to Goldman (1996: 94) Mexico's political system is failing to work as it should. 'An out-of-control power play among different political groups dominates Mexican politics.' Goldman blames a large part of Mexico's problems on the breakdown in the taxation system.

18 Opponents to the US/IMF bailout of Mexico argue that the Mexican devaluation led to a vast US$15 billion US trade deficit with Mexico. According to them, the bailout has gone further than just 'stabilising' a regional economy; it has significantly aggravated the US trade deficit. They also argue that American jobs are increasingly moving south to Mexico.

19 The IMF loan amounts to over seven times Mexico's IMF quota of $2.4 billion, and at the time, were unprecedented in the history of the IMF.

20 However, according to Rogers *et al.* (1997: 147) the Mexican banking system continues to struggle with the economic effects of the December 1994 devaluation of the peso, and since January 1997 it has faced the further challenge of conforming to US generally accepted accounting principles (GAAP). Restructuring is under way: by the end of 1995, eleven banks, holding more than 70 per cent of the banking system's assets, had been recapitalised.

21 In retrospect, the Financial Instability Hypothesis can explain a large part of the Asian crisis. For a good review of Minsky's hypothesis see Minsky (1982).

22 According to Aghevli (1999: 28) the 'massive capital inflows and weakening exports were reflected in widening current account deficits. To make matters worse, a substantial portion of the capital inflows was in the form of short-term borrowing, leaving the countries vulnerable to external shocks.'

23 Aghevli (1999: 28) believes that domestic allocation of the huge amount of foreign investment was inefficient because of 'weak banking systems, poor corporate governance, and a lack of transparency in the financial sector'.

Weakening exports combined with increased foreign borrowing cause a deterioration in current account deficits.

24 According to the IMF (1999), some US$35 billion was approved by the IMF in 1997 for Indonesia, Thailand and Korea, while the IMF arranged another US$77 billion of additional funding from the major supporting economies. In July 1998, a further US$1.3 billion from the IMF and US$5 billion from other sources were arranged specifically for Indonesia.

25 See Ariff (1996) for discussion on how Indonesia, Malaysia, Singapore and Thailand liberalised their financial markets.

26 In retrospect, the initial policies recommended by the IMF were based on false information and unrealistic expectations that proved to be inappropriate. The cause of the crisis had little to do with fiscal thriftiness and moves to tighten fiscal spending proved to exacerbate the problems.

27 The IMF also did not know that the South Korean government has also been propping up their own currency and that the country's foreign reserves were slowly being used.

28 According to Aghevli (1999: 30) had the 'IMF known how rapidly international reserves were falling in Thailand, and subsequently in Korea, policy adjustments could have been made earlier'.

29 According to Cohen (1998: 1) the Asian crisis was not the only factor in the decline in market confidence. Foreign investors became extremely cautious when the Russian parliament passed legislation prohibiting foreign ownership of more than 25 per cent of the national electricity monopoly that at that time already had foreign ownership of over 28 per cent. The state owned Oil Company, with oil reserves worth ten of billions of dollars, was suppose to be privatised but was unable to attract the US$2.1 billion asking price.

30 Oil and gas are responsible for up to 75 per cent of Russia's foreign currency earnings. Oil prices dropped approximately 30 per cent between 1997 and 1998, severely decreasing the earnings of Russia-based companies as well as government receipts.

31 The IMF had already loaned Russia over $18 billion since 1992. Then the reforms that the IMF demanded Russia adopt were either never carried out or done so half-heartedly.

32 The IMF has been highly critical of the way the Russian government has been tackling the economic crisis so far. IMF deputy director Fischer (1998) lashed out against the Russian government, which, he said, had misinformed the IMF about the size of Russia's reserves in gold and hard currency back in 1996. In addition, Russia had not done enough to restructure the country's banking system, and has not shown the political will to tackle these and other sensitive problems.

33 A large percentage of payments to the IMF are used to repay the fund on previous loans. The yearly interest payment on Russian loans amounts to approximately US$17.5 billion.

34 This is not to say that the IMF was without fault in its dealings with Russia. The IMF should have encouraged the Russian government more to adopt the changes necessary. In addition, the revaluation of the currency was probably set too high, making Russian goods less attractive compared to those being supplied in Asia and elsewhere.

35 See Crook (1991) for a concise account of the criticism directed against the IMF.

36   Mexico is now the largest borrower from both the IMF and World Bank with debts exceeding $180 billion. Mexico must meet interest repayments of the order of $25–$30 billion each year.

37   This argument is not without substance. India has been the highest benefactor from the IMF, receiving about US$55 billion since 1955, but still today over 40 per cent of the population still lives in severe poverty.

38   Italy and the United Kingdom were the last industrial countries to receive IMF funding in 1977. Both countries sought help from the IMF after the first oil shock to control their balance of payments following the move to flexible exchange rates.

39   After two decades of development planning financed largely by the IMF and World Bank, sub-Saharan Africa today has a lower per capita income than it did when the aid started.

40   Taylor (1997: 149) believes that IMF reform agendas are often 'intellectually ill-informed and counterproductive in practice'. He questions the advantages of adopting Anglo-American policies in many economies. For instance, in Chile, Mexico, Turkey and Eastern Europe, such policies have benefited 'industrialists who gain from liberalisation, financial speculators, households in the top 10–20 per cent of the income distribution who can afford to pay for an array of new consumer goods and the economic technocracy which puts new policies in place'. The rest of the population, including the other 80 per cent of the workforce, are losers.

41   Taylor (1997: 150) supports less IMF conditionality and a greater sympathy for individual circumstances. Taylor even suggests reverse conditionality, where domestic governments propose suitable economic policies to the IMF that are ideally suited to their own individual requirements.

42   According to Bird (1996) the demand for IMF assistance is inversely related to economic growth and development. If economists want to encourage less IMF lending, they should favour helping recipient economies to expand their productive capacity. Many who oppose IMF lending also support trade practices that favour large industrial economies and prevent smaller economies from growing.

43   Rowlands (1996) reports that empirical evidence suggests that IMF lending can actually help restore investor confidence and reduce the flight of foreign capital during a crisis. As such, IMF lending to vulnerable economies can help attract additional private investment.

44   For detail on more recent changes to the global financial achitecture, see O'Hara (forthcoming).

References

Aghevli, B.B. (1999) 'The Asian Crisis: causes and remedies', *Finance and Development*, June, pp. 28–31.

Ariff, M. (1996) 'Effects of financial liberalisation on four South East Asian markets, 1973–94', *ASEAN Economic Bulletin*, vol. 12, no. 3, pp. 325–37.

Bird, G. (1996) 'Borrowing from the IMF: the policy implications and recent empirical research', in *World Development*, vol. 24, no. 11, pp. 1753–60.

Boothe, B.B. (1995) *'Texas and Mexico, immediate impact of the Mexican Crisis'*, Fort Worth, Texas: Ben Boothe and Associates.

Camdessus, M. (1995) 'Drawing lessons from the Mexican Crisis: preventing and resolving financial crises-the role of the IMF', Address at the 25th Washington Conference of the Council of the Americas on 'Staying the Course: Forging a Free Trade Area in the Americas', Washington, DC, 22 May.

Cohen, A. (1998) 'Russia's meltdown: anatomy of the IMF failure', *Backgrounder*, no. 1228, The Heritage Foundation, 23 October.

Crook, C. (1991) 'Survey: The IMF and the World Bank', mimeo, University of California, Berkeley.

Dell, S. (1981) 'On being grandmotherly: the evolution of the IMF conditionality', *Essays in International Finance*, no. 144, Princeton: Princeton University Press.

Fieleke, N.S. (1994) 'The International Monetary Fund 50 years after Bretton Woods', *New England Economic Review*, September/October, pp. 17–30.

Fischer, S. (1995) 'The IMF and the World Bank at fifty', in H. Genberg, *The International Monetary System: Its Institutions and its Future*, New York: Springer-Verlag.

Gaidar, Y. (1997) 'The IMF and Russia', *American Economic Review: Papers and Proceedings*, vol. 87, no. 2, pp. 13–16.

—— (1999) 'Lessons of the Russian crisis for transition economies', *Finance and Development*, June, pp. 6–8.

Gil-Diaz, F. (1997) 'The Origins of Mexico's 1994 financial crisis', *The Cato Journal*, vol. 17, no. 3, pp. 51–63

Goldman, D.P. (1996) 'Under the volcano', *Forbes*, vol. 158, no. 10, pp. 94–103.

Guitian, M. (1994) 'The IMF as a monetary institution: the challenge ahead', *Finance and Development*, September, vol. 31, no. 3, pp. 38–41.

Horsefield, J.K. (1972) *The International Monetary Fund 1945–1965: Twenty Years of International Monetary Cooperation*, vol. 1, Washington, DC: International Monetary Fund.

Hoskins, W.L. and J.W. Coons (1995) 'Mexico: policy failure, moral hazard, and market solutions', *Policy Analysis*, no. 243, October.

IMF (1992) *International Monetary Fund Annual Report – 1992*, Washington, DC: International Monetary Fund.

—— (1998) *IMF Bulletin*, Washington, DC: International Monetary Fund.

—— (1999) 'The role of the IMF: financing and its interactions with adjustment and surveillance', Pamphlet Series no. 50, Washington, DC: International Monetary Fund.

Krueger, A. (1998) 'Whither the World Bank and the IMF?', *Journal of Economic Literature*, vol. 36, pp. 1983–2020.

Lane, T. (1999) 'The Asian Financial Crisis: what have we learned?', *Finance and Development*, September, pp. 44–7.

Martinez, G.O. (1998) 'What lessons does the Mexican Crisis hold for the recovery in Asia', *Finance and Development*, vol. 35, no. 2.

Mayer, M (1998) 'The Asian disease: plausible diagnoses, possible remedies', *Working Paper No. 232*, The Brookings Institution.

Meyer, L.H. (1999) 'Lessons from the Asian Crisis: a central banker's perspective' *Working Paper No. 276*, The Jerome Levy Economics Institute.

Minsky, H.P. (1982) 'The financial instability hypothesis: a restatement', in author's *Can It Happen Again*, New York: M.E. Sharpe, Inc., pp. 90–115.

Niskanen, W.A. (1999) 'Reshaping the global financial architecture: is there a role for the IMF?', *Cato-Journal*, vol. 18, no. 3, pp. 331–4.

O'Hara, P.A. (forthcoming) 'Recent changes to the IMF, WTO and FSP: a new global social structure of accumulation for long wave upswing?', *Review of International Political Economy*.

Peach, J. and R. Adkisson (1997) 'Enabling myths and Mexico's economic crises: 1976–1996', *Journal of Economic Issues*, vol. 31, no. 2, pp. 567–74.

Rogers, J.E, A. Zubikarai and R.H. Muhlestein (1997) 'Mexico', *International Financial Law Review*, July, pp. 147–8.

Rowlands, D. (1996) 'New lending to less developed countries: the effect of the IMF', *Canadian Journal of Economics*, vol. 29, pp. s443–s446.

Sanders, B. (1998) 'The IMF's disastrous plan for Russia', *The Christian Science Monitor*, Vermont.

Soros, G. (1999) 'Capitalism's last chance?', *Foreign Policy*, no. 113, Winter, pp. 57–65.

Taylor, L. (1997) 'The revival of the liberal creed – the IMF and the World Bank in a globilised economy', *World Development*, vol. 25, no. 2, pp. 145–52.

Williamson, J. (1982) *The Lending Policies of the International Monetary Fund*, Washington, DC: Institute For International Economics.

—— (1983) *IMF Conditionality*, Washington, DC: Institute for International Economics.

—— (1995) 'Causes and consequences of the Mexican Peso Crisis', remarks made to the *Institute for International Economics*, 14 March.

10 Economic development and environmental problems

John Asafu-Adjaye

Introduction

The effect of human beings' activities on the environment has been the subject of much debate and controversy over the past three hundred years. In 1798, Thomas Malthus argued in *An Essay on the Principle of Population* that food production increases in arithmetic progression whereas the human population increases in geometric progression. Therefore, over time, population growth would outstrip food supply leading to famine, starvation, disease and death (Malthus 1872). All of these factors would serve as a 'natural' check on population, resulting in a drastic reduction in population growth (Figure 10.1). To avoid this calamity, he proposed solutions such as drastic reduction in the reproductive rate, delay in marriages and sexual abstinence. Malthus' predictions earned the economics profession tags such as the 'profession of doom' and 'dismal science'.

The rise of modern 'environmentalism' can be traced to the 1960s when the increase in environmental pollution led to a rise in public environmental awareness. After the energy crisis of the 1970s, the Malthusian debate was resurrected with neo-Malthusians launching an attack on the virtues of economic growth. In 1972, the neo-Malthusian group 'The Club of Rome' published the results of a study entitled *The Limits to Growth* (Meadows *et al.* 1972), which attracted extensive media coverage. The study reached three major conclusions. First, at the prevailing annual rates of consumption the world would run out of mineral resources within 100 years, resulting in a sudden collapse of the world economic system. Second, this calamity would not be averted by piecemeal solution to the myriad of problems. Third, the only solution to the collapse would be an immediate reduction in economic growth, population growth and pollution.[1]

Environmentalists argue that international regulation of trade is necessary to 'build environmental responsibility into economic activity' and to ensure that 'trade meets the goals of environmentally sustainable development' (Hair 1993). As trade has become globalised, environmentalists claim that the magnitude of environmental degradation has worsened. According to Herman Daly, 'further growth beyond the present scale is overwhelmingly

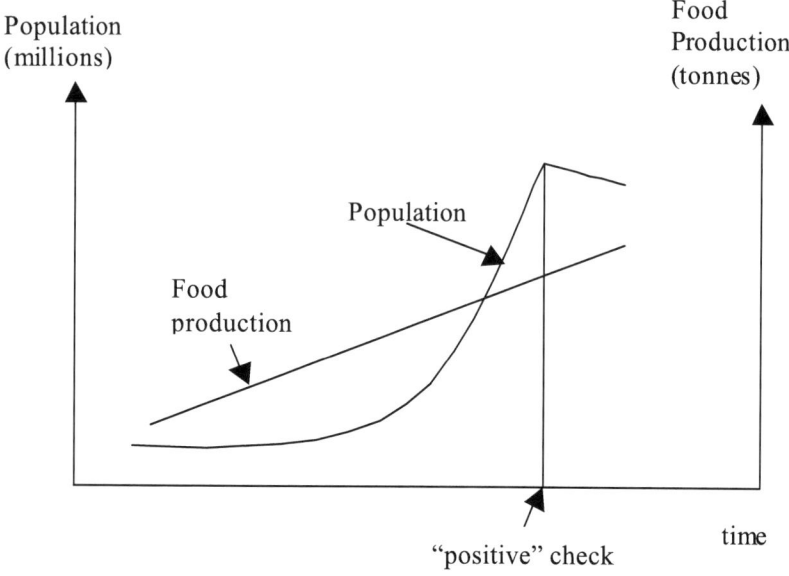

Figure 10.1   The Malthusian population model.
Source: Adapted from Asafu-Adjaye (2000).

likely to increase costs more rapidly than it increases benefits, thus ushering in a new era of "uneconomic growth" that impoverishes rather than enriches' (Daly and Cobb 1989).

Environmentalists are opposed to the concept of free trade on the basis of 'market failure'.[2] According to this view, since the market 'fails' to protect environmental values to the desired degree, there is a need for government to intervene in the market place. Most environmentalists view economic growth as incompatible with environmental quality and therefore advocate political constraints on economic activity both domestically and internationally. It is true that all economic activities do impact on environmental quality to some degree. However, government intervention in every case would be impractical and may be sub-optimal in some cases.

On the other side of the debate, there are those who believe that economic growth is necessary in order to achieve economic development and a cleaner environment. Numerous empirical studies have been conducted to prove that there is a positive link between economic growth and environmental quality.[3] In this chapter, we review the relationship between economic development and the environment. In light of the evidence presented, we address what policy measures could be taken to mitigate the environmental impacts of economic growth.

The chapter proceeds as follows. The following section sets the discussion in context by briefly reviewing global economic and environmental trends.

The third section addresses the contentious issue of whether economic development can only be achieved at the expense of environmental quality. Empirical research on the relationship between economic growth and environmental quality is briefly reviewed. The fourth section section addresses the policy implications of the environment–development debate, while the fifth section concludes.

Global economic and environmental trends

Economic trends

The global economy has witnessed a boom during the past thirty years. Total global output of goods and services increased from US$9.4 trillion to over US$25 trillion between 1960 and 1990 (UNDP 1996). Table 10.1 indicates that the world economy grew steadily between 1965 and 1997 at a rate of just over 3 per cent per annum. However, there was regional imbalance in the distribution of this growth. In particular, the East Asian (and Pacific) region economies grew at an average rate of 7.3 per cent per annum. In contrast, the sub-Saharan African countries grew at a rate of 2.6 per cent per annum.

Table 10.1   Global economic trends, 1965–1997

	% GNP growth p.a.		% value added growth p.a.		
	Total	*Per capita*	*Agriculture*	*Industry*	*Services*
World	3.2	1.4	2.2	–	–
East Asia and Pacific	7.3	5.4	4.0	9.5	7.8
Latin American and Caribbean	3.5	1.3	2.6	3.2	3.9
South Asia	4.6	2.3	2.8	5.5	5.6
Sub-Saharan Africa	2.6	−0.2	1.9	2.3	3.2

Source: World Bank (1999).

Table 10.2   Real annual domestic product growth

	1991–7	*1998*	*1999*	*2001*[a]
World	2.3	1.9	1.8	2.8
East Asia[b]	7.2	7.7	0.3	4.5
Latin American and Caribbean	3.4	2.0	0.8	3.9
South Asia	5.7	5.2	4.4	5.2
Sub-Saharan Africas	2.1	2.1	2.5	4.0

Source: World Bank (1999).

[a]Forecast.
[b]Includes Indonesia, Republic of Korean, Malaysia, the Philippines and Thailand.

Large parts of the developing world have missed out on the past three decades of economic growth. For example, since 1980, about a hundred developing countries have experienced economic decline or stagnation; in seventy of these countries, average incomes in the late 1990s were below 1980 levels (UNDP 1997).

Much of the rapid growth of the global economy has been brought about by globalisation. Globalisation has created a near 'borderless' world and has facilitated free trade and flows of private capital between countries. Global trade increased from US$4,345 billion to US$6,255 billion between 1990 and 1995. Transfers of net private capital into low-income and middle-income countries amounted to US$180 billion in 1995, compared to official development assistance of US$64 billion (World Bank 1999).

The growth of the global economy has brought with it several benefits such as improvement in health and living conditions. For example, in many developing countries, infant mortality rates have declined, life expectancy has increased and illiteracy rates have declined over the past three decades. However, disparities in poverty and income distribution persist between regions and within countries. Absolute poverty in parts of Africa, Latin America and the Caribbean has increased, and the gap between the developed and developing countries has widened. According to the 1998 Human Development Report, of the 4.4 billion people in developing countries, nearly three-fifths lack basic sanitation; almost a third have no access to clean water; a quarter do not have adequate housing. A fifth have no access to modern health services; a fifth of children do not attend school to grade 5; and about one-fifth do not have enough dietary energy and protein (UNDP 1998).

Within some regions and countries, the gap is increasing as well. In Latin America and the Caribbean, the richest 20 per cent of the population have average incomes of more than US$17,000; for the poorest 20 per cent, the average income is US$930 (UNDP 1997). Even in the relatively well off East and Southeast Asian countries, income gaps appear to be widening. Wealth disparities between urban and rural areas are growing in China, Indonesia and the Philippines. In Thailand it is estimated that gap between the rich and the poor more than doubled between 1981 and 1992.

Economic growth is required to meet the needs of a growing population. However, rapid growth has serious implications for our physical environment. Expansion of agricultural land is essential to produce more food.[4] Activities such as land clearing and the use of pesticides have potential adverse environmental impacts. Industrial production is required to house, clothe and feed the population. However, some industrial processes result in the production of air and water pollution, as well as the generation of toxic waste products.

Environmental trends

Energy is a vital input to transportation, industrial production and agricultural production. It also provides other important domestic services such as heating, cooling and lighting. Currently, the industrialised countries are responsible for most of the increase in manmade greenhouse gases in the atmosphere, accounting for about 70 per cent of carbon dioxide (CO_2) emissions even though they account for less than 20 per cent of global population (UN 1997). However, energy demand is projected to increase rapidly in the developing countries. It is estimated that developing country share of world energy demand will increase by almost 40 per cent by 2010, which will be more than double that of total OECD energy consumption.

Figure 10.2 shows that there is a strong correlation between energy use and economic growth, while Figure 10.3 reveals a similar relationship between energy use and social indicators such as life expectancy. Based on these facts, it can be concluded that in order not to retard social and economic development, energy consumption in the developing countries will need to increase. It is instructive to note, however, that per capita consumption in the developing countries will still be lower than in the advanced countries. To achieve sustainable development, there is the need to search for efficiencies in energy use and to gradually move towards renewable forms of energy such as wind, thermal and solar energy.

Is economic growth compatible with environmental quality?

Since the early 1990s, the economic growth–environment debate has been resurrected again with the emergence of empirical studies that indicate that environmental quality can eventually decrease with increase in economic growth. These studies argue that there is an inverted U-shaped relationship

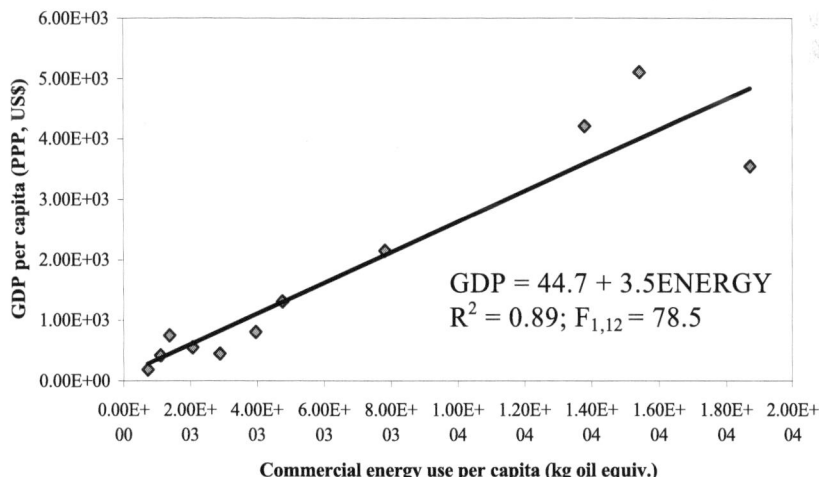

Figure 10.2   Gross domestic product and energy use in selected Asian countries.
Source: World Bank (1999).

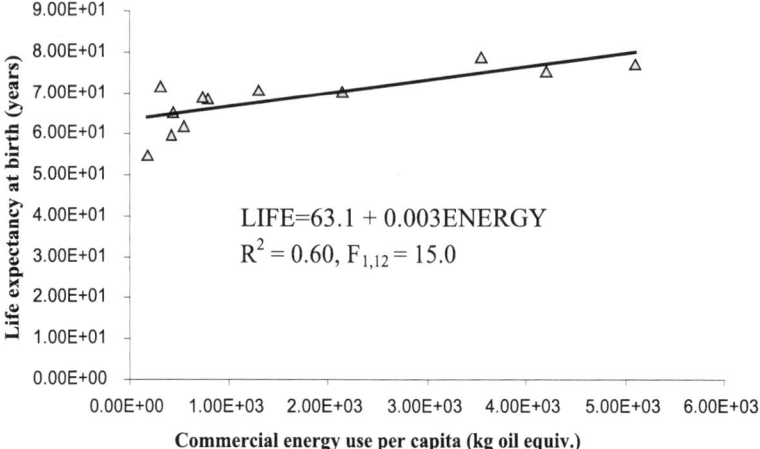

Figure 10.3   Life expectancy and energy use in selected Asian countries.
Source: World Bank (1999).

between pollution levels and income growth. That is, there is an increasing level of pollution for people living in lower income countries. However, as incomes rise, pollution levels decline. This phenomenon has been named the *environmental Kuznets curve* (EKC) after Simon Kuznets who postulated a similar relationship for income inequality and income levels (Kuznets 1955).

The basic premise of the EKC is that at very low levels of economic growth, environmental effects are low. However, as development proceeds, the rate of pollution increases. At higher levels of economic development, various factors (e.g. structural change, improved technology) cause pollution levels to decline. An example of an EKC for sulphur dioxide is shown in Figure 10.4. A typical feature of the EKC is the inverted U shape which suggests that pollution levels reach a maximum level with respect to income levels, after which it begins to decline. The maximum level of pollution is referred to as the 'turning point' and forms the focus of the debate about pollution control. If it is a fact that the EKC hypothesis is true, then one must expect developing countries to increase pollution levels at early stages of development.

Economists have proposed various theoretical models to explain the inverted U shape of the EKC. These models include: (a) overlapping-generations models; (b) production/consumption models of pollution and (c) political economy models.

Overlapping-generations models

John and Pecchenino (1994) employ the overlapping-generations framework of Samuelson (1958) and Diamond (1965) to offer a theoretical explanation

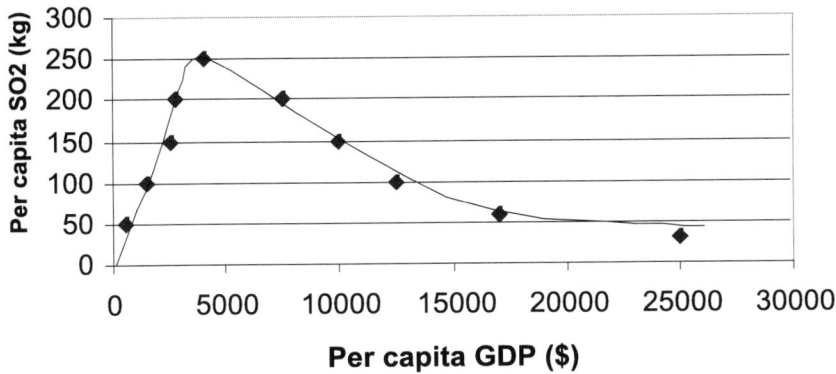

Figure 10.4   A hypothetical EKC for suplhur dioxide.
Source: Asafu-Adjaye (1999).

for why an inverted U relationship might exist between economic growth and environmental quality. In this approach, short-lived individuals make decisions about the accumulation of capital and the provision of a public good, environmental quality, where the decisions have long-lasting effects.

In the stylised model, economic agents live two periods, working young and consuming while old. The young allocate their wages between investment in capital goods and investment in environmental goods, which is a public good. Economic agents derive utility from consumption and environmental quality. Their consumption degrades the environment which is left to future generations. However, investment in capital improves the technology available to future generations.

John and Pecchenino (1994) show that economic agents in economies with little capital (or high environmental quality) may choose not to maintain the environment. As agents accumulate capital, the consumption externality causes degradation of the environment, resulting in a negative correlation between economic growth and environmental quality. On the other hand, in economies with high capital levels, agents can choose a mix of savings and maintenance such that a higher capital stock is associated with a higher level of environmental quality.

Under their framework, it is also possible for some environmental problems to improve at low-income levels, while others worsen even in rich economies. For example, in the case of water quality, returns to maintenance are high and agents may be willing to give up large amounts of consumption in return for improvements in quality. On the other hand, for other pollutants (e.g. carbon dioxide), returns to maintenance may be low and agents may value environmental quality relatively less.

Production/consumption models

Pollution can arise from consumption and production of goods and services or the use of environmental inputs in either of these activities. Lopez (1994) presents a very simple model comprising two production sectors, weak separability between pollution and other inputs, constant returns to scale, exogenous prices and technical progress. In this model, when private producers consider only their marginal costs (MPC) (i.e. do not pay for pollution), increased output levels lead to increase in pollution levels regardless of technological progress and preferences. However, when producers pay the marginal social cost (MSC), that is, MPC plus the price of pollution, then the relationship between output and pollution levels depends on preferences and technology. If it is assumed that preferences are non-homothetic, the change in pollution, with increasing output, depends on the elasticity of substitution in production between pollution and other inputs, as well as the degree of relative risk aversion. In this case, the degree of relative risk aversion is defined as the rate at which consumers' marginal utility declines as they increase their consumption of goods and services. For certain plausible values of these two parameters (i.e. elasticity of substitution and risk aversion) pollution levels may rise at low-income levels and decline at high-income levels, leading to the inverse U shape.

McConnell (1997) has proposed an EKC model in which pollution is generated by consumption but reduced by abatement. In this model, utility is defined as an additive function of consumption (C) and pollution (P). That is,

$$U = U(C, P) \tag{1}$$

where pollution is a function of consumption and abatement (A). That is,

$$P = P(C, A) \tag{2}$$

It is assumed that output is equal to consumption plus abatement. That is,

$$Y = C + A \tag{3}$$

McConnell (1997) assumes that a social planner maximises Equation (1) subject to the constraint, Equation (3). He goes on to demonstrate conditions under which an inverted U curve may or may not be generated by changes in the sign of the income elasticity of demand for environmental quality. McConnell shows that it is possible for pollution to decline with a zero-income elasticity of demand for environmental quality, or to increase with a high-income elasticity of demand for environmental quality.

Antle and Heidebrink (1995) have used the concept of the production possibilities frontier (PPF) to show why economic growth and environmental quality may not necessarily be mutually exclusive. They define an economy that produces two goods, market goods (x) and environmental services (e). The production functions are defined as

$$x = x(L, K, Z) \tag{4}$$

$$e = e(E) \tag{5}$$

where L is labour and other variable inputs used to produce market goods; K is environmental capital stock used to produce x; Z is conventional capital stock (e.g. structures, machinery, etc.) and E is environmental capital stock (e.g. forests, soil, water) used to produce environmental services. Both production functions are assumed to be concave. The marginal product of E is assumed to be negative for the production of market goods (Equation 4) at high levels of capital utilization, but is always positive for the production of environmental services (Equation 5).

Figure 10.5 shows a PPF generated from Equations 4 and 5. According to neoclassical economic theory, equilibrium is achieved when the marginal rate of technical substitution is equal to the price ratio of E and x. Assuming E is a pure public good, which is often the case with environmental services, this equilibrium will occur at point B, where the slope of the PPF approaches infinity. The rational producer will only apply units of the environmental capital stock beyond point B where its marginal productivity is zero. That is, there is no economic incentive to totally exhaust the environmental capital stock.

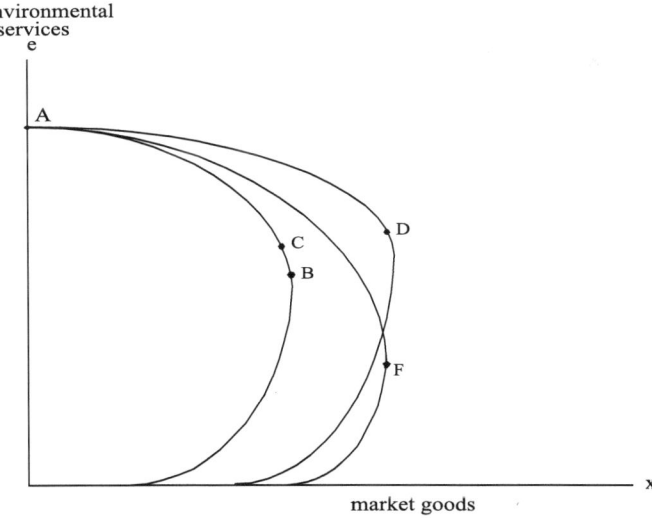

Figure 10.5   Production possibilities frontier for market goods and environmental services.

Source: Adapted from Antle and Heidebrink (1995).

Technological change shifts the PPF from ACB so that a higher level of market goods production could correspond to either more (point D) or fewer (point F) environmental services in a market economy. The main implication of this theory is that, even if environmental quality is a pure public good, economic growth and environmental quality improvement are not necessarily mutually exclusive if there is technical change. In this framework, it is possible for public policies (e.g. environmental regulations) to move the economy to point D, where more market goods and more environmental services are produced. However, it is also possible for some government policies (e.g. large-scale dam projects) to move the economy to say, point F, where the level of environmental services is reduced.

Political economy models

Many EKC studies model pollution levels as a function of per capita income without specifying the links between these two variables. According to Grossman and Krueger (1991), the strongest link is an induced policy response, which is, in turn, induced by popular demand: to quote Grossman and Krueger

> As nations or regions experience greater prosperity, their citizens demand that more attention be paid to the non-economic aspects of their living conditions. The richer countries tend to have relatively cleaner urban air and relatively more stringent environmental standards and stricter enforcement of their environmental laws than middle-income and poorer countries.
>
> (Grossman and Krueger 1991: 372)

Most environmental goods and services display public goods characteristics. That is, they are often zero-priced or underpriced. The solutions to environmental problems therefore require the issue of market failure to be addressed. According to the political economy approach, as a country's per capita income increases, it becomes better able to address the issue of market failure through the political process.

To conclude this section, the point needs to be made that there is not much difficulty in constructing a model that would generate EKC-type characteristics. The challenge is to find empirical evidence that backs up the theory. In the following section we review a selection of various empirical studies, which have attempted to support or refute the EKC hypothesis.

A review of EKC studies

Grossman and Krueger (1991) conducted the path-breaking study in the EKC literature as part of a wider study to assess the environmental impacts of the North American Free Trade Agreement (NAFTA). The study utilised panel data from the Global Environmental Monitoring System (GEMS) project to estimate EKCs for SO_2, dark matter, and suspended particulate matter (SPM) for a number of cities worldwide.[5] Regression variables including a cubic function of per capita GDP (PPP dollars), a time trend and trade intensity were used. The analysis confirmed that ambient concentrations of SO_2 and dark matter exhibit EKCs with turning points lying between \$4,000 and \$5,000 in 1985 US dollars (see Table 10.3). Although they found that economic

Table 10.3 A selection of EKC studies[a]

	Study	*Environmental indicator*	*Turning point (US\$ per capita)*	*Countries/cities/ time period*
1	Grossman and Krueger (1991)	SO_2 Dark matter	4,000–5,000	Cities worldwide
2	Shafik and Bandyopadhyay (1992)	SO_2 SPM Deforestation	3,000–4,000	149 countries, 1960–90
3	Panayotou (1993, 1995)	SO_2 NO_x SPM Deforestation	3,000 5,000 4,500 823	55 developed and developing countries, 1987–8
4	Panayotou (1997)	SO_2	5,000	Cities in 30 developed and developing countries, 1982–4
5	Cole *et al.* (1997)	Carbon monoxide Total energy use CFCs and halons	25,100 22,500 15,400	7 regions, 1960–91, 24 OECP countries, 1970–90, 38 countries, 1986, 1990
6	Cropper and Griffiths (1994)	Deforestation	4,760 5,420	64 countries in Africa, Latin America
7	Antle and Heidebrink (1995)	Afforestation National parks	2,000 1,200	93 countries, cross-section, 1985 82 countries, cross-section, 1985
8	Asafu-Adjaye (1998)	Reforestation	5,000	83 countries, cross-section, 1985
9	Wackernagel *et al.* (1997)	Ecological footprints	21,587	52 countries, 1985
10	Asafu-Adjaye (1999)	Energy use	22,218	4 Asian countries, pooled cross section-time series, 1971–95

Source: Asafu Adjaye (1999)
Note: [a]SO_2 = sulphur dioxide
   SPM = suspended particulate matter
   NO_x = nitrous oxide
   CO_2 = carbon dioxide
   CFC = chlorofluorocarbons

growth at middle-income levels was associated with improved environmental quality, growth at higher income would be detrimental.

An EKC study conducted by Shafik and Bandyopadhyay (1992) was used as a background study for the 1992 World Development Report (World Bank 1992). They estimated EKCs for ten different indicators of environmental quality: SPM, ambient SO_2, deforestation, lack of clean water, lack of urban sanitation, dissolved oxygen in rivers, faecal coliforms in rivers, municipal waste per capita, CO_2 emissions per capita and change in forest area between 1961 and 1986. They carried out panel and cross-section regressions using data from 149 countries for the period 1960–90. The two air pollutants, SO_2 and SPM, were found to conform to the EKC hypothesis with turning points at $3,700 and $3,300 respectively (Table 10.3). Deforestation was not significantly related to income, while river quality worsened as income increased. Finally, both CO_2 emissions per capita and municipal waste increased significantly with increase in income.

Panayotou (1993, 1995) conducted cross-sectional EKC regressions using data for 1987/88 for fifty-five developing countries. All the indicators, including emissions per capita for SO_2, SPM, NO_X and deforestation, were found to conform to the inverted U shape. The turning points were $3,000, $4,500, $5,500, and $823 respectively (Table 10.3). Panayotou updated his study in 1997 by explicitly accounting for the underlying determinants of environmental quality. In order to gain a more comprehensive understanding of the income–environment relationship, he incorporated a variety of policy instruments into the analysis. This involved 'decomposing' the structural economic factors influencing the emissions of SO_2 into its pure income, scale and sectoral composition effects, as well as testing independently for the impacts of the rate of growth and a policy variable. The results indicated that both the growth rate and the policy variables were highly significant, with ambient SO_2 concentrations turning upwards at just below $5,000.

Grossman (1993) undertook a comprehensive EKC study using data from up to 488 monitoring stations from sixty-four countries for the period 1977–90. U-shape relationships were observed for SPM, NO_2, CO, faecal coliform, biological oxygen demand (BOD)[6] and chemical oxygen demand (COD)[7] with turning points of $16,000, $18,500, $22,800, $8,500, $10,000 and $10,000 respectively.

In a departure from the aforementioned studies, Cropper and Griffiths (1994) estimated EKCs for deforestation for African, Latin American and Asian countries using time series data for a thirty-year period. Deforestation in African and Latin American countries displayed inverted U shapes with turning points of $4,760 and $5,420 respectively. However, there were no significant relationships for Asian countries.

More recently, de Bruyn (1997) used decomposition analysis[8] to determine whether structural change or technological innovation was a major factor in the decline in SO_2 emissions in the Netherlands and West Germany during the 1980s. Although he failed to find evidence supporting the significance of structural change, he found that environmental policy fostered by international agreements provides a better explanation of why pollution tends to decline as income levels increase. It is significant to note that de Bruyn (1997) found income to be only a minor determinant of environmental policy.

Cole *et al.* (1997) used more recent data encompassing a wider set of environmental indicators including CFCs, halons, methane, nitrates, municipal waste, carbon monoxide, energy consumption and traffic volumes. They found the turning points for per capita emissions of total NO_X, SPM and carbon monoxide to be comparable to earlier studies, implying that per capita emissions of these pollutants are beginning to decline in many advanced economies (Table 10.3). However, both CO_2 and energy use were found to increase monotonically with income. CFCs and halons, although predicted to follow a similar path as CO_2 in 1990, were found to have flattened out and decreased slightly.

Other environmental indicators for which turning points were reported (Table 10.3) were afforestation/reforestation (Antle and Heidebrink 1995; Asafu-Adjaye 1998 (see Box 1)), and ecological footprint (Wackernagel *et al.* 1997). Wackernagel *et al.* estimated the EKC for a sample of fifty-two countries using 'ecological footprints' as an indicator. The ecological footprint estimates the land and water required to sustainably provide for the average per capita consumption in each country, including the following: food, wood, energy and built area. Using a quadratic specification, the estimated turning point of $21,587 was outside the data range and the log-quadratic specification did not indicate a turning point.

Some studies have attempted to investigate the effect of political factors on pollution. However, the evidence so far has been inconclusive or contradictory. For example, Shafik and Bandyopadhyay (1992) tested for the influence of political and civil rights[9] on concentrations of various air pollutants (including SO_2) and found evidence that air quality is worse in more democratic countries. On the other hand, Torras and Boyce (1998) found evidence to support the view that less 'power-equal' countries (both with respect to democracy and income equality) have higher SO_2 emissions.

To conclude this review of EKC studies, it must be emphasised that the empirical evidence in support of the EKC hypothesis is mixed. The EKC hypothesis seems to hold across studies for air pollution indicators, with the possible exception of CO_2. The most consistent results are for SO_2 and SPM. However, even where the EKC appears to be valid, there are doubts about the stability and hence the reliability of the turning points. For example, in Cole *et al.* (1997) most of the turning points were outside the income range of the countries analysed. In Cropper and Griffith (1994) the per capita income levels of most of the African and Latin American countries were below the EKC turning points. The main implication of these observations is that environmental quality could worsen even in cases where EKC relationships exist.

Box 1 An empirical test of the environmental transition hypothesis

A test of the environmental transition hypothesis was carried out using average annual reforestation (REFOR) in the 1980s and annual per capita CO_2 emissions (CO_2) as indicators of environmental quality. These two variables were regressed against the following variables using cross-section data for 83 countries: total land area (AREA); total forested area and woodland (FOR); real gross domestic product per capita (GDP) for 1985; population (POP); and the number of riots per year (RIOTS).

The results of the estimations were as follows (t-ratios are in parenthesis):

$$REFOR=15.72-32.84GDP+4.482GDP2+0.45AREA+0.60FOR$$
$$(0.54)\ (-2.08)\quad (3.19)\qquad (2.57)\qquad (1.53)$$
$$+0.28POP-16.23RIOTS$$
$$(1.67)\quad (-1.65)$$
$$R^2=0.69;\ \bar{R}^2=0.67;\ F=28.32$$

$$CO_2=0.480+0.16GDP-0.01GDP2-0.005AREA+0.006FOR$$
$$(2.51)\ (1.50)\quad (-1.08)\quad (-0.42)\qquad (2.28)$$
$$-0.001POP-0.03RIOTS$$
$$(-1.03)\quad (-0.54)$$
$$R_2=0.28;\ \bar{R}^2=0.18;\ F=3.91$$

The results for REFOR indicate a convex function of GDP (i.e. U-shaped). On the other hand, the results for CO_2 suggest that GDP increases with income. The R^2 statistics suggest that the quadratic form fits the data better for REFOR than for CO_2. In both equations, the coefficient of RIOTS has the expected sign but is significant at the 10 per cent level for the REFOR equation only.

The major policy implication of these results is that economic growth may not necessarily lead to increasing damage to the environment over time. Some environmental indicators may initially deteriorate as growth occurs due to pressure on natural resources. However, the evidence suggests that as income increases there is an improvement in some indicators.

Source: Asafu-Adjaye (1998).

A critique of the EKC

The EKC hypothesis has come under heavy attack from both economists and non-economists alike. The EKC seems to suggest that countries can simply 'grow out' of any limitations brought about by the depletion of natural resources and increased environmental degradation. This view was put even more forcefully by Beckerman (1992) who said, *inter alia*, that 'the best and probably the only way to attain a decent environment in most countries is to become rich'.

Eminent scholars such as Arrow *et al.* (1995), Rothman (1998), and Stern *et al.* (1996) have critiqued the EKC. Special issues of the following journals have been devoted entirely to the subject: *Ecological Economics* (1995), *Ecological Applications* (1996) and *Environment and Development Economics* (1996). A panel of economists, led by Kenneth Arrow, met in Sweden to consider the relationships between economic growth and environmental quality. They concluded, *inter alia*, that an inverted U curve does not constitute evidence that environmental quality will improve in all cases or that it will improve in time to avert the adverse impacts of economic growth (Arrow *et al.* 1995). They argued that in most cases where emissions have declined with increasing income, the reductions have been due to local institutional reforms such as environmental legislation and market-based incentives, although such reforms have tended to overlook international and intergenerational consequences.

From the current empirical evidence, it is unclear whether the EKC is the result of economic growth and therefore best tied to income increases, or whether it is merely a symptom of other underlying exogenous changes. Consequently, some of the more recent studies have attempted to find alternative approaches for analysing EKC relationships. For example, Unruh and Moomaw (1997) and Moomaw and Unruh (1997) have disputed the EKC conclusion that increase in income results in emissions reduction. Instead, they argue that reductions in emissions are triggered by specific historic events such as the 1973 oil crisis. They find that the transition to lower per capita CO_2 emissions can occur at different income levels and can occur rather abruptly. They demonstrate that, in the case of countries as different as Spain and the United States, the transitions occurred soon after the oil price shocks of the 1970s.

McConnell (1997) has suggested that although income is an important factor in explaining the EKC-type relationship, other factors such as abatement costs, or the impact of pollution on production may override the effects of income. He therefore investigates the relationship between the demand for environmental quality and income by considering the combined effect of preferences, increasing costs of pollution abatement and the marginal utility of consumption in a growing economy in order to decompose the reduced form effect of income on pollution. He concludes that a high-income elasticity of demand for environmental quality is neither necessary nor sufficient to yield an EKC-type relationship.

Some studies (e.g. Liddle 1996; Asafu-Adjaye 1999) have found no evidence of trade playing a major role in determining the EKC. On the other hand, others (e.g. Suri and Chapman 1998) find the opposite result.

Policy implications

In the last few years, progress has been made in understanding the relationship between the environment and development. A number of clear trends have emerged from the research conducted to date:

1   There is a U-curve relationship between environmental quality and income. However, this does not apply to all environmental indicators. The foregoing review has demonstrated that the indicator which consistently displays such a relationship, based on the number of studies confirming it, is SO_2. A few studies have found the EKC hypothesis to hold for SPM, deforestation, afforestation and energy use. However, these results cannot be generalised.
2   Even where a U-curve relationship is found, the turning points tend to be much higher than the per capita incomes of the countries involved. For example, in Asafu-Adjaye (1999) the turning point for energy was US$22,218 for a sample of four countries comprising, India, Indonesia, South Korea and Japan. However, real per capita income for India, the least well off in the sample based on GDP, is US$439. These results imply that, for many developing countries, environmental problems may worsen in the foreseeable future.
3   It has been suggested that trade openness could help in reducing environmental pollution. However, there is no overwhelming evidence in the literature to support this proposition.
4   Many of the studies that have found a U-shaped relationship between economic growth and the environment do not convincingly explain how growth affects the environment. The empirical evidence supporting the existence of an EKC relationship is not clear-cut. This implies that the relationship between the environment and development is too complex to be adequately represented by simple economic models.

A general conclusion that can be reached is that developing countries will not automatically grow out of their environmental problems. However, economic growth is necessary for developing countries to make a dent in their environmental problems. The fact that many countries' per capita incomes are below potential turning points supports the view that restricting economic growth to save the environment may not be a socially optimal decision. Progress towards the turning point can be boosted by a combination of prudent economic policies and environmental regulations.

Some of the studies reviewed above indicate that institutional factors do exert a significant influence on the relationship between income and environmental degradation. Barbier (1997) argues that policies that aim to improve the operation of markets are more likely to reduce the 'environmental price' of economic growth, thereby flattening out the income–environment relationship and possibly achieving a lower turning point. Such policies include the removal of distortionary subsidies, introduction of more secure property rights over resources and implementation of economic instruments to internalise externalities. Some of these policies are briefly discussed in the following section.

Furthermore, a poorly developed institutional framework may affect the ability of authorities to monitor environmental degradation and/or pollution and, in turn, retard the development of effective environmental policies. In his EKC study of SO_2 emissions, Panayotou (1997) found that improved policies and institutions in the form of more secure property rights, better enforcement of contracts and effective environmental regulation could assist in making the EKC flatter. For example, reductions in SO_2 emissions in the Netherlands and West Germany have been brought about by tougher environmental regulations requiring better end-of-pipe technology. Komen and others' research indicates that increased public spending on environmental research and development, while possibly leading to environmental improvements, may also act as a catalyst for private investment in cleaner technologies (Komen *et al.* 1997).

In the following sections, we examine policy responses to the environmental degradation problem at the local/national and global levels.

National and local level policy response

At the local and national levels, there are a variety of options for dealing with the problem of environmental degradation. In Chapter 4, we discussed a number of market-based instruments including standards, taxes, subsidies and marketable permits in relation to solving problems based on gender disparities. In this section, we will take a brief look at a different set of options for tackling the pollution problem – voluntary incentives.

Most pollution policy instruments rely on coercion (e.g. fees or penalties) or some form of financial incentives. As the name suggests, voluntary incentives rely on voluntarism and self-regulation. There are two major categories of voluntary incentive mechanisms – voluntary agreements and voluntary, incentive and community-assistance programs.

Voluntary agreements

A voluntary agreement (VA) is basically a 'contract' between a government agency and industry in which environmental goals and deadlines have been negotiated and subsequently agreed upon by both parties (Barde 1995;

Carraro and Sinisalco 1996). In a VA, the industry is self-committed to taking appropriate measures to meet these goals. In the event of non-compliance there are no real sanctions, except that regulations and coercive measures may be imposed at the end of the contract period. One important feature of a VA is that although pollution levels may be fixed within a geographical area, the industry is free to pursue the most cost-effective measures to achieve the agreed objective. One advantage of VAs is that they can be combined with regulatory requirements in two different ways: (1) they can be implemented before any subsequent regulations; and (2) they can reinforce existing regulations that may be poorly enforced.

Like most other policy instruments there are arguments for and against VAs. For example, it has been argued that voluntary agreements reduce government control over industry, or that it could encourage 'collusion' between government and industry. In practical terms, voluntary agreements may become difficult to manage when there are many sources requiring regulations, and when pollution spillovers affect communities who are not party to the voluntary agreement. However, on the positive side, voluntary agreements are flexible, transparent and could provide incentives for technological innovation.

Voluntary, incentive and community-assistance programs

Voluntary, incentive and community-assistance programs depend on the commitment, enthusiasm and goodwill of local community groups to undertake conservation projects. As the name suggests, this approach is purely voluntary, although, in some cases, grants may be advanced to facilitate the initiatives. This approach has been recommended as a mechanism for conserving biodiversity on private property (OECD 1996). The main attraction of such programs is that they are non-interventionist in nature and require minimal administrative costs. A disadvantage is that they can be difficult to target and monitor without incurring high administrative costs. Schemes like these work best in cases where the participants have a genuine interest in the goal of the project.

Global policy response

If the EKC relationship is true, then countries in early stages of development will, as a result of lack of access to technology and capital, adopt industrial processes that are polluting, or will mine their natural resources. In this respect, it is self-serving for the rich nations to demand that the poorer nations cut back on pollution or natural resource use. Therefore, it has been proposed that the rich nations could compensate the poorer ones for foregoing income from natural resource exploitation. Various forms of transfer mechanisms have been proposed. including international financing of conservation projects and debt-for-nature swaps.

International financing of conservation projects

A number of initiatives by which advanced countries can assist developing countries to reduce environmental degradation have been proposed. These include using savings from military expenditure made since the Cold War to retire debt in developing countries and to fund conservation projects, and flexible interest repayment terms on debt for sustainable development projects. Another initiative already underway is the Global Environmental Facility (GEF). The GEF was established by the World Bank and the United Nations Environment Program. The GEF aims to provide concessional loans to developing countries for projects associated with protection of the ozone layer, reduction of greenhouse emissions, protection of international water resources, and protection of biodiversity.

Specific projects that are eligible for assistance under the scheme include development of alternative energy sources, afforestation, conservation of tropical forests, and investments to prevent oil spills and ocean pollution. Although the scheme is a worthwhile one, some countries have complained about inadequate funds. It would appear that the issue of financing the recurrent expenditure for the fund has not been properly worked out.

Debt-for-nature swaps

The concept of debt-for-nature swaps has been proposed as a way of assisting developing countries to protect their environment and at the same time reduce their foreign debt. The idea originated from the concept of debt conversion. After Mexico's 1982 financial crisis, it threatened to default on its foreign debt. This threat forced international banks to accept the fact that some debt-ridden countries were incapable of fully repaying their debts. Consequently, banks began to minimise their risk by selling high-risk debts to other banks at discounted values. Such debts became known as secondary debts or loans, and soon a market for these loans began to develop. A typical debt conversion consists of swapping secondary debt for equity in the debtor country and offers a low-cost way of investing in a developing country. For example, in 1986, Chrysler Motor Company bought off Mexico's foreign debt with a face value of about US$108 million for US$65 million. In return, the Mexican government provided about US$100 million in pesos for the manufacture of a car manufacturing plant.

Debt-for-nature swaps[10] operate along the same lines as debt-for-equity swaps, except that, as the name suggests, the investments are targeted at preserving the environment. For example, the US environmental lobby group Nature Conservancy bought about US$2.2 million of Brazil's foreign debt for US$850,000. Most of the money has been paid into a fund to be used to conserve a tropical rain forest in the country. The World Wildlife Fund for Nature has been involved in debt-for-nature swaps in a number of developing countries. By 1991, about nineteen debt-for-nature swaps worth over US$100 million had taken place. However, this amount is miniscule in comparison to total developing country debt of over US$1.3 trillion in the same period.

Although well intentioned, debt-for-nature swaps have been criticised on a number of grounds. Some people are of the view that a good proportion of foreign debt has been incurred by totalitarian or corrupt governments and that using debt-for-nature swaps to retire such debt is tantamount to legitimising illegal or immoral transactions. For example, it has been alleged that the former president of the Philippines, the late Ferdinand Marcos, incurred millions of dollars of national debt which were improperly used and as such the people of the Philippines should not be held accountable for such debts. Another argument against debt-for-nature swaps is that they interfere with national sovereignty in the sense that they allow foreigners to dictate how governments in developing countries should allocate their expenditures. It has been alleged that some of the debt-for-nature swap projects are designed more for research and exploitation of natural resources than for conservation (Mahony 1992).

The number and size of debt-for-nature swaps, to date, have been such that none of these criticisms have been proven beyond doubt. Realistically, it is unlikely that this approach will make any significant dent in Third World debt. It would appear that the major benefit of these schemes is in raising awareness of sustainable development issues and making some contribution towards the achievement of that goal.

Conclusions

This chapter has tackled the complex subject of the relationship between economic development and the environment. After describing some general trends in economic and environmental indicators in the last few years, the discussion focused on various dimensions of the trade–environment relationship, resulting in a set of policy recommendations on trade and the environment. The discussion of the trends suggested that increase in population will increase the demand for food, clothing and shelter. The consumption of resources such as energy will continue to escalate because energy is a major input in industrial production. Energy use was found to be highly correlated with economic growth and social indicators such as infant mortality and life expectancy, implying that energy is vital for development. However, to achieve sustainable development, there is a need to develop alternatives forms of energy (e.g. renewable energy).

A considerable part of the discussion centered on the relationship between trade and the environment at different stages of development or income. At issue was the environmental Kuznets U-curve hypothesis which stipulates that, as the per capita income of a country increases, environmental degradation will initially increase, but then will eventually decline once a maximum level has been reached. The maximum level of pollution at which degradation begins to decline is referred to as the turning point. A review of empirical studies revealed that there is mixed support for the EKC hypothesis. The EKC relationship appears to hold consistently for SO_2. In the case of CO_2, all the studies indicate that it increases with income, and has no turning point. Other environmental indicators for which the EKC hypothesis appears to hold include carbon monoxide, CFCs and halogen, energy use, and deforestation/reforestation. Another important observation about the EKC is that in some cases where turning points have been observed, the turning point is much higher than per capita incomes of the countries involved.

In conclusion, much still remains to be accomplished in explaining why EKCs arise. In the meantime, it is clear that countries will not automatically 'grow' out of their environmental problems. The role of institutions in countries that have obtained low levels of environmental pollution was found to be significant. Policy responses to environmental degradation were discussed, with emphasis on voluntary incentive mechanisms. In general, these approaches could offer a cost-effective and flexible means of reducing local and global pollution.

Notes

1   The model follows the basic premises of the Malthusian Theory. Several re-sources are fixed in supply and growth increases exponentially. These assump-tions and the absence of technology ensure the exhaustion of resources.

2   According to Herman Daly 'a more accurate name than the persuasive label "free trade" is "deregulated international commerce"' (Daly 1993).

3   We make a distinction here between economic growth and economic develop-ment. The former strictly refers to increase in economic indicators such as GDP and GNP, while the latter is a broader concept involving improvement in quality of life indicators, poverty and income distribution.

4   Of course, with improved technology more food could be produced without necessarily expanding agricultural land. However, the fact of the matter is that most developing countries do not utilise high technology in agriculture.

5   The GEMS is a joint project of the World Health Organisation and the United Nations Environment Program.

6   BOD is the amount of natural oxidation that occurs in a sample of water in a given time period.

7   COD is the amount of oxygen consumed when a chemical oxidant is added to a sample of water.

8   De Bruyn (1997) and Panayotou (1997) both advocate decomposition analysis as a preferred alternative to the reduced-form approach. This is because an expansion of the reduced-form model to include further explanatory variables increases the possibility of serious multicollinearity problems.

9   The political liberties index measures rights such as free elections, the existence of multiple parties, and decentralisation of power. The civil liberties index measures freedom to express opinions without fear of reprisal.

10 See Hansen (1989) for an overview.

References

Antle, J.M. and G. Heidebrink (1995) 'Environment and development: theory and international evidence', *Economic Development and Cultural Change*, vol. 43, pp. 603–25.

Arrow, K., B. Bolin, R. Costanza, P. Dasgupta, C. Folke, C.S. Holling, J. Bengt-Owe, S. Levin, K.G. Maler, C. Perrings and D. Pimentel (1995) 'Economic growth, carrying capacity, and the environment', *Science*, vol. 268, pp. 520–1.

Asafu-Adjaye, J. (1998) 'An empirical test of the environmental transition hypothesis', *Indian Journal of Quantitative Economics*, vol. XII, pp. 67–91.

—— (1999) 'The environment and development: theory and empirical evidence', *International Journal of Development Planning Literature*, vol. 14, pp. 117–34.

—— (2000) *Environmental Economics for Non-Economists*, New York, London, Singapore: World Scientific Publishing Ltd.

Barbier, E.B. (1997) 'Environmental Kuznets curve', Special Issue, *Environment and Development Economics*, 2, pp. 369–81.

Barde, J.P. (1995) 'Environmental policy and policy instruments', in H. Folmer, J.L. Gabel and H. Opschoor (eds) *Principles of Environmental and Resource Economics: A Guide for Students and Decision Makers*, Aldershot, UK: Edward Elgar.

Beckerman, W. (1980) 'Economic growth and the environment: whose growth?', *World Development*, vol. 20, pp. 481–96.

Carraro, C. and D. Sinisalco (1996) 'Voluntary agreements in environmental policy: a theoretical appraisal', in A. Xepapadeas (ed.) *Economic Policy for the Environment and Natural Resources: Techniques for the Management and Control of Pollution*, Cheltenham, UK: Edward Elgar.

Cole, M.A., A.J. Rayner and J.M. Bates (1997) 'The environmental Kuznets curve: an empirical analysis', *Environment and Development Economics*, vol. 2, pp. 401–16.

Cropper, M. and C. Griffiths (1994) 'The interaction of population growth and environmental quality', *American Economic Review*, vol. 84, pp. 250–4.

Daly, H and J.B. Cobb (1989) *For the Common Good: Redirecting the Economy Toward Community, the Environment and a Sustainable Future*, Boston: Beacon Press.

Daly, H.E. (1980) *Economics, Ecology, Ethics*, San Francisco: Freeman.

—— (1993) 'The perils of free trade', *Scientific American*, November.

De Bruyn, S.M. (1997) 'Explaining the environmental Kuznets curve: structual change and international agreements in reducing sulphur emissions', *Environment and Development Economics*, 2, pp. 485–503.

Diamond, P. (1965) 'National debt in a neoclassical growth model', *American Economic Review*, vol. 55, pp. 1126–50.

Grossman, G. (1993) 'Pollution and growth: what do we know?', CEPR DP-848, London: Centre for Economic Policy Research.

Grossman, G.M. and A.G. Krueger (1991) *Environmental Impacts of a North American Free Trade Agreement*, National Bureau of Economic Research Working Paper 3914, Cambridge MA: NBER.

Hair, J.D. (1993) 'GATT and the Environment', *Journal of Commerce*, December.

Hansen, S. (1989) 'Debt-for-nature swaps: overview and discussion of key issues', *Ecological Economics*, vol. 1, pp. 77–93.

John, A. and R. Pecchenino (1994) 'An overlapping generations model of growth and the environment', *Economic Journal*, vol. 104, pp. 1393–410.

Komen, M.H.C., S. Gerking, and H. Folmer (1997) 'Income and environmental

R&D: empirical evidence from OECD countries', *Environment and Development Economics*, vol. 2, pp. 505–15.

Kuznets, S. (1955) 'Economic growth and income inequality', *American Economic Review*, vol. 49, pp. 1–28.

Liddle, B.T. (1996) 'Environmental Kuznets curves and regional pollution', Paper presented to the 4th Biennial Conference of the International Society for Ecological Economics, Boston University, Boston, MA.

Lopez, R. (1994) 'The environment as a factor of production: the effects of economic growth and trade liberalization', *Journal of Environmental Economics and Management*, vol. 27, pp. 163–84.

McConnell, K.E. (1997) 'Income and the demand for environmental quality', *Environment and Development Economics*, vol. 2, pp. 383–99.

Mahony, R. (1992) 'Debt-for-nature swaps: who really benefits?', *Ecologist*, vol. 22, pp. 97–103.

Malthus, T.R. (1872) *An Essay on the Principle of Population*, 7th Edition, London: Reeves and Turner.

Meadows, D.H., D.L. Meadows, and W. Behrens (1972) *The Limits of Growth: A Report to the Club of Rome's Project on the Predicament of Mankind*, New York: Universe Books.

Moomaw, W.R. and G.C. Unruh (1997) 'Are environmental kuznets curves misleading us? the case of CO_2 emissions'. *Environment and Development Economics*, vol. 29, pp. 451–63.

Organisation for Economic Co-operation and Development, OECD (1996) *Making Markets Work for Biological Diversity: The Role of Economic Incentive Measures*, Paris: OECD.

Panayotou, T. (1993) 'Empirical tests and policy analysis of environmental degradation at different stages of economic development', Working Paper, WP238, Technology and Employment Programme, ILO, Geneva.

—— (1995) 'Environmental degradation at different stages of economic development', In I. Ahmed and J.A. Doeleman (eds), *Beyond Rio: The Environmental Crisis and Sustainable Livelihoods in the Third World*, London: Macmillan.

—— (1997) 'Demystifying the environmental kuznets curve: turning a black box into a policy tool', *Environment and Development Economics*, vol. 2, pp. 465–84.

Rothman, D.S. (1998) 'Environmental Kuznets curves – real progress or passing the buck? A case for assumption-based approaches', *Ecological Economics*, vol. 25, pp. 177–194.

Samuelson, P. (1958) 'An exact consumption-loan model of interest with or without the social contrivance of money', *Journal of Political Economy*, vol. 66, pp. 467–82.

Shafik, N. and S. Bandyopadhyay (1992) 'Economic growth and environmental quality: time series and cross country evidence', Background Paper for *World Development Report*, WPS, The World Bank, Washington DC.

Stern, D.I., M.S. Common, and E.B. Barbier (1996) 'Economic growth and environmental degradation: the environmental kuznets curve and sustainable development', *World Development*, vol. 24, pp. 1151–60.

Suri, V. and D. Chapman (1998) 'Economic growth, trade and energy: implications for the environmental Kuznets curve', *Ecological Economics*, May, 195–208.

Torras, M. and J.K. Boyce (1996) 'Income inequality and pollution: a reassessment of the environment Kuznets curve', *Ecological Economics*, special issue on EKC.

United Nations (UN) (1997) 'Kyoto Protocol to the United Nations Framework Convention on Climate Change', Article 3, Annex B, UN, New York.

United Nations Development Program (UNDP) (1996) *Human Development Report,* New York and Oxford: Oxford University Press.

—— (1997) *Human Development Report,* New York and Oxford: Oxford University Press.

—— (1998) *Human Development Report*, Oxford University Press, New York and Oxford.

Unruh, G.C. and W.R. Moomaw (1997) 'An alternative analysis of apparent EKC-type transitions', *Ecological Economics*, special issue on EKC.

Wackernagel, M., L. Onisto, A.C. Linares, I.S.F. Lopez, J.M. Garcia, A.I.S. Guerrero and M.G.S. Guerrero (1997) 'Ecological footprints of nations: how much nature do they use? How much nature do they have?', The Earth Council, San Jose, Costa Rica, 10 March.

World Bank (1992) *World Development Report 1992: Development and the Environment*, New York: Oxford University Press.

—— (1998) *World Development Indicators 1998*, CD-ROM Version, Washington, DC.

—— (1999) *World Development Indicators 1998*, CD-ROM Version, Washington, DC.

11 Globalization as Westernization

A post-colonial theory of global exploitation

Ozay Mehmet

Introduction

Globalization, defined here as Westernization (i.e. the spread of Western economic techniques, political institutions and norms), is a system that enriches the West while impoverishing the Rest (Huntington 1993; Mahbubani 1992). The Western economic ideology is capitalism, a market-centred system of resource allocation dominated by owners of capital. In its latest manifestation, capitalist ideology has joined neo-liberal and neo-conservative camps on the basis of a common belief in the universal supremacy of market forces (Fukuyama 1992; Huntington 1996). While the market has been enthroned, the power of the state has declined. This puts the wellbeing of the vast majority of people around the globe at risk. The chief villain is a globalizing capitalist ideology. What is this ideology?

The capitalist ideology has evolved in the West as a cumulative process, but it had its roots in the era of imperialism based on colonial exploitation of the Rest for the material benefit of the West. As such, it is not a new phenomenon. What is new, however, is the emergence in the post-1945 period of a new sub-ideology of international development, engineered in the West, ostensibly for narrowing the gap between the rich and developing worlds, but, in reality, to globalize Western capitalism.

The core of the international development ideology was a Eurocentric worldview (Mehmet 1995, 1999), based on the idealization of Western economics and politics matched by a presumed inferiority of non-Western norms and institutions. This post-Westphalia worldview is a hierarchical ordering of inter-state relations. At the bottom of the system was the Third World, invented around 1950 (Harris 1987: 18). The Third World was conceived as primitive and under-developed. But the idea of development, closely linked to progress, reflected capitalism's 'great ascent' (Heilbronner 1963). National development was led by a generation of Western-educated leaders such as Nehru of India (Mehmet 1995: 61), willing to bank on Western know-how and technology transferred from the First World. Rejecting endogenous development options (e.g. Gandhian economics), these post-colonial leaders believed that they could copy and learn from the West and, in time, catch up to the rich countries, in line with the 'trickle-down' theory (Todaro 1981: 68, 131). Naively they accepted Western aid and technical assistance inflows intended to reconstruct the Third World just as Marshall Plan had reconstructed Europe.

From the Western donors' perspective, the key motivation behind the ideology of international development was a deliberate aim of winning 'the hearts and minds' of the non-Western people for capitalism in a global strategy of containment of Communism threatening it from the Second World. Thus, Walter Rostow, the author of the influential 'stages of growth' theory (Rostow 1960), expressed the dominant ideology of international development as a 'non-Communist Manifesto' and massive Western aid and technical assistance flowing into the Third World were justified as strategic instruments of the Cold War. With these hidden agendas and conflicting expectations between donors and recipients, it is no wonder that both Western aid programs and development theories have failed.

This chapter is an attempt to seek the deeper causal factors behind this failure. It is organized in five parts. Following this introduction, the second part will sketch out the ideology of international development in the post-war period when Westernizing donors and technocrats promoted the idea of mass prosperity for all in previously colonial territories, now renamed the Third World. However, as explained in the third part, globalization of capitalism has worked as a tool of global inequality since it is a system of monopoly-monopsony exploitation on a global scale. Therefore, the fourth part argues that Western capitalism is inherently unfit for the Global Village. The final part will highlight some of the main conclusions of the paper.

The ideology of international development

The West pursued the ideology of international development at two diametrically opposed, indeed contradictory, planes, one theoretical/analytical, and the other practical/policy. At the theoretical/analytical plane, a brand new discipline called 'Development Economics' was introduced and promoted in Western universities in order to legitimize Third World development as a scientific field. The scientific basis of this new discipline was a 'Perfect Competition Model', derived from mainstream economics. It was a deductive construction, resting on highly individualistic behavioural assumptions, entirely reflecting European experience, in particular the Weberian Protestant Ethic.

What are these behavioural assumptions? How are they manifested? They are derived from market forces of supply and demand on the basis of revealed preferences that are supposed to be 'rational.' Consumers are supposed to be utility-maximizers constrained by their tastes and incomes, while producers are profit-maximizers influenced only by production costs and technology. Social values such as cooperation, sharing and solidarity are irrelevant in market relations. These assumptions, however, even if valid in the West, can hardly be claimed to be universal.

Yet market ideology has been vigorously globalized in the post-colonial period since 1950 in a process dominated by economists. Western economics, its inherent flaws and all, was utilized in this period by development practitioners and technocrats churning out blueprints, to put forward wave upon wave of theories of international development. These included capitalist growth models assuming perfect capital–labour substitution (Harrod 1939; Domar 1946); two-sector theories of migration built on income-maximizing rational behaviour (Lewis 1954; Harris and Todaro 1970); balanced versus imbalanced theories of industrialization designed to create new industries and markets all based on the universality of the profit motive. The chief underlying premise in all these theories and models of international development was the imperative of transfer of Western technology, know-how and aid in a top-down replication of the Western capitalist achievement in an imagined 'Third World' stylized into an abstract and uniform category for textbook analysis. Little heed was given to the fact that these imported abstractions hardly fitted the actual cultures, capabilities or requirements of the developing countries.

Worse still, at the practical/policy plane, trade and aid policies were utilized to globalize Western production on a global assembly line. Initially, local industries were built under the protectionist 'import-substitution industrialization' (ISI) strategy favouring capital-intensive consumer goods for the local market. American-style marketing and advertising slowly but surely began to erode local cultures in a new brand of consumerism connecting the global assembly line with the global 'supermarket' (Barnet and Cavanagh 1994).

Arguably, the most Eurocentric industrialization theory was the famed 'two-sector' model by Arthur Lewis, the author of *Theory of Economic Growth* (1955), who subsequently was honoured with a Nobel Prize in Economics. The highly influential Lewis model aspired to industrialize a low-income, labour-surplus economy by massive transfers of the 'disguised unemployed' into urban sectors. This would have two simultaneous positive effects, both reinforcing each other to generate higher GNP. First, it would reduce excess surplus in agriculture, thereby automatically resulting in higher productivity. Second, it would create industrial employment. In fact, neither of the predictions materialized. The assumption of 'disguised unemployment' in agriculture was counter-factual since it was based on abstract theorizing, not hard empirical evidence. Neither was the predicted industrial job creation realized owing to the pro-capital bias of industrialization.

The Lewis model, however, was adopted and popularized by Western donors and experts as the new gospel of development. Its main effect was a huge rural–urban exodus of poor migrants looking for jobs and better economic opportunities in urban sectors. The slums and urban poverty, which are now the dismal realities of many Third World cities, are the direct consequence of this kind of faulty theorizing.

In retrospect, it would have been far more effective to invest in rural and agrarian development, but that would have gone against the grain of pro-urban growthmanship of the period. Western extension workers, pushing inappropriate farm technologies more suitable for temperate climates than tropics, declared that Third World peasants and farmers were 'irrational' merely because they resisted high-risk experiments.

While Third World agriculture and food sectors were neglected and sacrificed for the sake of pro-urban industrialization, world trade was liberalized and entered a period of unprecedented expansion. Trade expansion benefited the West, enabling its major corporations to go international. The ISI strategy, then in vogue in the Third World, contributed to this globalization. Subsequently 'export-oriented' industrialization replaced ISI under global sourcing and product standardization. Under both scenarios, however, the big winners have been the profit-seeking corporations which have 'gone international' to become global companies, transforming themselves into multinational corporations (MNCs), sometimes referred to as multinational enterprises. Why and how these companies from the West, and subsequently from Japan and to a lesser degree from other countries, have emerged as MNCs has been extensively studied, from Vernon (1971) to Dunning (1992). Whatever their motives, MNCs are global monopolies and oligopolies, dominating capital and technology markets. As a result, they exercise market power and, thanks to this power, routinely exploit developing countries by a systemic under-pricing of human and natural resources. This global exploitation enriches the First World while impoverishing the Third, an outcome imbedded in the way capitalism works.

This unequal outcome is not the result of some conspiracy, but rather the consequence of the natural tendency of capitalist market forces. The forces work, in a huge, largely decentralized, system of production and consumption relations, toward the goal of capitalization on a global scale. Under capitalism, all production and consumption decisions have an inherent pro-capital bias. The end-result of these decisions is slowly but surely to convert every productive resource, whether physical or natural or whether in nature or imbedded in humans or families, into a new form of capital, ultimately to be owned and controlled by capitalists. We shall explain how this global *capitalization* works in the next part of this chapter.

Capitalization: how monopolistic exploitation works globally

Monopolies, oligopolies and cartels driven by monopoly profit dominate the real market system. This is especially true for international trade dominated by MNCs, the chief instruments of capitalization. Although international trade is subject to rules such as those managed by the World Trade Organization (WTO), negotiated multilaterally, these rules reflect the interest of dominant trading powers, principally the USA, European countries and Japan. Unlike anti-trust, anti-monopolies and unfair trade laws, as for example found in the USA, international trade regulation is silent on monopolistic practices and monopoly profits in the global marketplace.

Monopoly profit rests on exploitation of labour and natural resources and it is a positive function of the rate of exploitation. The higher the rate of exploitation, the greater the monopoly profits. There are two kinds of monopoly profit, direct and indirect, although both are, essentially, a return on market control.

Direct monopoly profit is extracted by monopolists' market control of factor or product markets and it reflects the ability to fix prices for inputs or products. A good example is the wage of a worker hired in the labour market in which the employer is a monopsonist (i.e. single employer in the local labour market), whereby the value of the worker's output far exceeds the wage paid to the worker. The difference is exploitation accruing to the monopolist as a return on market power, the ratio of the exploitation margin to the value of worker's output being the rate of exploitation of the worker by the monopolist. A different kind of monopoly exploitation occurs in product markets (e.g. manufacture of sport shoes) whereby a monopolist derives large monopoly exploitation by maximizing the difference between prices paid to workers (e.g. in Vietnam or Indonesia) and prices for which it sells to consumers in rich countries in North America.

Indirect monopoly profit occurs as a result of accounting manipulation. Transfer pricing is an important example of such manipulation. Intra-corporate sales and purchases are not real, but artificial accounting prices used for bookkeeping purposes. It is used extensively by MNCs with branch-plants or subsidiaries in different countries to escape tax liability in foreign jurisdictions and help shift income from periphery to the home country. Thus, a subsidiary in Guyana, producing bauxite, may intentionally under-price its sales to the parent company in the USA, thereby declaring 'loss' in Guyana while simultaneously maximizing corporate earnings in the USA. Loss-making operations in Guyana then may be used to justify exploitation of Guyanese workers and resources by means of under-payment of Guyanese labour and resources in addition to tax evasion and avoidance.

Besides transfer pricing, market control to extract monopoly profits includes forcing prices to rock-bottom in long-term contracts for the purchase of raw materials such as petroleum in pre-OPEC days, or cheap electricity or logs from countries rich in rain-forest. In plantation economies, an important tool of exploitation by Western plantation companies is strategic stockpiling to buy cheap and sell dear, the basis of global profit-seeking.

The inner logic of the global profit-seeking behaviour of MNCs is global exploitation based on *capitalization,* i.e. to enlarge the capital stock, heavily concentrated in the West, through conversion of non-capital resources into new forms of capital along the global assembly line. Thus, labour in one period becomes human capital in the next as a result of investment in education and training. New knowledge becomes intellectual property transformed by modern technology. Environment becomes ecological assets by monetizing natural resources. All these are privatized and controlled by capitalists constantly enriched by *capitalization.*

All these forms of market power exploitation by MNCs work to enrich the West by impoverishing the Third World. This global inequality is not the result of some corporate conspiracy theory. Rather it is the natural outcome of capitalist market forces, although, of course, the effects are no less disturbing.

The converse of Third World impoverishment by exploitation is income and wealth concentration in the West. Again, due to the operation of capitalist market forces, economic concentration in the North is always pro-rich. Capitalism is a non-national, non-egalitarian ideology: it is a system based, not on nationalism, but on market inequality. It thrives in the West, as in the rest of the world, on inequality or polarization between the rich and the rest.

Western capitalism is risky and speculative, sharing many common similarities with gambling: a few win, but most lose. At a global level, the West wins under capitalism, because market forces are Western-biased. Fundamentally, this stems from the fact that economics, as a body of scientific knowledge, is pro-capital and anti-labour. While capital and technology are priced in the West at high levels, Third World resources are under-priced, either by treating environment as a free good, labour as plentiful and cheap, or by such indirect means as intra-corporate transfer pricing as observed above. Unions and social safety nets ensure workers in the West decent wages, but few Third World workers enjoy such protection.

Under-pricing Third World labour and environment overstates the rate of return on capital, over-values capital assets. It encourages speculation rather than steady growth, finally leading to the collapse of financial markets as happened in the case of the Asian currency meltdown in 1997/8. Instability of markets is the very essence of capitalism. Cyclical as well as short-term swings in commodity markets, in foreign exchange markets and in other markets create opportunities for windfall gains and supernormal profits for speculators and capitalists. If markets remained always in stable equilibrium, there would be merely normal returns for capitalists who drive the market.

In the nineteenth century the search for profit converted England from a closed, agrarian economy into the 'workshop of the world', a world dominated by aggressive 'captains of industry'. Despite the initial success of industrialization, classical economists were pessimistic about the long-term sustainability of capitalism. John Stuart Mill predicted the ultimate collapse of the system due to vanishing profits in a stationary state. Malthus, the prophet of doom, was even more pessimistic, predicting a population explosion owing to ever-worsening population–food balance (Mehmet 1999: Chapter 2).

Going international with free trade and colonial expansion has postponed the collapse predicted by nineteenth-century economists; it has not eliminated the inherent danger. England, a small island, could ship its excess population to the colonies. But mankind has nowhere to go to escape the law of diminishing returns on a global scale. Imagine how sustainable it would become if all the Indians and Chinese were to emulate the Western ideal of consumerism by becoming two-car owning families, living in 3,000 sq. ft. homes, complete with microwaves, dishwashers, etc.

To date, globalization, or a universalized market economy, has meant trade liberalization and free capital mobility in financial flows and diffusion of modern technology. Who has benefited from this unprecedented growth? MNCs, since they control much of these capital and technology flows, especially in modern computer, information and communication sectors. In 1992, there were some 37,000 MNCs compared to only 7,000 just twenty years ago, with annual sales of US$5,500 billion, a figure considerably greater than the value of total world trade of US$4,000 billion (ILO 1994: 13).

While trade liberalization, actively pursued by the WTO, has promoted capital mobility, there is no parallel freedom for labour. The International Labour Organization (ILO), the oldest UN specialized agency responsible for worker rights, has been comparatively weak, and its labour standards have had virtually no impact on international trade. Ironically, in the period of rapid trade expansion and liberalization, there have been increasing barriers for migrants in high-income countries, with extensive visa and citizenship regulations and restrictive occupational licensing.

This asymmetry in the way capital and labour are treated in market economies is a major bias of Western capitalism. While financial markets are being globalized, and the rights of capital protected under international rules (such the OECD-sponsored but ill-fated Multilateral Agreement on Investment), there is no parallel concern about worker rights and the rights of migrants. At best only lip service is being paid to international labour standards while often 'social clause' debates in the USA or EU disclose strong domestic protectionist interests. Meanwhile, labour-abundant regimes in the Third World notable by the absence of labour and environmental standards are becoming magnets for Western capital in search of profits in a 'race to the bottom' whereby there is global downward pressure on wages and an onslaught against social safety nets.

The capital–labour asymmetry is creating blockages in labour markets in the Third World, and preventing the evolution of an orderly global labour market. The labour market imbalances are, in turn, pushing excess numbers of job seekers into the arms of unscrupulous labour contractors operating an expanding trade in the trafficking of human beings (Mehmet *et al.* 1998: Chapter 2). Illegal networks of crime–prostitution–drugs now operate globally, sometimes linked to international terrorism. Insufficient job prospects and capital-biased macroeconomic policy management (largely based on imported Western advice), are also generating social conflict (Thurow 1996; Rodrik 1998), riots and wars, always resulting in new waves of refugees and displaced persons.

To illustrate these negative consequences of Western capitalist development, we shall now construct a simple model of export-oriented industrial estates (IEs). Sometimes called export-processing zones (EPZs), these are special-purpose development schemes, created by host countries in the hope that they will operate as regional growth poles. A notable example is the Batam Island scheme between Indonesia, Singapore and Malaysia (Lee 1991). Host countries actively seek to attract MNCs or their branch-plants with a wide range of tax and tariff incentives along with such anti-labour guarantees as prohibition of unions or strikes on IEs and EPZ (Hadiz 1997). The IEs and EPZs facilitate the MNCs, global production and sourcing activities. There is now a global assembly line along which parts and components are produced, and final products assembled, in a multiplicity of national jurisdictions that effectively subordinate national interest to global profit-seeking by MNCs. This is because MNCs are typically 'foot-loose' and generate relatively low levels of retained value-added locally. In such labour-intensive sectors as electronics or garment industries, female workers work under exploitative conditions and live in poverty (Buvinic 1997; Aslanbeigui *et al.* 1994). In sweat-shops, out-sourcing for the global marketplace, often children are similarly exploited (Mehmet *et al.* 1998: 50–3).

Yet, production on IEs and EPZs is high value-added activity. How are these value-added benefits distributed, specifically between resident and non-resident parties? This is the question which our simple model seeks to answer.

In Figure 11.1 the IE/EPZ represents a meeting-place of two resource flows: foreign capital and technology, denoted by K_f, and domestic resources

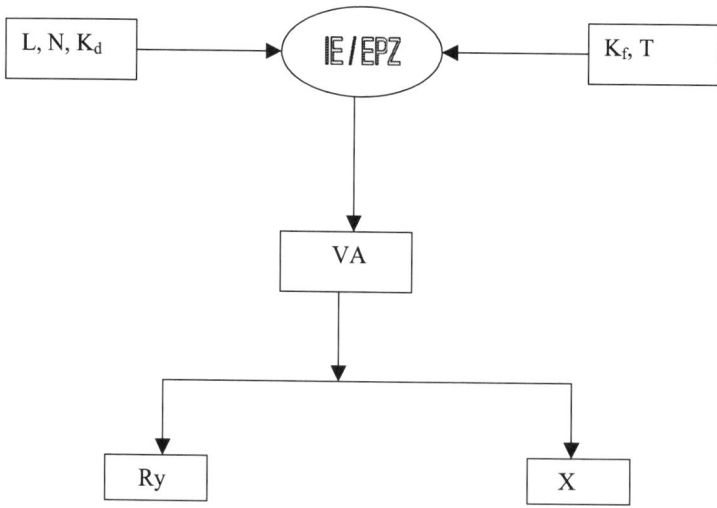

Figure 11.1 A model of exploitation on the IEs/EPZs.
Source: Mehmet 1986: 84.

consisting of labour, L, land, N, and capital, K_d. These resources create value-added, VA, which is distributed amongst owners of resources. If perfect competition prevailed, VA would be distributed in direct relationship to their contribution to the VA produced. However, since non-resident owners of resources (i.e. MNCs or their affilitiates) enjoy monopoly–monopsony powers, they extract the lion's share of VA. Thus domestic workers, without any rights or protection under social security laws, are subject to exploitation. This implies that wages paid to these workers are only a fraction of their marginal product, the difference being rents collected by MNCs and their affiliates as monopoly profit. By contrast, payments for imports of technology typically entail over-payment to non-resident investors at the expense of domestic parties. Consequently, retained income, RY, is a relatively small percentage of total VA, in contrast to X, the percentage share realized by non-residents in the form of payments for royalties, management fees as well as profits.

Overall, the IE/EPZ model demonstrates the unequal distribution of the gains of economic growth between resident and non-resident actors. MNCs or their branch-plants are the principal gainers, at least in the early stages of industrial development, thanks to their monopoly–monopsony powers in labour, capital and technology markets. In time, there may be long-term benefits in the form of 'learning by doing'. But these benefits may be eroded by new concession agreements between host governments and MNCs. Typically, these agreements favour the latter thanks to their monopoly–monopsony powers, e.g. their ability to threaten host governments with 'foot-loose' investment strategies of relocating to alternative regimes unless they get their way.

Is capitalism fit for the Global Village?

An economic system is founded upon the twin principles of efficiency and equity. The efficiency rules govern the transformation of inputs into outputs of goods and services, subject to cost and technology constraints. Equity rules relate to the distribution of rewards.

Capitalism is an efficiency-oriented system, which fails badly on equity. In fact, Kuznets (1955) has articulated in a classic contribution a hypothesis that economic growth worsens income distribution. This stems from the fact that inequality is embedded in capitalism, more specifically in market forces of supply and demand centred exclusively on ability to pay or 'effective demand'. Ability to pay favours the rich, while ignoring basic human needs. How the rich acquire their income and wealth is immaterial for market forces. Fruits of exploitation and other unfair practices are treated at par with the productivity of honest work and fair means. These same market forces dismiss totally human need, even when occasioned by hunger caused by famine, or by prevailing norms of justice and fairness, and biological factors of human existence. The Kuznets inequality hypothesis, at first thought to be temporary and expected to vanish under a 'trickle-down' process (Mehmet 1999: 13–14), underscores the inappropriateness of Western capitalism for the developing world.

The capitalist system is unfit for the Global Village, which requires not only efficiency, but equity and sustainability as well. It is no accident that the West holds the largest stock of capital assets in the world. This outcome is the by-product of the unequal operation of market forces. These forces concentrate wealth and productive assets in the West at the expense of the Rest. According to the latest *Human Development Report* (UNDP 1999), the richest 20 per cent of the world population living in high-income countries had 86 per cent of the world GDP compared to just 1 per cent share of the bottom 20 per cent (UNDP 1999: 3). In fact, these global inequalities have steadily worsened in recent decades.

There is a huge chasm between Third World realities and idealized market forces as they are presented in textbooks on economics. The textbook version is built on a utopian concept of 'perfect competition', based on perfect foresight and information, absence of government and many buyers and sellers. The economic ideal of perfect competition is an impossible abstraction far removed from how real markets work. As shown in the preceding part, the real market is a system of monopoly exploitation impoverishing the majority of humankind for the benefit of the few rich in capitalist economies in great affluence. Thus, again citing from the UNDP *Human Development Report 1999*:

> The world's 200 richest people more than doubled their net worth in four years to 1998, to more than $1 trillion. The assets of the top three billionaires are more than the combined GNP of all least developed countries and their 600 million people.

The Global Village must be built on social justice. As such, the Global Village would require not only efficiency rules, but also equity and sustainability rules as well to ensure the welfare of all members of the Global Family. In an inherently unequal and unjust world, it is futile to advocate and prescribe 'civil society' reforms for the Rest. Civil society reforms must be tied to global governance effective reforms in the global trading and financial system to ensure sustainable and equitable world development. In this spirit it is time to phase out conventional aid programs by international taxation to generate autonomous resource flows for investment in sustainable development in the South. Logically these taxes should be levied on MNCs as a counter for their monopoly/monopsony powers (Mehmet 1980).

Conclusion

Free trade cannot be free for all. Otherwise new rounds of crises will follow the Asian currency collapse. Unregulated capital movements may be good for speculators, but they undermine sustained economic development. There must be agreed international regulation of international trade and capital emanating from the principle of equality of all stakeholders in the North and South, with global equity emerging as much a cornerstone of WTO as trade liberalization.

Western capitalism is too pro-capital and too exploitative to fit the Global Village. Equitable distribution of global wealth and sustainable development must be the foundations of the Global Village. The efficiency gains of economic growth must be equitably distributed for the benefit of the Global Family. A.K. Sen's theory of entitlement based on expansion of human capabilities (Sen 1998) is a good ethical system for guiding transition to a more just and egalitarian global governance (UN Commission on Global Governance 1995). A good starting point in this direction would be major reform of international financial institutions and development agencies now some 50 years old and outmoded. In the global marketplace, *capitalization* and monopoly/monopsony exploitation by MNCs and other forms of unfair trade practices must be brought within the WTO regime, and trade liberalization must be linked to core ILO labour standards and other 'best practice' guidelines collectively agreed for sustainable development to benefit present as well as future generations.

In the twenty-first century, Western economics, and in particular the sub-discipline of economic development, will need to transform itself in three particular respects. In the first place, it must become more inter-disciplinary and more normative by linking itself to international ethics representing a blend of Western and non-Western ethical values (Goulet 1997). This is how economics can begin to cast off its Eurocentric (or neo-mercantilist) bias. In particular, aid programs based on donor interest must be replaced by autonomous resource flows financed from taxes levied on MNCs and such innovative mechanisms as the Tobin Tax on speculative currency movements.

Second, globalization of trade and finance must be accompanied by international social policy (Mishra 1997) to ensure a level playing field in labour markets by protecting vulnerable groups such as children and women, now subject to exploitation along the global assembly line. Similarly, it is vital to universalize basic worker rights everywhere in an integrating world economy. The ILO Declaration on Fundamental Principles and Rights of Work, adopted at the June 1998 International Labour Conference, is a promising start in this direction (ILO 1998).

Thirdly, global development needs to evolve from multicultural consent. Rules of international trade, aid and investment must be determined on the basis of global dialogue, not imposed by Western powers alone. It is time to democratize such agencies as the WTO, WB and the IMF which are now under the domination of Western powers. *Economic* development must give way to *human* development so that people become ends, not means. This should also apply to measurement of economic performance, in particular poverty reduction.

References

Aslanbeigui, N. (1994) *Women in the Age of Economic Transformation,*London and New York: Routledge.

Barnet, R.J. and J. Cavanagh (1994) *Global Dreams: Imperial Corporations and the New World Order*, New York: Simon & Shuster.

Buvinic, M. (1997) 'Women in poverty: a new global underclass', *Foreign Policy*, no. 108, Fall.

Domar, E. (1946) 'Capital expansion, rate of growth and employment', *Econometrica,* April.

Drydyk, J and P. Penz (eds) (1997) *Global Justice, Global Democracy,* Society for Socialist Studies, vol. 12, Winnipeg/Halifax, Canada: Fernwood Publishing.

Dunning, J. (1992) *Multinational Enterprises and the Global Economy*, Don Mills, Ontario: Addison-Wesley.

Fukuyama, F (1992) *The End of History and the Last Man*, London: H. Hamilton.

Goulet, D. (1997) 'Development ethics: a new discipline', *International Journal of Social Economics,* vol. 24, no. 11.

Hadiz, V.R. (1997) *Workers and the State in New Order Indonesia*, London and New York: Routledge.

Harris, J.R. and M. Todaro (1970) 'Migration, unemployment and development: a two-sector model', *American Economic Review,* March.

Harris, N. (1987) *The End of the Third World: New Industrializing Countries and the Decline of an Ideology*, Harmondsworth: Penguin.

Harrod, R.F. (1939) 'An essay in dynamic theory', *Economic Journal,* vol. 49.

Heilbronner, R. (1963) *The Great Ascent: The Struggle for Economic Development in our Time*, New York: Harper & Row.

Huntington, S. (1993) 'The Clash of Civilizations?', *Foreign Affairs,* Summer.

—— (1996) *The Clash of Civilizations and the Remaking of World Order*, New York: Simon & Shuster.

ILO (1994) *Defending Values, Promoting Change: Social Justice in a Global Economy, An ILO Agenda,* Geneva.

—— (1998) *ILO Declaration on Fundamental Principles and Rights at Work and Its Follow-Up,* Geneva, 18 June.

Kuznets, S. (1955) 'Economic growth and income inequality' *American Economic Review,* March.

Lee, T.Y. (ed.) (1991) *Growth Triangle: The Johor-Singapore-Riau Experience,* Singapore: ISEAS.

Lewis, A. (1954) 'Economic development with unlimited supplies of labour', *Manchester School,* May.

—— (1955) *The Theory of Economic Growth*, London: Unwin.

Mahbubani, K. (1992) 'The West and the Rest' *The National Interest,* Summer.

Mehmet, O. (1980) 'An interntional levy on multinational corporations' *International Interactions*, vol. 7, no. 2.

—— (1986) *Development in Malaysia, Poverty, Wealth and Trusteeship,* London: Croom Helm.

—— (1995) *Westernizing the Third World, the Eurocentricity of Economic Development Theories*, London and New York: Routledge.

—— (1999) *Westernizing the Third World, the Eurocentricity of Economic Development Theories,* 2nd Edition, London and New York: Routledge.

Mehmet, O., E. Mendes, R. Sinding (1998) *Towards a Fair Global Labour Market, Avoiding a New Slave Trade*, London and New York: Routledge.

Mishra, R. (1997) 'Globalization and social policy: defending social standards', in Drydyk and Penz, *op. cit.*

Rodrik, D. (1998) 'Globalisation, social conflict and economic growth' *The World Economy*, vol. 21, no..2, March.

Rostow, W. (1960) *The Stages of Economic Growth, A Non-Communist Manifesto*, Cambridge: Cambridge University Press.

Sen, A.K. (1998) 'Human development and financial conservatism' *World Development*, vol. 26, no.4

Thurow, L. (1996) *The Future of Capitalism: How Today's Forces Shape Tomorrow's World*, New York: Marrow.

Todaro, M. (1981) *Economic Development in the Third World*, 2nd edition, New York: Longman.

UN Commission on Global Governance (1995) *Our Global Neighbourhood*, New York: Oxford University Press.

UNDP (1999) *Human Development Report*, New York: Oxford University Press.

Vernon, R. (1971) *Sovereignty At Bay*, New York: Basic Book.

Index